GARY MACKAY'S
HEARTS DREAM TEAM

Gary Mackay's
HEARTS DREAM TEAM

GARY MACKAY
WITH ROB ROBERTSON

BLACK & WHITE PUBLISHING

First published 2012
by Black & White Publishing Ltd
29 Ocean Drive, Edinburgh EH6 6JL

1 3 5 7 9 10 8 6 4 2   12 13 14 15

ISBN: 978 1 84502 453 6

Typeset by Iolaire Typesetting, Newtonmore
Printed and bound by MPG Books Ltd, Bodmin, Cornwall

CONTENTS

FOREWORD
BY DAVE MACKAY

To be asked to contribute the foreword to *Gary Mackay's Hearts Dream Team* is an absolute privilege. As a lifelong Hearts supporter to be part of a publication that honours the greatest players, management and backroom staff in the history of the club is a joy indeed.

Now can I say that although Gary and I share the same surname – both went to Balgreen Primary School in Edinburgh and went on to captain Hearts – we are not related. My nephew Colin was a few years below Gary at primary school but that is as close as our families ever got. What we do share is a love of Hearts and when Gary approached me to write this foreword I didn't hesitate.

My health isn't what it once was so can I thank my lovely wife Isobel for helping me out, not just with this foreword, but also all during my life. She has been a tower of strength through the years even although she comes from a Hibs supporting family! I managed to get over that hurdle pretty quickly but through the years we have had a right few good-natured arguments while watching derby games. To this day she always says to me that the best result to ensure peace in the Mackay household is for a draw between Hearts and Hibs.

When Gary mentioned his book idea to Isobel and myself memories of the good old days came flooding back. It was great fun just thinking back to some of the super players I watched when, as a young boy growing up in Edinburgh, I used to go along to Tynecastle every week to watch my heroes in action.

For all the roads and the miles I have travelled in football one of the best journeys I ever made was the relatively short one from my front door at 18 Glendevon Park to Tynecastle. When I was small enough I used to sneak under the big gates of the stadium and simply stand on the terraces looking in awe and wonder at my field of dreams. Watching some of the all-time greats such as my own hero Bobby Baxter, who used to come off his shift at Gilmerton Colliery on the Saturday morning and turn out for Hearts in the afternoon, strengthened my love affair with the club that lives on to this day.

I first fulfilled my ambition to play at Tynecastle when I turned out for Saughton High School against Kings Park School from Glasgow in the final of the Scottish Schools Cup way back in 1949. We had drawn the first match at Hampden, which was the right result for me as it meant the replay would be at my beloved Tynecastle.

To be in the home changing room where the great players of my youth used to get stripped was a dream come true. What happened out on the pitch was even more so. I scored the winning goal in a 2-1 win following a cross from my brother Tom. It was my first ever goal at Tynecastle. What a thrill!

To then sign for the club and make my debut against Clyde at Tynecastle on 7 November 1953 just before my nineteenth birthday was a great moment. Although we lost 2-1 and I didn't play particularly well, running out on the hallowed turf alongside the likes of Jimmy Wardhaugh and John Cumming in front of 16,000 fans was a great moment for me.

My six years at Hearts remain among my happiest times in football. The record books state that from 1953 to 1959 I started

179 games and scored 29 goals. Trophy wise I was fortunate enough to lift the Scottish Cup in 1956 when we beat Celtic 3-1 at Hampden in front of 132,840 fans.

I was also part of the team that won the Scottish League Cup by beating Motherwell in 1954 and was involved again when we won the same trophy in 1958 after we beat Partick Thistle in the final. The biggest honour was being captain of the side that won the 1957-58 Championship by 13 points from Rangers. With Jimmy Wardhaugh, Jimmy Murray and Alex Young banging in the goals, Gordon Marshall keeping clean sheet after clean sheet and Bobby Kirk, George Thomson, Andy Bowman, Bobby Blackwood, Jimmy Milne, John Cumming, Fred Glidden and Ian Crawford, among others, in top form, it was the greatest Hearts team I ever played in. Although Willie Bauld started just nine matches that season and Alfie Conn and Johnny Hamilton only four each, they also made a big contribution to our champion-ship-winning team.

And that is the problem Gary faces in naming his Hearts Dream Team. He has so many candidates to pick from! I don't envy him the task, as there are several names in that Scottish League-winning side alone that would grace any Hearts Dream Team. There have been many other top-class players who have turned out for Hearts through the years and it is a tough decision Gary has to make to pick the best of the best.

I can't think of a better person to make that call as Gary, a lifelong Hearts supporter who played for the club longer than anybody else, knows the club inside out and is well versed in its history.

Whether I make your starting eleven or not, Gary, can I wish you the best of luck in your deliberations and long may the Hearts remain glorious!

Dave Mackay
Nottingham, July 2012

1

PICKING MY DREAM TEAM

From virtually the day I fell in love with football I fell in love with Hearts. Even although my father's family had an affiliation with Hibs, it was relatives on my mother's side who guided me towards the best team in Edinburgh. My grandfather Jimmy Munro and my mum's uncle Bill used to have me kicking a football and wearing my Hearts strip as soon as I could walk.

I first played with my grandfather in the big, long hall of his house. It had a cupboard at the top of the hall and the front door was at the other end and these were our makeshift goals when we used to play shooting. I was Donald Ford at that time. When I was out playing with my mates a few years later I was my hero, Ralph Callachan.

My family would constantly talk to me about the players they loved such as Donald Ford, Jim Cruickshank and Eric Carruthers. The love of the Hearts was in their blood and pretty soon was in mine too. My grandfather and great uncle would always speak so vividly and passionately about the players they had witnessed when they stood on the Tynecastle terraces cheering on the team. No matter how great the Hearts teams I was involved in during my playing career, they always used to say they were never as good as the sides that they had seen play.

That is an example of how every Hearts fan will have their own opinion as to who should be in their Dream Team and why I did not have an easy task on my hands in picking my best starting eleven. I took the task very seriously and read a lot of books on the club and spoke to many people for advice and information on the greats of Tynecastle. Many of the players I considered for my Dream Team played long before I was born, while others graced the club after I retired after seventeen proud years with Hearts. Hopefully the joy I got from being involved in the writing of this book will be shared by Hearts supporters from all eras, who will enjoy reading it and remembering all the great stars who have graced our club.

Through the years Heart of Midlothian Football Club has played a part in so many people's lives, with the highlight for many being our famous 5-1 Scottish Cup win over Hibs at Hampden in 2012. The club takes a real hold of you and you can never let go. For instance, I was at a function on 7 April 2012 to celebrate the sixtieth anniversary of Tollcross Hearts. The guy who is chairman of that group, Brian Ross, has been in charge for forty years, which shows the lifelong allegiance Hearts inspires in people.

Now I'm not going to give away my Dream Team, but I will tell you that they will play in a slightly unusual attacking formation. I could have gone 4-3-3, 4-4-2 or 4-1-4-1 before I decided I wanted to go for a set-up that allowed me to pick the greatest players in the history of the club in the same team, and I will unveil my special formation later in the book. The reason for my chosen formation was because I feel, in the tradition of Heart of Midlothian, I want my players to get forward and attack the opposition. That is what I associate most with the maroon and white. A 6-5 win against Dundee United; beating Rangers 4-2 in a Scottish Cup game at Tynecastle; beating Lokomotiv Leipzig 5-1 – those score-lines off the top of my head show what Hearts are about. When I was a player it was all about getting about teams and getting the ball up to wee Robbo to score. Especially against the Hibs! In my grandparents' day the Terrible Trio used to score goals for fun and in recent years men like Rudi Skacel have scored vital goals at vital times for the club, especially in the winning Scottish Cup run of 2012. Others in our famous fan section have gone for different formations, some a bit more defensive than mine, but I am happy with the one I have picked although it wasn't easy choosing the personnel.

I may have picked eleven starters plus seven subs but I must have looked at around eighty serious contenders for my Dream Team before coming to my final decision. There has been some outstanding talent that has represented our club and, by the way, I don't think it is wrong for all Hearts supporters to call it 'our club'. It means that much to us all. The players and management may change but the great support from the fans at Tynecastle remains forever.

There is something magical about Hearts that affects everybody who becomes involved at Tynecastle. Even foreign players like Gilles Rousset look upon Heart of Midlothian as being 'his club'. Move on fifteen years and at that very same Tollcross function I mentioned I heard Marion Kello talking about Hearts as 'his club', despite the fact he had been there only a short amount of time. Maybe it is the same elsewhere but I think there is a romance about Heart of Midlothian Football Club that very few other clubs in the world can match. Hopefully this book can capture some of that romance and magic that surrounds Tynecastle and the greatest football club in the world.

Can I, at this stage, thank Rob Robertson of the *Scottish Daily Mail* for his help in writing this book. Can I also apologise to Rob's partner Claire and his children Kirsten, Clare and Bruce for his prolonged absences late in the evening when we would sit at my kitchen table with a cup of coffee, surrounded by Hearts history books, evaluating the players I would consider for my Dream Team. Also Mark Stanton of Jenny Brown Associates did a power of work to bring this book to fruition.

Can I also thank Davy Allan of London Hearts for all the statistics that are included in the book and who kept me right on the facts and figures. Also can I praise the magnificent contributions made in the famous fans section of the book. Everybody went out their way to make reasoned arguments for choosing their Dream Teams and going through them made fascinating reading.

Can I thank the politicians who contributed and whose love of Heart of Midlothian crossed party lines: First Minister Alex Salmond; Tory MSP David McLetchie; Labour Peer George Foulkes; and former Lord Chancellor Charlie Falconer, who is a huge fan, as is his brother David. Although they may not always see eye to eye with each other on politics, they are united when it comes to Hearts.

John Jeffrey may be one of Scotland's 1990 Grand Slam heroes and a real rugby legend but he has shown in this book he can pick a top-class Hearts Dream Team and knows a thing or two about football tactics. The same goes for my good friend, actor Ken Stott, who put his Dream Team together while filming his latest movie *The Hobbit* in New Zealand. Top ITN correspondent Martin Geissler worked on his Dream Team while filming with British troops in Helmand province in Afghanistan and did a grand job.

I can't thank enough three of Scotland's top sportswriters who have followed Hearts closely through the years. Stuart Bathgate is chief sportswriter at *The Scotsman* newspaper, a role that Mike Aitken used to hold before his retirement, although Mike still has a column in the Hearts programme every other week. Like Mike, Brian Scott has retired from his regular beat on the *Scottish Daily Mail*, but still writes a superb column in that newspaper every Saturday. All three of these distinguished journalists have watched Hearts for decades and know more about the club than most people and can I thank them all for their contributions.

The same applies to Iain Mercer, a former broadcast journalist who now runs the property company started up by his dad Wallace, the former Hearts chairman. Iain and his family still retain a great affection for Hearts and if he had his way, as his Dream Team shows, I would have lost my place back in the early 1990s to a world-famous player!

Also to Campbell Brown and his team at Black & White Publishing, thanks for coming up with the idea for my Hearts Dream Team book, and again thanks to Rob for helping to make it happen.

And finally . . .

When you've finished reading my Dream Team, come and join this debate on my Facebook page, GARY MACKAY'S HEARTS DREAM TEAM, and have your say on the greatest players and managers of the greatest team there is.

2

MACKAY'S MILESTONES AND SOME TYNECASTLE TALES

Born: Edinburgh, 23 January 1964 to Sandra and Peter

Schools: Balgreen Primary School and Tynecastle High School

Boys club: Salvesen Boys Club

Signed for Hearts: July 1980

Matches played: Including challenge matches, testimonials and friendlies as well as competitive games the total reached 737 – 656 starts and eighty-one times coming on as a substitute.

Goals scored: Not as many as I would have liked but I still got ninety-one in total in all competitions, ten of them coming from the penalty spot.

Height: 5 feet 9 inches

Playing weight: 10st 5lb (a bit more than that now)

Competitive debut: Came on as a substitute against Ayr United in a 4-0 away Scottish League Cup defeat on 24 September 1980

Favourite boots: I wore the same pair of Adidas Montevideo for six seasons. Can you imagine a player doing that nowadays?

Three years into my career, after I broke a bone in my foot (or after David Beckham did it I should say I broke my metatarsal) I wore them all the time in games and in training because they had solid Achilles support. There was a shoe repair shop at the top of Haymarket and I went in there with them all the time to get them patched up. I kept getting my Montevideo boots repaired up until they were literally hanging together.

Favourite boot boy: I had a few. Scott Crabbe, Mark Bradley, Gary Naysmith, Paul Ritchie. I maybe gave them a bit of a hard time because I wanted my training kit laid out properly and my boots polished to perfection but it was all part of their apprenticeship.

Nowadays there are kit men doing absolutely everything for the young pros which I feel is very wrong. I always felt that for an apprentice to sweep the Tynecastle terraces on a Monday morning before training was character building and kept their feet on the ground.

Pre-match meal: When I first started at Hearts we always had steak on a Saturday three hours before a game which was crazy as it takes longer than that to digest. Now you would not have steak three days before a game, let alone three hours. When I came to my senses later in my career I would have scrambled egg on toast or grilled fish and then fruit salad.

Pre-match rituals: I would have to sit under the same peg in the corner of the dressing room. On a match day if the strips had been laid out a different way I would ask whoever was sitting where my usual peg was to swap seats. I also never put my strip on in the dressing room, only when I was running down the tunnel.

Half-time rituals: There was one that I nearly started but then thought the better of it. At half time in an Edinburgh derby under Jim Jefferies I was having a pee and Robbo, who was using the urinal next to me, gave his little man a shake and soaked my right boot. I went straight out as a second-half sub with Robbo's pee on my boot, equalised against Hibs at the Gorgie Road end and played a fantastic forty-five minutes of football that helped Hearts come away with a draw. Because it worked once I did think of asking Robbo to pee on my boot every half time but then I realised that wasn't the sort of thing you asked one of the greatest-ever Hearts players of all time to do on a regular basis.

Goal celebration: It all depended on who we were playing. I would kiss the badge against the so-called bigger teams in front of their fans. Especially Hibs. I loved doing that.

Favourite team-mate on the pitch: Not because of his magic pee but because we had a great understanding, it has to be wee Robbo.

Favourite team-mate off the park: Kenny Black knew exactly what it took to be a top professional. He worked as hard as he could in training and gave it his best shot when he played. He also knew because of the pressure you were under you had to enjoy yourself off the field too and, by hell, Kenny knew how to enjoy himself. A great guy. I am sure his involvement with Motherwell and Scotland will have a positive effect on both sets of players.

Best dressing room tipster: Willie Johnston passed around the dressing room some great tips in his day. The best was on one nag called Springle that came in at 33/1. It was my first ever bet and I put a tenner on it and won back £330 plus my stake. Wee Bud got his tip about Springle when we were staying at the Marine Hotel in North Berwick and four of us went in at the same time to the local bookmaker's in the High Street to collect total winnings of £1,360. Can I say we had a good night after our win and wee Bud bought quite a few drinks.

Hardest opponent domestically: The legendary Tommy Burns by a mile. We were beaten 6-0 by Celtic at Parkhead on 1 April 1981 and the Celtic fans in the jungle were calling us April Fools. From start to finish Tommy Burns had me spinning like a top. I did not know if it was New York or New Year. He tore me apart. I did not enjoy the experience but it proved to be an important lesson for me.

Hardest foreign opponent: Safet Susic may not be a well-known name in Scotland but he is a legend in his own country of Bosnia and also in French football. He was an attacking midfielder when we were beaten 4-0 by Paris Saint Germain in France in 1984 and he gave me the run around. I noticed that the readers of *France Football* magazine years later named him PSG's greatest-ever player ahead of the likes of Ronaldinho and George Weah, which made me feel a bit better.

Best international memory: Scoring on my international debut against Bulgaria in 1987, which made me a hero in Ireland as it meant Jack Charlton's team qualified for the European Championships. The fact I was the first Hearts player in thirteen years to pull on an international jersey since Donald Ford made it extra special. My next game after I came back from playing in Sofia was at Pittodrie and the reception I received from the Hearts fans because of my winning goal for Scotland was fantastic. The roars when I ran out on the pitch that day from the Hearts fans will live with me forever.

I didn't go on to have the international career I would have liked but after me John Colquhoun, Henry Smith, Dave McPherson and John Robertson all went on to play for Scotland. Having more and more Hearts players representing their country was a major part in restoring pride in Heart of Midlothian.

Choice of karaoke song: I tried to vary it between 'The Hearts Song' and 'Things' by Bobby Darin. The Hector Nicol version of 'The Hearts Song' is a traditional favourite that highlights what I think is the romance and spirit of Heart of Midlothian. The Bobby Darin song is simply a good one to sing. Sadly, I used to murder them both at team nights out.

Favourite Hearts memory as a player: Any time we beat the Hibs!

Favourite Hearts memory as a fan: I have two. As a lifelong supporter it was the team lifting the Scottish Cup after the win over Rangers at Celtic Park in 1998 that ended years without a trophy and then again at Hampden after the 5-1 win over Hibs in 2012. The feeling when Hibs were beaten was fantastic and a moment to treasure forever. The Scottish Cup win over Gretna in 2006 cannot be forgotten and was another great time for all Hearts fans but I didn't feel the same emotion I did after the wins in 1998 and 2012. I have to admit that I did have a bit of envy, especially after the 1998 win, because I had only left the club the previous year but that is part and parcel of life. I may not have won anything with the club I loved but it was great to see them lifting the Scottish Cup, not once but three times as a fan.

Abiding memory of the 2012 Scottish Cup final win over Hibs: I had hired a mini-bus for my family and friends and drove it to and from the game. On the way back on the M8 near Harthill we found ourselves in the outside lane with the Hearts team bus – with the Scottish Cup proudly on display – on our inside. Gary Locke, Ian Black and a few others did a double-take when they saw the mini-bus alongside them was being driven by me. They gave me a wave and brought the Scottish Cup to the nearside window so I could get a good look. There were lots of big smiles across the motorway lanes and it took the police outriders to move me along as I would have driven beside the bus all the way back to Edinburgh.

Worst Hearts memory: That final league game against Dundee at Dens Park in 1986. I don't have to say any more.

Final game for Hearts: Against Celtic at Parkhead on Saturday, 1 March 1997. The saddest day of my professional life.

3

THE CHAIRMAN AND HIS BOARD

Hearts have had some fantastic chairmen and some top-class directors through the years, most of whom had the best interests of the club at heart. Others may have taken over important roles at the club with the best of intentions but have made a real hash of things and taken us to the brink of extinction. Others have made some crazy decisions without due consideration of the fans, the players or the management team. They all know who they are, and as I like to think this is an upbeat book about the best that Heart of Midlothian has to offer, I am not going to dignify them by mentioning their names. I want to accentuate the positive and nobody did that off the field more for Hearts than the man who I have chosen as my Dream Team chairman.

When Wallace Mercer took over the club in the 1980s the role of the club chairman was becoming more and more significant and demanded a much higher profile than had been the case in the past. The media focused much more on the running of football clubs and the fans wanted their chairman to stand up for their team. Hearts could not have had a better man in that role than Wallace Mercer. He was larger than life. As football players we all had big egos but can I say probably nobody's was as big as Wallace's. He described himself as a controlled egomaniac, and who am I to argue? He was a showman, a leader, an entertainer,

11

an impresario. Just the sort of man Hearts needed to promote and run the club that had been in the doldrums before he strode into Tynecastle. He would beat the drum for Hearts and was never a shrinking violet when it came to making his views known.

Wallace was a very successful businessman before he bought into Hearts but he had a low profile. That was to change over-night when he arrived in Gorgie. Throughout his time at the club he was charismatic and had a good way with people but like all successful businessmen he could be a ruthless bugger at times. He could be very confrontational but I suppose he needed that in-your-face approach in the first place when he was fighting his way up from the bottom of the business ladder. He increased the profile of the club going forward into the 1980s to a level never seen before and, at times – actually make that most of the time – it was great fun to be involved at Tynecastle when he was in charge.

What many people don't remember about Wallace was that a lot of his success came about because he surrounded himself with good people, and I don't just mean on the football side. In the commercial department he employed guys like Robin Fry and Charles Burnett, who were innovators in coming up with new money-spinning ideas. For instance, along with Wallace they came up with the idea of giving away a car donated by Alex-ander, the Ford dealers, through a half time draw. Later they also entered into promotions with Miller Homes for fans to win the incredible prize of a house in the same way.

On top of that Hearts were one of the first Scottish team to come up with the idea of getting a shirt sponsor. Looking back, some of the things they did at Hearts through Wallace's business connections were incredible and innovative. It is fair to say he turned the club around. No disrespect to Bobby Parker when he was chairman in the 1970s, but he did not have the financial acumen to take the club forward and neither did Archie Martin, who I will discuss later. The difference with Wallace was that he came with a bit of money and knew how to use it to benefit the club, although he had a tough time clearing their debts early on in his time in charge.

Now he would be the first person to tell you he was not a great Hearts fan before he bought the club. He wasn't even a football man, as rugby was his game. He used to play for London Scottish when he was based down south and if he had an affiliation to any club it would be Rangers and there was a time he owned shares in them. In fact, when he first became majority share-holder at Hearts he was clever, as he knew he didn't have a huge football knowledge so appointed Edinburgh publican Alex Naylor as the club chairman for an interim period until he learned the ropes. Naylor left in less than a year and then the Mercer era really kicked in.

Although he was a supporter of the Tory Party he had empathy with the fans and on more than one occasion when the British unemployment rate in the 1980s topped the three million mark he let those out of work into Tynecastle for free. I remember one game in particular against Motherwell which ended in a boring no-scoring draw. I remember that match because it was so bad one newspaper did a piece saying it was lucky that Wallace had let half the crowd in for free as the other half had been robbed after having to pay to watch such rubbish.

I was a young apprentice when Wallace and Kenny Waugh were fighting it out to take over at Tynecastle and, to be honest, out of the two I had a better feeling about Kenny. That was because he made an effort to speak to us apprentices, whereas Wallace didn't. Kenny was higher profile than Wallace as he was an Edinburgh publican, but the down side was that his family had strong links to Hibs.

I must admit I could not have told you what Wallace looked like until his picture appeared in the paper a few days before he took over at Hearts. He was only in his thirties and was not well known at all to me or our fans. It was only when Donald Ford enlisted him to the consortium he was forming to try and take over the club did the name of Wallace Mercer start to make headlines.

From the off he was a real showman, going as far as introducing 100 metre Olympic Gold medallist Allan Wells to the fans at Shandon Snooker Club on Slateford Road as part of his campaign to win control. In the end he narrowly won the boardroom vote 3-2, ahead of Kenny Waugh, and the Mercer revolution started to happen. He showed his early ruthlessness by sacking Bobby Moncur after just thirteen days because his gut instinct was he was not a man he could work with.

Wallace always aimed high and I remember he was knocked back by both Jim McLean and Jock Wallace as he tried to find a replacement for Bobby. With the best will in the world, giving the manager's job on a short-term basis to Tony Ford who had been first-team coach under Bobby Moncur was not his greatest decision, but he soon saw the error of his ways and Tony didn't last long.

When you look at Wallace's overall record in charge it is clear he was a major force for good for Hearts. I accept things did not start well when Alex MacDonald took charge but remember he had only taken over from Tony Ford in March so did not have a full season to work with the players. Things were bad that season as the club was in turmoil because Wallace's rebuilding plans were at an early stage. That season the club declared a loss of over £380,000 with gate receipts only totalling £144,000 but Wallace's brain was working hard at new fund-raising ideas.

I remember clearly the second leg of the Scottish League Cup semi-final against Rangers on 27 October 1982, but not because of the result. We had lost the first leg at Ibrox 2-0 and knew we would struggle to overturn that deficit. Wallace wanted to boost the crowd so a week before he announced he would be introducing his first-ever half time draw where a £35,000 house and a Ford Sierra car were up for grabs. We got 19,000 in that night for a publicity stunt that got huge coverage in papers all over Britain as no club had ever done anything like it before. Unfortunately the result was not as good as the half-time promotion, as we lost 2-1 to go out on a 4-1 aggregate.

I had very few dealings with the Hearts board directly as I always kept a respectful distance as I was a young player. The most memorable meeting I ever had with Wallace and his gang was at a lunch that I will never forget. When I was away on honeymoon in 1987, the Hearts directors accepted a bid of £500,000 for me from Dundee United. It was a decent amount of money back then, probably too much for my signature! Hearts had sold Dave Bowman to Coventry City for £200,000 three years before, which helped keep the club afloat, so there was no pressure on me to leave. I spoke to club secretary Les Porteous and told him I would rather stay than go and soon afterwards I was taken to a top-class restaurant with him and Wallace to discuss my future.

The swanky joint, called Rafaeli's, has long since changed its name but it was just around the corner from where Harry's Bar is in the west end of Edinburgh. We went there and over lunch I negotiated, on my own, a new four-year contract. Les and Wallace had more than a few glasses of wine but I kept a clear head to do my deal. No agents for me in those days. Everything I did, I did myself. I would never have thought I would be negotiating a contract with someone with the business experience of Wallace at a posh Edinburgh restaurant where the deal was sealed with a handshake. To be fair, he did not take advantage of my lack of financial acumen and I felt he gave me a decent deal. He was good at pulling out all the stops with players when he wanted you to stay and would treat you like royalty to get you to sign a new contract. As well as signing a new deal to stay at Hearts I got the best meal of my life into the bargain. Not a bad afternoon's work, if I do say so myself.

My abiding memory of that meal, apart from the final bill for it, which was enormous, is that I saw for the first time someone snapping their fingers to get the attention of the waiter. Wallace only did it once but I felt a bit uncomfortable at his actions, but it wasn't done in an arrogant way, as that was just the way he was. It was his way of drawing attention to himself. It was just Wallace being Wallace. It wasn't the sort of thing I would do, but Wallace was a man who didn't think twice about snapping his fingers and expect people to come running.

Apart from that top-class lunch that secured me a new four-year deal, I didn't have a personal friendship with Wallace in that we never socialised together, but that was the same for most of the players, particularly the younger ones, because he was our chairman and there was a gap between us. I never knocked on Wallace's door in anger on a matter involving myself, although I did protest to the board, along with wee Robbo, about Alex MacDonald being removed from his job.

The only other time I nearly came close to battering down his door was when Sandy Clark was manager for about a year before Wallace sold out to Chris Robinson and Leslie Deans. I felt it would have been beneficial for Heart of Midlothian Football Club if Wallace had put a clause in the contract he drew up when he sold the club that made it clear Sandy had to be retained as manager under Robinson and Deans. The work Sandy did at the club at the time made me think it would have been common sense to have kept him on rather than get rid of him for no good reason, which is what happened in the end. To this day I regret not banging on Wallace's door on that issue before he sold the club and left Tynecastle for good.

By the same token, after being in contact with Wallace's wife Anne in researching this book, I am satisfied Wallace fought as best he could to keep Sandy in a job and was deeply upset when Robinson dismissed him so quickly.

Apart from those few isolated incidents I got on pretty well with Wallace, who gave me a few laughs along the way. I remember in particular in February 1989 being in Germany for the UEFA Cup quarter-final second leg against Bayern Munich. An Iain Ferguson goal had given us a 1-0 lead to defend in the Olympic Stadium and we were confident going into the match. At the official reception the night before, Edinburgh Lord Provost Eleanor McLaughlin was walking about in her chains of office. Jimmy Caldwell, a friend of our sprint coaches Bert Logan and George McNeill, asked to borrow her chains to put round the neck of Wallace and as he did he called him the true Provost of Edinburgh. Did Wallace love being called that! He walked about proud as punch with a big grin on his face. You know something? I could never begrudge Wallace's bits of fun as he had worked hard to earn his time in the sun. With Wallace in charge we had every right to think the sky was the limit in terms of ambition. He always aimed high in life, so why should we not as players do the same? Having such a confident chairman gave the players confidence too.

It would only really be the fans who had followed the Hearts in the 1970s through very bad times who would be able to put into context the pride Wallace brought back to the club. He was the leader of the renaissance of Hearts and laid the platform for future success. He was a people person and learned early on how to keep the media on side, as he knew their important role as opinion formers. I have heard stories from journalists about Wallace bringing champagne into the press room after big wins and being a great host to them.

As players that extravagance was never splashed out on us because he could never have allowed himself to get too chummy with the players like he did certain members of the press, as there could come a day he would be telling us we were leaving the club against our will. According to Mike Aitken, the hugely respected former chief football writer of *The Scotsman*, Wallace called more press conferences than any other chairman in the history of Scottish football. Hardly a day went by when Wallace's name wasn't in the papers. The papers called him 'The Great Waldo', while Mike, who was one of Scotland's finest sportswriters, kept comparing Wallace to Phineas T. Barnum, the great American showman.

I will remember Wallace as a man who kept the vast majority of the promises he made. He did his best not to sell off our best players for short-term gain, helped stabilise the club when it was going to rack and ruin, and built a real family atmosphere at Tynecastle. Wallace boosted the profile of Hearts and himself no end throughout Scotland. He even had his own television show on BBC Scotland for a while and also hosted a chat show on Radio Forth where his guests included Malcolm Rifkind, who was the then Secretary of State for Scotland. Because of all his radio work he got one of his nicknames: 'Wireless Mercer'.

In 1984 we had a total home gate of 125,000, which was the first year after we made it back into the Premier League. By the end of the 1988 season we had 450,000 fans through the doors of Tynecastle. These figures tell their own story. Wallace always did his best to look after the players financially and ironically the season we were paid the most is the one I always want to forget but sadly the memories never die.

Before the 1985-86 season we came to an agreement that bonuses would only be paid after every four games, rather than on a simple win bonus per game. At a time when it was two points for a win we received next to nothing if we did not take at least six out of eight points. That season because of our great league run we regularly got at least six points out of every four games, sometimes eight, and Wallace gladly put his hand in his pocket to pay us. There was a big bonus paid for four wins in a row, and we got a few of them. That season when we played thirty-six league games we lost just six – all away from home – and drew ten. It may have been a lucrative year financially but it goes without saying I would have gladly given all the money back to Wallace in return for a championship medal.

The one matter that caused controversy during Wallace's time in charge was his attempt to take over Hibs. Because my father's family were always big Hibs fans I was never sure trying to unite Edinburgh in football terms by creating one big team would have worked. Then again, there were a lot of things I wasn't convinced would work under Wallace and they did, but I always had a gut feeling from the start this would not be one of them. As a Hearts player I always wanted the opportunity to take on Hibs in an Edinburgh derby. I used to dream about playing in such a game as a kid and to achieve my aim was a privilege. To take that away from me, from a professional point of view, would have disappointed me greatly. It would have also disappointed the Hearts fans who always love to beat Hibs.

In a way, what Wallace's attempted takeover of Hibs did, in a similar way that Save Our Hearts did for our club, was to galvanise their supporters into realising things had to change at their football club because they were being mismanaged. That is the complete opposite of where they are now as they are as professionally well run within the boardroom as any club in Scotland. Back then it was maybe a hunch Wallace had to try and buy over Hibs and he maybe reacted too quickly to that hunch. Nobody really had thought long-term about it before his plan became public and I always felt everything had been a bit rushed.

With hindsight, after the troubles it caused – what with people running onto the pitch at games, us having to get police escorts and having to stay at a hotel across in Fife before the first derby after the takeover plan was announced – the whole thing left a bad taste in the mouths of a lot of people. But what I would not want it to do, and Hibs supporters have to understand this as well, is to detract from what Wallace did for Hearts. If Wallace had not stepped in during the early 1980s we would not have had so many great memories. For example, lifelong fan ITN correspondent Martin Geissler remembers elsewhere in the book Hearts playing Bayern Munich in the Olympic Stadium. Getting to that level of competition would not have happened unless Wallace had taken the club by the scruff of the neck.

Trying to take over Hibs for £7.5 million wasn't his finest hour but he did far, far many more good things for Hearts that should not be overshadowed by one of the few things he, in my opinion, got wrong. Looking back, I firmly believe that Wallace Mercer and the board he appointed were the men that put the heart back in Heart of Midlothian Football Club and in hindsight it turned out to be a dark day when he sold out in June 1994.

He may have been an unknown thirty-three-year-old when he took over Hearts but when he left thirteen years later after selling out to Chris Robinson and Leslie Deans for £2 million, he was known throughout Scotland.

Football finance is something I know little about but Wallace was always proud of the fact that if you had bought one hundred Hearts shares for £100 back in 1981 they would be worth £750 when he left. It was only right that he was made an Honorary Life President of Hearts in May 1994 but I found it sad that he had to fight through the courts at a later stage to be allowed into the boardroom on match days, which should have been his automatic right.

He always kept pictures of his beloved Hearts at his home in North Berwick and in the south of France and his passing in January 2006 at the age of just fifty-nine was a sad day for the club. In a way, Wallace was a benevolent dictator, although in the boardroom he had top-class lieutenants who were Hearts men through and through to try and keep him under control. His board members make up the majority of my Hearts Dream Team board, with a couple of very important additions.

Pilmar Smith, a lifelong Hearts fan, will be my Dream Team vice chairman, with Les Porteous being the club secretary. Douglas Park, who although he wasn't a Hearts fan was another larger than life character, and he also gets a seat at the table. He owned Park's of Hamilton, the bus company that is still well respected to this day, and I noticed that Douglas was one of the names linked with The Blue Knights consortium that tried to take over Rangers.

Pilmar, who was a self-employed bookie and a lifelong Hearts fan who was at the club morning, noon and night, did his best to keep Wallace focused as his mind could wander a bit as he had so many different interests outside the club. Pilmar's role on my Hearts Dream Team board would be to represent the interests of Hearts fans, as he did that superbly when Wallace was in charge. He also supervised the redevelopment of Tynecastle and through his links with the Scottish Labour Party brought some high-profile guests to our games.

I remember Neil Kinnock, who was the then leader of the Labour Party, being at one of our matches against Falkirk at Brockville when he sat next to Wallace. Obviously the television cameras and photographers were crowding round them and it has got to be said Wallace loved it. I'm not sure if Kinnock ever realised that in the eyes of the Hearts fans Wallace was the more famous of the two of them! I remember Wallace being very polite to Mr Kinnock after the game, although clearly he must have realised Wallace was a big Tory and voting Labour was something he would never do.

Les Porteous used to be involved with Newtongrange Star before he was taken on as club secretary in 1980. He was the man Wallace used to describe as his rock because he was always so dependable and he would definitely ensure everything runs smoothly off the field in my Dream Team. Les used to describe himself in football parlance as the sweeper because he was always mopping up behind everybody else, especially Wallace who wanted his orders carried out to the letter. He was the practical type who was an incredibly efficient and able club secretary.

Douglas Park could be as loud and abrasive as Wallace could be, and one thing is for sure, Wallace could be loud and abrasive. Not surprisingly, I was told some of the board meetings were absolute humdingers when the pair of them were in the same room and going at it hammer and tongs. These guys were never 'yes' men and Wallace had hand-picked them for his board because of it. Wallace was aware of his tendency to go over the top and try and push through even the craziest of plans. These directors were hand-picked by him to make sure some of his more madcap schemes never got off the starting blocks and that trio would keep him in check in the Dream Team boardroom.

Les and Pilmar had ideas themselves and would put them forward to the board and then the directors would discuss them, with Wallace trying his best to have the final say. When I used to think of Wallace's style as chairman I used to remember one of Brian Clough's famous sayings which was, 'If I had an argument with a player we would sit down for twenty minutes, talk about it and then decide I was right!' I always felt the Hearts board meetings would be held along those lines, with Wallace's strength of personality dominating proceedings, although I don't think he got his way all the time like the legendary Mr Clough.

When he took over, Wallace kept Bobby Parker around the club, the only member of the previous board he retained, and I want him on my Dream Team board. Wallace's decision to keep Bobby made perfect sense to me as he provided a link with the past in that he had been a great player and former chairman. He also had great boardroom experience at Tynecastle before Wallace came on the scene. He became a director from 1970, chairman from 1974-80 and then remained a director for three years under Wallace. I like to think Bobby would be an influential father figure to Wallace in my Dream Team boardroom. I remember in the early days of Wallace's time in charge he always sat next to Bobby at first-team games. Bobby was also a regular at reserve matches when I was coming through the system and Wallace was clever enough to realise it was in his benefit to keep such a Hearts legend on side. Bobby was also instrumental in Alex MacDonald becoming Hearts manager. Alex was having so many injury problems when he was a player at Hearts that he was nearly swapped for Lex Richardson of St Mirren.

It was only after a chat with Bobby Parker did Wallace decide to keep him on and he went even further than that. On Bobby's recommendation he made Alex player/coach six months after he arrived at Tynecastle.

The final two members of my Heart boardroom are men who, in their own special way, made major contributions to the club. One came before Wallace, the other years later, but both have a place in the history of Hearts. Archie Martin, who was one of the unsung heroes of Tynecastle, is a former club chairman who deserves to be remembered for his contribution to the club. He was a Hearts supporter who came onto the board at the end of Bobby Parker's time as chairman and subsequently took over from him although, as I mentioned earlier, Bobby remained on the board.

I have chosen Archie to be part of my board because he, like Wallace, had the best interests of the club at heart. Archie was not a flamboyant character, although he was always well turned out and his style of dress is what I remember about him more than anything else. He had real class and he spoke and explained things in laymen's terms, which was helpful to young players like me. His forte when he was at Hearts was to bring in younger players to the club who were Edinburgh boys that other clubs from both sides of the border were trying to sign. The first group he convinced to sign for Hearts included Ian Westwater, David Bowman, Stuart Gauld who had a good career in Ireland, myself and Robbo at a slightly later date.

When Archie was trying to convince me to sign when Bobby Moncur was manager, he took my mum and dad out for dinner to discuss things. He told them straight how much they would pay me as an apprentice and they were impressed by his honesty and caring attitude. I had other offers on the table and I am sure I would have taken one of them up if it had not been for my love of Hearts and the persuasive powers of Archie on my mum and dad. Although Archie was pushing at an open door when he made me an offer to sign for Hearts, it was one simple act by him that made me certain I would join my boyhood heroes.

When I was a youngster Ian 'Boobs' Brown took us for training but it was always at venues away from my beloved Tynecastle. I had been inside the stadium before but had never set foot through the front door and turned left to go towards the changing rooms before I signed. I may have gone in occasionally through a different door on the way to what was called 'the Brown gymnasium' at the club but never walked down the tunnel or onto the pitch. Taking me out onto hallowed turf and showing me round the stadium should have been part of Hearts' attempts to sign me, or any other player for that matter, but only when Archie came along and intervened personally at the eleventh hour did it happen.

It was ironic that I trained at Hibs for a year, been on trial at Celtic and also Rangers, had interest from Manchester United but I had not been allowed in the changing room or out onto the pitch of the team I supported until Archie showed me round the stadium and made my mind up for me to sign. On the day I put pen to paper Archie made it clear I would have a chance of making it into the first team early if I was good enough. He explained he didn't really want to pay lots of money for journeymen players who had been round the block a few times and instead wanted to invest in youth and give youngsters he thought could go all the way to the top a chance in the first team and, to be fair, he was true to his word.

It would be fascinating to be a fly on the wall at a Hearts Dream Team board meeting with Wallace as chairman and Archie also on the board. My instinct is that the pair would get along but Wallace, being the stronger character, would rule the roost.

My final member of my Hearts Dream Team board is a man who was important in our Save Our Hearts campaign and came through some tough times when he was chairman with his dignity intact. George Foulkes came onto the Hearts board as chairman after the Bank of Scotland, to whom Hearts owed lots of money, demanded a fair-minded and independent man to try and guide the team through troubled times. They could not have chosen a better person.

George did his best in difficult circumstances and was kept on in the role by Vladimir Romanov when he arrived at Tynecastle. His time as chairman under him was short and not terribly sweet. George has admitted to me through the years that he should have resigned in protest when George Burley was sacked rather than toe the party line. When Romanov went on to sack Hearts chief executive Phil Anderton that proved to be the final straw and George resigned then in protest.

I have put George on my Hearts Dream Team board because he knows the club inside out and would do a great job. He has stood on the terraces as a fan, spent time in the boardroom as chairman, and knows what it takes to ensure the club remains on an even keel. He was also vital in the Save Our Hearts campaign that kept the club at Tynecastle as I mentioned earlier and for that I will be eternally grateful.

George would be a major off-the-field figurehead for my Dream Team as he understands the history of the club and remains a great ambassador for Hearts. George has a real sense of fun and enthusiasm about him and I think he would get on well with Wallace and the rest of the Dream Team directors.

Wallace always used to describe his board members as his best of friends and also his best of enemies. He respected them all as men but he used to joke they were a pain in the neck when they didn't agree with him. I think the Dream Team directors I have chosen to work with him would not agree with him all the time but he would have great fun working with them, of that I have no doubt.

4

THE BEST BOSSES

Compared to some Hearts players who have been at the club over the past decade I suppose I played under relatively few managers during my seventeen years at Tynecastle. Nowadays the merest suggestion that results are going against a team and the pressure is on the manager immediately. In fact, even when results were going in Hearts' favour during George Burley's managerial reign he still lost his job.

Make no mistake, it takes a certain type of person to be a good manager and to withstand the pressure that goes with the job. I had a stab at it with Airdrie and it didn't really work out. I was an example of a player who didn't make the grade as a manager but in the history of Hearts that hasn't always been the case. Take for example the first person I considered for the role of my Dream Team manager. I never saw Tommy Walker's team in action but my grandfather Jimmy Munro spoke warmly of that trophy-laden era. He remembers the discipline and the fitness all the players had in what was mostly a golden time for the club. They would go into most seasons under Tommy thinking they had a good opportunity to win trophies because of the quality of the squad that he had assembled.

Tommy was in charge for the most successful period in the history of the club and an indication of the importance of his success came from the fact that after the Scottish Cup victory of 1956 we did not win it again for another forty-two years. Tommy put a squad together that was so talented that my grandfather used to say it was a privilege to watch them in action. There were always goals in the team; they were always attacking and always a joy to watch.

I will mention Tommy's playing career in a different chapter but here I will concentrate on his managerial career. Many will feel that he should have been an automatic choice for my Dream Team manager and I can understand their thinking. He picked up more trophies than any other manager, spent more time in the hot seat than any other coach and came back as a director where he did a lot more great work for the club. I have huge respect for Tommy but I will explain later why he isn't my choice, although many in the famous fans section of the book have named him as their Dream Team manager.

He had returned to Hearts from Chelsea in 1948 where he assumed the dual role of player and assistant to manager David McLean. David had taken over in 1941 from Frank Moss, the ex-Arsenal and England goalkeeper who had been in charge for three and a half years previously.

Tommy only played one game, against Dundee, before hanging up his boots for good and becoming David's full-time number two. Before Tommy came on board, David had done a great job bringing young players through the system at Tynecastle, especially during the war years.

Other teams used to bring in high-profile guest players to boost crowds to keep the money coming in during the Second World War. David was a huge believer in giving youth a chance and turned his back on such a short-term fix to give youngsters a chance in his team, like Jimmy Brown, Tom Mackenzie, Charlie Cox, John Urquhart and a certain young man called Alfie Conn. It paid dividends and David was building a great young team in the years immediately after the Second World War. Unfortunately he did not have the chance to see the fruits of his labour as he died after a long illness in 1951 just as his young players were reaching maturity.

Tommy Walker was thrust into the hot seat immediately and when he became Hearts manager he already had the Terrible Trio – Alfie Conn, Willie Bauld and Jimmy Wardhaugh – at the club, as well as top players like Freddie Glidden and John Cumming. With Dave Mackay also around, along with Willie Duff and Ian Crawford, it isn't surprising that Tommy was spoiled for choice when it came to choosing his starting eleven.

When the League Cup was won in 1954 under Tommy it was Hearts' first trophy in forty-eight years. An indication of how many great players David McLean had brought through beforehand came from the fact that eight of the winning team had been recruited by him. It was a fact Tommy Walker readily acknowledged at the time. That was just the start of Tommy's successful spell as Hearts manager as under him his team also won the Scottish Cup in 1956 then the league title in 1957-58.

Now for me it is always a sign of a top-class manager that he knows when time is up for his more senior players. Tommy had the guts to phase out the Terrible Trio and bring in players like Jimmy Murray, Alex Young and Gordon Smith and he still managed to win another league title in 1959-60 and two League Cups, but sadly the league title was lost in a last-day defeat to Kilmarnock in 1964-65. He resigned in 1966 after a few bad results but returned in our centenary year of 1974 to take up a position on the board where he stayed until 1980.

Tommy seemed to have his famous fans, even in Parliament. Shortly after Tam Dalyell was elected as an MP he was interviewed by the editor of the *Linlithgow Gazette* and was asked: 'And who was your hero?'

'Frankly, Tommy Walker,' was the reply from the highly respected politician.

Willie McCartney was another whose team caught the imagination of a previous generation. He had joined the club in 1919 and had taken over from his father John, who had been in charge of Hearts for the ten years previous. John McCartney did a grand job and reports at the time suggest that his team would have won major honours if it had not been for the outbreak of the First World War. His son Willie had the task of rebuilding the side that had lost many of their players during the conflict.

The blackest day in the history of Hearts came at the Battle of the Somme in 1916. The 16th Royal Scots, which became known as the legendary McCrae's Battalion, lost almost three-quarters of their men, including several Heart of Midlothian footballers. A memorial in the honour of the fallen, paid for by public subscription, has since been erected at Contalmaison in northern France near to where the fighting took place. I had the privilege of laying a wreath there with my friend, actor Ken Stott, and it was an emotional experience for both of us.

Losing so many of his top players in such tragic circumstances meant that Willie McCartney had a difficult task on his hands in 1918 when the war came to an end. Things did not start well for him, and although Hearts drew big crowds during the early 1920s, results did not go their way and they were nearly relegated in 1922. To be fair to the Hearts board, they persevered with Willie and he turned the club around. One of the most famous players ever in the history of Hearts has to be Barney Battles junior, who I discuss elsewhere in the book, as he scored goal after goal for Hearts when Willie was in charge. Although no trophies were won the crowds were growing and McCartney brought a feel-good factor to Tynecastle.

Back then a manager did absolutely everything at a club. Willie asked in 1933 to pass on some of his administrative duties to a chief executive type, which was granted. Unfortunately having more time with the players had no real impact and in June 1935 he resigned but he did a lot for the club before leaving and has to be congratulated for guiding them so well over such a long period.

I am told Willie left under a cloud, which would have been a shame. It seems the chairman gave him a new contract but he then tried to interfere with his team selections. A chairman meddling in team affairs? Now where have I heard that before at Tynecastle? It was a real body blow for Hearts supporters that he left to go to Hibs, which made the situation even worse.

During my research for this book I felt that the men who were technically the first two managers of Hearts deserve an honorable mention. Up until 1901 when Peter Fairley was appointed, team affairs were run by the Hearts board of directors. Peter was called secretary–manager and although administrative work took up most of his time he had a say in who played on a Saturday, although ultimately the final decision still lay with the all-powerful board of directors. When he left in 1903 his attempts to get more involved in picking the team made it easier for the new manager William Waugh to put more pressure on the board to do the same. William was actively involved in advising the board on how the players were doing in training and recommended who should play on a Saturday. He seemed to have had very big ideas because he applied unsuccessfully to manage Arsenal and by all accounts was so devastated at getting a knock back he left Hearts in 1908, never to return to football. Instead he bought and ran a bar in Broxburn.

Hearts have had so many good managers through the years and it was difficult to pick out the ones who deserved a mention and some, like the next man, you may not agree with. I accept that the name of Bobby Moncur being mentioned in the same breath as some of our greatest managers is something that many true Jambos will struggle to comprehend, but please let me explain.

Although Bobby never made a big impression on the fans he had a big impact in the dressing room. He was certainly a big influence on me when I was starting out and also did a lot for the club in the short time he was there in terms of taking on the old guard and improving the all-round professionalism at the club. I was slightly in awe of him to begin with, as he was an experienced Scotland internationalist and famous for being the only Newcastle United captain to lift European honours when his team won the Fairs Cup back in 1969. It was Bobby who signed me, Ian Westwater, Dave Bowman and John Robertson when Archie Martin was chairman. We got £3,000 each in total to sign. One thousand five hundred up front and the rest when we made our debut and I think Archie paid that out of his own pocket, at least that is what I am led to believe.

Bobby had a great presence about him but like a few of the managers who were at the club during my time he was in the wrong place at the wrong time. I felt sorry for him because he was up against it from the start. No disrespect to a lot of the players who were at Heart of Midlothian when I started out, but the term 'professional' would have been used very loosely in relation to most of them. There were a lot of really good lads but the professional element was not there.

Too many people did their own thing off the pitch and they could not, or would not, adhere to the discipline Bobby tried to instil in them. The way Bobby tried to bring them into line was probably good for the young guys there like me and Robbo because it gave us an idea of the discipline needed to succeed at the top level. Being told that was the way to do things by such a hugely respected figure as Bobby Moncur taught us good practice early on. As impressionable young lads he made a big impact on us.

There were some who wanted to work against Bobby's discipline and the structure of how he wanted Heart of Midlothian to be as a club. He brought Tony Ford in as his coach and assistant and Tony was not a man who would ever turn away from verbal confrontation if it came his way. Both were good operators but neither of the two had a hands-on feel of Scottish football. That did not help them because they could not work the transfer system in Scotland because ultimately the aim for Hearts when he came was to get out of the old first division but by spending as little money on new players as possible.

I know Wallace Mercer never saw eye to eye with Bobby and got rid of him just thirteen days after he took over the club but I think that might have come as a blessed relief for Bobby, as I firmly believe he was on the verge of chucking it anyway through frustration. He could not work in an environment where the level of professionalism and high work ethic that he was used to at Newcastle United was not shown by many of the players at Hearts.

Bobby was really into youth development and fully behind my signing and was aware Archie Martin was trying to bring in promising local lads. Ian 'Boobs' Brown, who was the Hearts youth coach, watched me playing and recommended me to the club in the first instance but it was no foregone conclusion I would sign for my boyhood heroes. Robbo, David Bowman and I all had a bit of press because we had represented Scottish schoolboys and Manchester United was among the clubs that were interested in signing me. It had been a while since Hearts had signed any schoolboy internationalists as they had all gone to other clubs with bigger budgets. I'm not saying schoolboy internationalists are better players than others of the same age who maybe were just overlooked but it did make a difference to me being part of the Scotland set-up when I was at school.

Luckily that international side I was in was full of good players and Bobby Moncur always felt playing alongside top-class talent as a youngster made you a better player yourself. I had guys like Paul McStay, Eric Black, and Brian Rice in the Scotland Under-15 team, which was top quality. During my school days, unless you were signed on an S Form you were not aligned to a professional club. Bobby encouraged me every step of the way in my early days at Hearts and I made my debut under him against Ayr United in a Scottish League Cup match down at Somerset Park on 24 September 1980 when I came on as a substitute. We were beaten 4-0 and although it was a thrill to play what happened afterwards left a bad taste in my mouth and was a graphic illustration of the lack of professionalism I was talking about earlier.

Some players were laughing and joking on the bus home to Edinburgh, having been well beaten by Ayr United. They were drinking beer, playing cards and all that. I am not decrying any individuals. It was just the way the club was at the time. Bobby was sitting in silence, probably disgusted, at the front of the bus. I think at that moment he realised he was going to struggle to get rid of all the bad habits.

Another indication of that lack of professionalism that I remember came when we were sent back from training at Saughton Enclosure because he was not happy with the attitude of some of the players. Jim Denny and Willie McVie were involved in a bust-up and he called a halt to training because of it. Some of the players were delighted training had finished an hour early as it meant they could get down to the bookies. That summed up the lack of commitment felt by some of the players to the football club and I found that disgraceful.

Through it all Bobby retained a dignity that was to be admired, even when he knew the fates were conspiring against him. I am not sure if some of the players were a bit jealous of Bobby because he was a Scots guy who had done well in England, unlike most of them. Or maybe the players had got used to running the changing room under previous manager Willie Ormond and didn't want to lose their power.

The feedback I get from my friends in the north of England is that Newcastle United officials still realise Bobby's importance to their club where he is still idolised and where he is currently a club ambassador. That is the way it should be for someone who deserves legendary status at Tyneside. When I look back at what he achieved as a player the respect that should have been afforded to him at Tynecastle was never given. He tried his best when he was in charge of Hearts and it took a brave man to take on the more experienced players in the dressing room. I put him in my Dream Team managerial discussions due to the fact he tried to introduce a more professional culture to Tynecastle. Those who did take on what he was saying, like myself and wee Robbo, became better players for it.

A few managers down the line Joe Jordan came in and I felt he freshened up Hearts although, again, I accept not everyone will agree. He had been at AC Milan and had some great qualities as a manager, although I did not like what he asked me to do as a player. He asked me to play as a wing-back in a 3-5-2 formation. Joe was a bit ahead of his time when it came to training, which was different than it had been under previous managers. It was more methodical and better thought out. It wasn't all about bursting your gut running around and a lot of our time we spent working on tactics. That was foreign to us but it paid dividends as we learned a lot.

What helped Joe was the fact he had Frank Connor as his assistant, who was an absolute magnificent football man and a great individual, but he couldn't take the physical side of training, like the warm-ups, because an old football injury meant he was not physically able to get about. I think he might have had a hip problem, so Joe was with us on the training field a lot more than most managers.

By the same token, Frank's role cannot be under-estimated. He was an honest man who was of the old school when it came to football matters. If you got on the wrong side of him or had a bad game you would beware of his tongue come Monday morning. Frank demanded respect and from day one, although he was the spitting image of the Reverend Ian Paisley and knew that himself, he warned us never, ever to call him Reverend as a joke. We didn't have the guts to do that to his face but muttered it under our breath if he was having a pop at us in the dressing room.

When I look back now I wish I had bought into a lot more of what Joe and Frank told me. In saying that, I was not the only one. Others took a dislike to the way he ran the club, which I never did. I just wanted to do my best for Hearts but I must admit I struggled by playing in the formation he put together. Joe, to be fair to him, was a bit ahead of his time not just in terms of training as I mentioned earlier but also in the way he prepared his team and set them up on a Saturday. The game was changing. It was about preparing properly, having a proper shape to the team and Joe was a master at that.

Under Alex MacDonald and Sandy Jardine we just sort of went out and played. Under Joe it was more structured and he took part in all the warm-ups and could have still played for us as he looked in great condition. I still have great respect for him and it is no surprise to me that he has helped Harry Redknapp mould Tottenham Hotspur into one of the top sides in England before he left the club at the end of the 2011-12 season. I am not sure he has the same respect for me and other individuals who played under him at Hearts, which is a source of regret. When you look at what Joe went on to achieve in the game, some of us could have given him that little bit more and tried harder to make Hearts a better side under him.

In a way it was not just the players who lost a bit of faith in him, as the actions of chairman Wallace Mercer suggested he had too. As far as I am aware, in the season when we were challenging for the 1991-92 league title and ended up finishing second, Joe had asked at Christmastime for a bit of money to sign Stan Collymore, but the club would not back him. He felt getting Stan would have taken the club to the next stage. When you look at what Stan achieved in the game as a player then it is obvious it would have.

Joe had an eye for players and brought in other guys like Glynn Snodin from Leeds United in 1992. For some reason the fans nicknamed him 'The Lord' and he paid back Joe with some decent performances and the winning goal against Slavia Prague in the UEFA Cup on 30 September 1992 when his thirty-yard free-kick went into the keeper's top right hand in front of the School End. Although Joe hadn't long finished playing when he took over at Hearts and had known some of the players from his time with Scotland, he was never close to us as a squad. Maybe that came from his experiences in Italy where I can't imagine the managers were ever that close to the players.

Two semi-finals and runners-up in the league was a good return for Joe but the writing was on the wall when we were beaten 6-0 by Falkirk at Brockville on 1 May 1993. The fans had clearly lost faith in Joe and the team because I remember Hearts reserves won the league at Motherwell the day we were beaten at Brockville. There was a bigger Hearts support at Motherwell than Brockville. I had the flu before the game and Frank Connor had asked me to take a flu jab because we were really struggling for numbers. I could look myself in the mirror after trying my best to play well while still being under the weather. Am I convinced others did that day? No. I maintain to this day some players were not too perturbed about Joe being sacked. I was never in that camp as I appreciated what he had tried to do. I was saddened every time a manager was sacked. If you are not as a player, there is something wrong with you.

Not many people can make the jump from player into the manager's chair but Sandy Clark did that pretty easily. He took over from Joe in April 1993 with three league matches to go and what Wallace Mercer saw in him was someone who knew the club well, who identified young players for the club and had a great eye for picking talent.

Sandy was a big personality who made a huge impact on the training ground at Roseburn and who brought on a lot of young lads that would go on to have long careers, as I mentioned elsewhere in the book. Sometimes things in football fit like a glove. I thought Sandy Clark and Heart of Midlothian fitted like a glove.

I accept his results were not brilliant near the end of his time in charge, but the way Sandy was removed was wrong. I don't know if Tommy McLean had already been earmarked to take over when the new owners Chris Robinson and Leslie Deans took control of the club, but either way the writing seemed to be on the wall for Sandy the minute they bought out Wallace Mercer. I felt the way that Sandy was removed was not done with any class befitting such a great servant of Hearts. The speed of his dismissal was very wrong. He had been at Hearts for a decade but the minute Robinson walked through the door he sacked him.

From a personal point of view, the men who came in to replace him may not have made much of an outward impact on Hearts but there was a wealth of experience among Tommy McLean and his assistant Tom Forsyth and first-team coach Eamonn Bannon. They had relative success at Motherwell before they turned up at Tynecastle but I have to admit it took me a while to overcome my disgust at the way Sandy had been sacked, but as a professional footballer in the end I just had to get on with things.

The summer before Tommy McLean got the job I ended up looking like a miniature version of Arnold Schwarzenegger, which did not endear me to him to begin with. I had built up the top half of my body so much during the pre-season I could not run like I used to. My reasoning had been that because I was getting older I had to build myself up more but I went a bit over the top and was too muscle bound. Tommy had a real clear-out in a short time and brought in various players like Jim Bett and Brian Hamilton who were near the end of their career but still did a decent job for us. A lot of the young players at Hearts at that time were told they were not good enough as he went for experience, which was the polar opposite view held by Sandy Clark, who felt that a lot of the young guys were ready to move into the first team.

Although Tom and his coaching team had a lot of experience I felt, and still do, that their stand on young players was flawed. For instance, Gary Locke was having a bad game at Pittodrie and was subbed at half time but doing that did his confidence no good. It was an indication of the strength of character that Gary had that he shrugged it off to get himself back into the team.

I liked Tommy and Tam but things happened that were not quite right. For instance, we played Rangers at Tynecastle in a Scottish Cup game and we were two goals up at half time and things were going swimmingly. Rangers did get back to 2-2 but we still went in at full-time victorious. We were all relatively pleased at the way we had regrouped and came away with the 4-2 win. To my surprise, when we came into the dressing room Tommy stripped the walls. As I was getting a bit older I realised when it is the time and the place for managers to respond negatively. After beating Rangers in the cup is not one of them. That worried me a bit. Yes, there was the negative of losing a two-goal lead but we showed a desire to win but he was still not happy. That was not good.

The three of them had great knowledge of football but there was nobody really there to lift us, nobody with the personality to give us a Churchillian-type speech. Also, I am not saying you need lots of humour in the dressing room but you do need a balance and that wasn't there at Tynecastle back then. It was under Tommy that I nearly for the first time ever decided not to play for Hearts. We were playing Hibs at Easter Road near the end of the 1994-95 season and I was sub. There were thirty seconds left, we were trailing 3-1, and he told me to go on. That moment was the closest I have ever come to saying no but I did. I had no idea why they put me on to this day. They knew I was a Hearts fan and I didn't want to run on just to see Hibs celebrating. I don't think I even touched the ball. I was furious.

On the Monday morning I asked Eamonn Bannon why I did not start that game and why I had been forced to come on. He said I had a poor game the week before against Airdrie in a Scottish Cup semi-final defeat, which was a fair enough comment. He also accused me of telling George Stewart, who used to play centre-half for Hibs, what the Hearts team would be for the derby game.

I was shocked. I had been up to George's pub in Juniper Green but told Eamonn his accusation was rubbish. George was a big pal of mine who had been on my testimonial committee. I had been up there delivering two tickets for a regular in his pub who used to go to the Hearts end for derby matches. All I said to him was that I didn't think I would be playing. That was not me telling him the team. I could not understand and still to this day cannot understand why Eamonn would have said that. As part of the Hearts coaching team he should have been standing up for me in the first place, as he knew me and should have told Tommy McLean there was no way I would give out the Hearts team to give Hibs an advantage.

That was the Monday. On the Tuesday we played three twenty-minute games on the pitch at Tynecastle. I was never in the first team once.

I never once chapped the manager's door up until then during my career, demanding to know why I was not playing, because most of the managers I worked under were respectful enough to pull me in and tell me why in the first place. But I chapped Tommy McLean's door that day and asked for a word. We were due to play Partick Thistle and I said to him he would be making a big mistake not to play me as I felt I had something to prove and had a big game in me, as did Gary Locke, who was also unlikely to be picked.

I told Tommy if he didn't pick the pair of us we would lose and head to the relegation play-offs, and he would be under pressure. He never said anything but I did end up playing on the Saturday and I had probably one of the best games I ever had in a Hearts jersey that day.

Tommy listened to me that day and I have the utmost respect for him because of that. In the end that turned out to be an amazing season and we stayed up but the writing was on the wall for him.

You may ask when I am being critical, although I would describe it as honest in my appraisal of him, why I even considered him in my Dream Team discussions. I have mentioned him in the book for the level of professionalism he tried to bring to the club, just as Bobby Moncur had done earlier in my career. Hearts needed hard taskmasters and Tommy fitted that mould. He could never be mistaken for a ray of sunshine but he pushed us hard and I liked that in a manager.

The next man up is someone I actually had a little bit of a hand in appointing. When Tommy McLean was about to be sacked we went up to the north east of Scotland for a few pre-season friendly games. The squad was split with one team playing Cove Rangers while the other went even further north to play a game against Fraserburgh. I was going to play Cove but I got a call from Chris Robinson on the Friday night asking if I knew Jim Jefferies. I said I knew of him as he had tried to sign me the previous season for Falkirk. He asked me to privately phone him because he wanted Jim to be the next Hearts manager.

I did call him and said to Jim that he could not miss the opportunity to go and manage the club he had supported all his life and played for and captained. We spoke about it for a long time and the phone call had an effect, albeit not immediate. It was only much later that Jim decided to become the next Hearts manager but he only made his decision after a lot of soul searching.

At the outset can I say my time with Jim and his assistant Billy Brown was mixed. A lot of highs and a lot of lows. He achieved the ultimate prize in winning the Scottish Cup and I was hugely disappointed that it was in the year after I left. Jim put a great structure in place that helped Hearts win the 1998 Scottish Cup and the team had paid its dues along the way with some heart-breaking League Cup final defeats. We had been beaten 5-1 in one cup final, 4-3 in another, both by Rangers.

What I enjoyed under Jim and Billy was the training and Paul Hegarty was instrumental in that. Paul was a massive part of the backroom team under Jim and Billy and a great coach and an important man to have in the dugout. Paul must have been really pissed off at me at times as he could run the legs off me in training. He had long since retired but he was still in great shape. He was still running marathons and expected you to have a similar standard of fitness to him at all times. By heck, that wasn't easy. You also had George McNeill and Bert Logan there as well, so it was always a tough shift out on the training ground.

There was a big turnover of players when Jim and Billy arrived at Tynecastle because both of them were really good at picking players they knew had potential. For instance, Stevie Fulton and David Weir blossomed under them at Hearts and both these guys have a lot to thank them for. Jim's philosophy was to have two players for every position and to begin with, as I mention in the midfielder chapter, it was Paul Smith and me who went head-to-head. Like me, Paul was a big Hearts fan and we used to go to games together as kids. It was a case that Jim and Billy's management style was having someone in your position breathing down your neck to keep your standard up. I loved playing under them when I was in the team. Hated it when I was out.

To begin with, Paul got in the team because I was not playing well and when he got injured and I thought I was in with a shout Brian Hamilton was brought into the squad and he kept me out as well then Stefano Salvatori came in and took my jersey. Jim and Billy were like that. They always kept you on your toes.

When I was going through all this time on the sidelines Billy was great with me and kept my spirits up. He was brilliant with all the psychological stuff. He pulled me aside and said he was pushing for me to play against Hibs one Saturday and not to let him down. Billy was the type of guy you wanted to please and I played out my skin for him and kept my place for a long while afterwards.

Chris Robinson and Leslie Deans backed them with money, which ultimately led to the downfall of the club as they spent too much and the books didn't balance, but at the time the investment was most welcome. For instance, guys like Pasquale Bruno, who I mention elsewhere in the book, who was a great influence on the likes of Paul Ritchie, did not come cheap. There was lots of money spent to achieve the Holy Grail of winning the Scottish Cup and pushing for the league title. Maybe a bit too much money, in my opinion, was splashed out on players on the way down in their careers. For instance, the Serbian centre-half Gordan Petric, who arrived at the club from Crystal Palace in 1999 for £500,000, maybe did not have the commitment to the club that he should have had for all the money he was on but he wasn't the only one.

Looking back, it was a bit weird for me working under Jim Jefferies because, as I mentioned elsewhere, I was the only one still on the playing staff who could remember him clearly as a player. Having him telling me what to do was a bit funny. In saying that I still have the utmost respect for Jim, although we did not part in the best of circumstances when I finally left Tynecastle. I am not trying to be a martyr but I gave seventeen years to the club and also worked with the late Brian Whittaker on the corporate side to try and bring more money into Tynecastle. Some people say I was bitter when I left and I might have been if it had not been for my former wife, Vicky.

At the centre of everything was the fact that Jim had said he was thinking of offering me a new contract but I might not play in the first team regularly. He said he would be operating an Under-16 team and would I be interested in running it, which I was. Then Airdrie came in for me with a £10,000 offer for me to go there as a player under Alex MacDonald. I thought about it but I expected and hoped that Jim would react by offering me a year's contract extension with some coaching with the main Hearts team as well as the Under-16 side. He went the opposite way and never mentioned the possibility of a coaching job with the Under-16s or any other team ever again. It was as if he wanted me out the door only a week or so after making it clear he wanted me to stay.

Hearts were playing Hibs on the Saturday but I did not go to training and Vicky went down to Tynecastle to meet Jim for a chat. I don't know what she said to him but it turned out I got a £10,000 golden handshake and was told I was free to go to Airdrie. That same amount of money turned out to be my contribution to the Save Our Hearts campaign.

I left with a heavy heart because I loved being at Tynecastle. I loved the history of the club, the people, the memories, being part of such a great Scottish institution. It was all I had ever known. I had loved every minute of being there and I was incredibly sad to leave. What turned out to be my final competitive game was two weeks previous on Saturday, 1 March 1997 against Celtic at Parkhead. Jorge Cadete and Paolo di Canio scored as we lost 2-0 and I got booked as well to add to my misery. I was thirty-two years old and had played my 640th and final competitive match for the club I loved to death. My final day at Tynecastle was on Thursday, 13 March 1997 when I packed everything away and walked out the front door one final time.

When I moved to Airdrie my boys Ryan and Nicholas continued watching the Hearts. They were not going to come to Airdrie to watch their old dad. My abiding memory of what they said about the team a few times was that some of the players brought in after I left were rank rotten. Being good boys, I am sure they said that to soften the pain I had felt leaving Tynecastle. To this day the pair of them think that Mo Berthe was the worst player to ever wear a Hearts jersey. I hardly saw him play because I was with Airdrie at the time. I would be interested to hear your thoughts on that one if you ever meet me after reading the book.

Although the way I left maybe caused a bit of a rift between me and Jim at the time, that was soon forgotten and we now get on fine. Off the park Jim can talk the hind legs off a donkey and has a dry sense of humour. Even in pressure situations he was always great with the one-liners. For instance, after Colin Cameron scored the penalty within the first minute in the 1998 Scottish Cup final against Rangers he turned to Chick Young of BBC Scotland who was sitting right behind the dugout and asked him, 'How long to go? Surely it must be nearly full time.'

Jim and Billy kept going long after our Scottish Cup win and to be honest I was surprised when they took up the offer to come back to Tynecastle after spells at Bradford and Kilmarnock. They did well, got us into Europe but were then out of the door as quick as you like after just nineteen months when things weren't going quite right. They offered Jim a director of football role at Hearts but he was right to turn that down. I felt sorry for Jim when he left second time around. What more could they have done for the club?

When Jim started his second spell at Tynecastle I am sure he was allowed to get on with his job but that may have changed as time went on. Football managers have huge workloads anyway without having to deal with influences outwith their control. Maybe Jim regretted a wee bit going back to Hearts for that second spell but that has not changed his status with the Hearts fans. They still love him, which is only right.

Another manager I feel deserves special consideration for my Dream Team is Craig Levein. A lot has been made of my relationship with Craig and, as I mention elsewhere, both of us would admit we are not close friends. We are both opinionated people. Craig has aspired to greater things in football management than I ever did and I credit him with that. We had a fall-out when I started my agency business, which involved Hearts player Graham Weir who was up for contract renewal, but things were not going well. I said the way that Chris

Robinson was running the club, what with the fear that Tyne-castle would be sold, that people should not buy season tickets. Craig was disgusted and he had every reason to feel that way from the perspective of his role as a football manager who needed the fans to back his team and also their money to maybe help pay for new players to strengthen his team.

I felt I had every right to say what I did because of my lifelong loyalty and devotion to Heart of Midlothian that Craig would be the first to admit he could not come close to matching. I am still falling out with people in this day and age and no doubt so is Craig. If you have the courage of your convictions there is nothing wrong in that.

There were some great times for Hearts when Craig was in charge. Yes it could be dour as it was based on a rock-solid defence, but people like Mark de Vries, John-Louis Valois and Patrick Kisnorbo shone brightly at Tynecastle – although in Valois' case not for too long. For all his football ability and top-class skill as a defender Craig liked to play with a big target man and it was de Vries that I remember as one of his best signings in July 2002. The big Dutchman still gets a hero's welcome at Tynecastle whenever he returns there, mainly because he scored four goals in the 5-1 win over Hibs on his first start in August 2002. On top of that less than a year later he scored the winning goal in Bordeaux to give Hearts one of their greatest ever away results in Europe.

Craig was brilliant at pinpointing talent like Mark and getting the best out of his players. I felt that he handled himself well when he was in charge and dealt with a difficult period at the club under Robinson superbly well. That experience stood him in good stead when he faced difficult times at Leicester City and he bounced back very well from there at Dundee United and now as Scotland manager.

Craig was always ambitious and although he will want to do well for Scotland I do think he has the talent to go on and have a managerial career elsewhere at club level once his time at Hampden comes to an end, which it obviously one day will. There is nothing wrong in that because if Scotland is successful other clubs will come for him.

Out of the other guys there were two I always felt sorry for but who deserve a mention for the sheer hard work they put in. One was my former team-mate John Robertson. Wee Robbo could have been a great Hearts manager if he had been given more time. Bringing in Donald Park, another guy who I have huge respect for, to be his assistant was a masterstroke. He could have built a great team ably assisted by Donald.

When the club got rid of Robbo I told Phil Anderton, the former Hearts chief executive, it was a very bad decision to lose both Robbo and Donald. If they had wanted to make the football club better from bottom up they could have done it, as Robbo could have been the figurehead with Donald working away with the young players. It had the potential to be a fantastic combination and early signs were good. He only returned as manager in November 2004 and despite making two cup semi-finals and doing reasonably well in Europe as well as finishing fifth in the league, he was sacked in May 2005. A disgraceful decision in my book.

The other man I will always feel sorry for and still have huge respect for as well is George Burley. After talking to Hearts fans since he was sacked I know I am not alone. I have heard people from within Hearts – and they know who they are – saying that the removal of George Burley had to happen. I have never heard such utter rubbish in my life!

When he was at Tynecastle there were people with agendas against him. I was working for Hearts at the time doing a bit of ambassadorial stuff and some commentary work for their internet site so had a bit of an inside track on things. If George Burley had stayed at Hearts they would have won the league that year. I have absolutely no doubt about that. He was appointed manager on 30 June 2005 and won eight out of his first ten games and took the club to the top of the table before he was crazily and stupidly given the boot.

George's managerial career would have gone a different route if he had not been sacked and his coaching career would have gone from strength to strength at club level as he had Hearts flying. It was the only time in my life that I was able to replicate what it must be like following Celtic or Rangers. At half time in some matches I used to think the game was won. Hearts was like a runaway juggernaut heading quickly towards huge success. George did not even have a full pre-season to work with his team as he only became manager at the end of June 2005 after being out of football for just twenty-three days after leaving Derby County.

What he had in his favour was the fact he was such a good coach that the Hearts squad bought into what he was trying to do immediately and the dressing room seemed to be united under him. It was the most scandalous decision taken in my lifetime at Hearts to get rid of him after just 114 incredibly successful days in the history of Hearts Football Club. I was at Tynecastle in hospitality and sitting at one of the tables when I heard the news before a home game against Dunfermline Athletic and I was stunned. In hindsight, this is one time that I should have spoken out but I didn't. I did consider not going back to Tynecastle but couldn't bring myself to do that.

The rumour mill was full of falsehoods, which even if some of them were true the individual welfare of the person would be far more important. My feeling is that George Burley was sacked because he was too popular. He was bigger than people at the club wanted him to be. They wanted him cut down to size. It was pathetic.

Valdas Ivanauskas I met a couple of times and the fact that he won the Scottish Cup will not be forgotten. What also should not be forgotten is the work carried out by his assistant John

McGlynn, who returned to the club in the summer of 2012 to replace Paulo Sergio. John has a work ethic second to none. He not only puts high demands on his players but demands a lot from himself. I am sure he was a huge help in the dressing room and on the training ground during their Scottish Cup run that ended with the penalty shoot-out win over Gretna. Now who can remember who all scored for Hearts in the penalty shoot-out that day? For the record the heroes were Steven Pressley, Robbie Neilson, Rudi Skacel and Michael Pospisil before Gavin Skelton missed to give Hearts the 2006 Scottish Cup.

Also nobody will ever forget the semi-final win over Hibs on that famous April weekend. That was a pivotal day in our history and Valdas was our manager so that also gives him a special place in my heart. In the semi-final I was close to having a tear in my eye because when I looked at the scoreboard at Hampden it said we were beating Hibs 4-0 in the semi-final of the Scottish Cup. That is something I would have loved to be part of. Paul Hartley scored a stunning hat-trick and Edgaras Jankauskas got the other, details of which I have mentioned elsewhere in the book but make no apologies for mentioning again. On top of that, Hibs' Ivan Sproule was sent off for stamping and Gary Smith was also dismissed in an incredibly one-sided derby.

The next man up is someone who will always be remembered for masterminding, in my view, the most famous-ever Hearts win. For Paulo Sergio to mould a side capable of winning the Scottish Cup in his first season in charge was an incredible achievement. Also remember Hearts didn't have an easy run to the final and played St Johnstone in the fifth round, St Mirren in the quarter-final and Celtic in the semi before they destroyed the Hibs. What made the victory even more impressive was the fact that Paulo had inherited Jim Jefferies' team three games into the season and realised he needed to make tactical changes. He made Hearts more robust at the back, put great faith in Ian Black in the midfield and kept the width in the team, which was vital.

As with all Hearts transfers I am not sure if it was Sergio's call to bring in Craig Beattie but if he did it was a masterstroke as he will always be remembered for that winning penalty over Celtic in the Scottish Cup semi-final.

Sergio had to work with the backdrop of having players' wages not being paid on time, an imposed media blackout that I don't think he was happy with, but through it all he kept his composure and Hearts on the right track. How focused and single-minded his players were in the Scottish Cup final win over Hibs speaks volumes for his style of management. He made the players get right behind him from the start and they bought into his style of play and gave the level of commitment he demanded. He managed to get Andy Webster, who had been injury prone, to play consistently throughout the Scottish Cup; he got the best out of Rudi Skacel and increased the confidence of Andrew Driver.

What also impressed me about him was that he is a humble man who was ice cool under pressure on Cup final day. I was watching him and it wasn't until the fourth goal went in that he started to celebrate. After the first three Hearts goals he was a picture of concentration as he talked to his assistants on the touchline and shouted instructions to his players as they ran back to the centre-circle. Although I was pleased for John McGlynn that he got his job, I thought it was a travesty that Paulo was forced into the position that he had to leave after the Scottish Cup win. Of course, maybe we don't know the full details, but surely when a manager wins silverware for the club and there's the chance to build on that into the future then he deserves to be offered a decent contract? As it is, we'll just need to wait and see how the new manager gets on, but I hope we don't lose the momentum that has been built over the last season.

Now before I come to naming my Hearts Dream Team manager can I pay tribute to all the thirty men who have held the hot seat for Hearts. It is an incredibly tough job but to hold that position is in my view the greatest honour in Scottish club football. As I said earlier, I must admit I did come very, very close to choosing Tommy Walker as my Hearts Dream manager based on his trophy-laden time at the club, but the man I have chosen is someone I felt helped put the heart back in Hearts.

It was a risky decision for Wallace Mercer to appoint Alex MacDonald as player–manager in place of Tony Ford back in 1982 but he took a chance. I don't think even Wallace would realise the impact Alex would have on Heart of Midlothian Football Club. Alex was there as a player for six months before he was made up to manager and I shared a dressing room with him but we didn't hit it off straight away. I was a pig-headed youngster who thought that because Alex had scored goals in cup finals against Hearts and I was a Hearts supporter that I should not like him.

I didn't even know him as a person, had met him for a few minutes, but had made my mind up from the start that he should not be at Tynecastle. Not to put too fine a point on it, I was acting like an arse. I should have given him instant respect but I didn't. He was in the Rangers team that won the European Cup Winners' Cup because of his footballing talent and tenacity out on the pitch. The way he played made him someone that other supporters loved to hate. And I used to love to hate him. I continued to hate him as I didn't want him there because I was a stupid, local boy who regularly asked myself, 'Why does my great club need Alex MacDonald?' We didn't need any Rangers old boy. We were the great Heart of Midlothian. I felt I was the only true Hearts supporter in the dressing room and had been following the team all my life. I had watched Jim Cruickshank make great saves and had been there to see us beaten 3-1 by Dunfermline in the 1967-68 Scottish Cup final.

What did Alex MacDonald know about Hearts? He was a man who stuck two fingers up at my club on a regular basis and now he was at MY club. As things turned out, I was made to eat humble pie pretty quickly as he turned out to be the man who would have a massive influence on the careers of lots of players, including myself, and who helped turn around a club that once was on its knees.

Within the first few days of being appointed manager the first thing Alex did was pass on two very important messages that I remember to this day. One was that I was always to look him in the eye when I spoke to him because that is the type of respect he would always give me. Secondly, no matter what happened at training or during a game, regardless of how much stick he had given me, the next day if he said good morning to me he expected me to say good morning in return. In other words, I was not to bear a grudge or sulk about the place like a spoilt brat.

It was like, wow, someone is giving me good advice and setting down boundaries. I was young, thinking I was going to be a professional footballer regardless who was manager and he was telling me things I had never heard before and things that had an everlasting effect on me. They may sound simple pieces of advice, good manners even, but looking back, they turned out to be important points, not just in my football but also my life development. I have never forgotten either point he made. When I walk into my local gym every morning I say good morning to people and I still make eye contact when I speak to them. It is something I am pleased Alex taught me.

With Alex in charge and Wallace running the boardroom Heart of Midlothian became a whirlwind of activity. When Alex brought in Sandy Jardine there was a real wow factor. Bringing in Sandy, someone who lived in Edinburgh and knew Hearts was okay by me. Yes he had played for Rangers too but he was an east coast man. He understood my club.

Alex also had the respect of other professionals, which allowed him to attract other top-class players like Willie Johnston who had a tremendous impact on the football club. If people wanted to work hard in training and run their guts out for him on the pitch they would survive under Alex's regime. He was never one to suffer fools gladly and over a four-year period there was only one full-time senior, by that I mean old professional, left from the time he took over and that was Walter Kidd because he bought into immediately what Alex was trying to do.

Walter took on board everything Alex, Sandy Jardine and other senior guys like Jimmy Bone and Sandy Clark and Willie Johnston said and learned from that. Others like Stuart McLaren moved on because of his age, which left Walter the only one of a particular vintage that survived the cull to hold down a first-team place.

The huge thing for me with Alex was that you did not know exactly what he had that made him such a great manager but if you could bottle it it would be like a magic potion. There was something about him that made him such a great motivator, such a fantastic man to work for. He also had a great knowledge of people's temperaments. He could relate to what young players, like myself and Robbo, were doing at the club and allowed us to grow as footballers and men. He didn't give us much rope and came down hard on us if we stepped out of line, but he did allow guys like Willie Johnston and Jimmy Bone a bit more freedom. He never let us young players get too big for our boots. After all, he had been nineteen once, he had played in top games as a teenager, and his picture had been in the paper for scoring goals. He never expected you to get too carried away and you couldn't really in relation to what he had achieved during his playing career.

If you look at his period of management from early 1982 to 1990 I would say it was a success, as we were just eight minutes away from winning the Scottish League and lost in the Scottish Cup final. People will say that still is failure but they are not looking at the bigger picture. Alex and that team helped restore pride in Hearts. As a manager he helped turn around a football club, along with great support from people such as Sandy Jardine and unsung heroes like second-team coach John Binnie. He helped Hearts gain respect from the football community and made them a force to be reckoned with once again. His judgement on the quality of players was amazing. Mike Galloway, signed from lowly Halifax Town for a minimal fee, did such a great job in the one and a half years at the club that he was sold on for £500,000 to Celtic.

What Alex put in shape at Hearts was vital for the future well-being of the club. Regularly getting to League Cup finals and semi-finals started to occur from Alex MacDonald's reign going forward. For me, Alex was a natural manager as he didn't turn just one club around, he turned around two as he did the same with Airdrie.

I have a lot to thank Alex for. I became an internationalist under him, for which I will be eternally grateful. I didn't get a cap until 1987 and the way Alex and Sandy ran the club helped in that honour coming my way as they improved my game no end, with their constant promptings and words of advice.

Alex did not seek publicity. He wanted the praise to be for the players. The biggest disappointment for the men who worked under Alex was that we did not reward him for all his hard work by winning a trophy.

I had been following my own career path so closely during my playing days that I didn't realise till years later the significance to Alex of us not lifting the league title or at least the Scottish Cup. If we had picked up either honour I am sure Alex would have gone on to manage his beloved Rangers. If I feel as an individual that I let Alex Macdonald and Sandy Jardine down in some way, it is that I did not allow them to follow their destiny which should have been at one stage sitting together at the top of the stair in the manager's office at Ibrox.

No disrespect to John Greig, who is a Rangers and Scotland football legend, but you could argue Alex may have been a better choice to run the club, bearing in mind his coaching experience at Hearts. To throw John in at the deep end was always going to be tough on him. Even a Scottish Cup win could have tipped the balance in Alex and Sandy's direction.

Alex made me feel wanted as a player throughout his time at the club and I was not alone. He had that uncanny knack of saying the right thing at the right time to help build your confidence. As I mentioned elsewhere in the book, Hearts had a bid of £500,000 on the table for me from Dundee United in the summer of 1987. I could have left but I wanted to stay and help Alex and Sandy build the club I loved and signed a new contract at Tynecastle instead. What Jim McLean achieved at Dundee United was phenomenal but would I have been able to work with him like I worked with Alex MacDonald? I am not convinced.

The writing was on the wall for Alex when they made him and Sandy co-managers because that didn't really work. Maybe six years is a long lifespan for a manager at the one club. Maybe it was the right time for a change, but Robbo and I went public with our criticism of the decision to get rid of Alex.

I accept it could not have been easy for Wallace sacking him but I like to think he could have understood why two young lads like Robbo and me, whose careers had been nurtured by Alex, were so upset about him leaving.

The mark of respect for Alex we all had comes from the fact that when he moved on to Airdrie and got them into Europe for the first time in their history and into Cup finals, some of his most important players had been with him previously at Hearts. Maybe some of them did not play regularly at Tynecastle, but he took them with him and made them part of a very good Airdrie team. People like Jimmy Sandison I am thinking about here, and he also brought Kenny Black back after selling him from Hearts to Portsmouth.

Alex may not have won anything as Hearts manager but he laid the foundation for the modern-day side and helped create a football revolution at the club. Tommy Walker may have won more trophies but Alex brought respect back to Tynecastle. That is something money can't buy and part of the reason why he is my Dream Team manager.

5

THE BACKROOM BOYS

When results are going well it is the players and the manager that get all the glory. Of course, when the reverse is true they also get it in the neck from the fans, which is only fair and proper as they are well paid for what they do. Below the level of the players and the manager at every football club is a group of unsung heroes that makes the football club tick. They may not grab the headlines but their input is vital. For my Hearts Dream Team I have put together a group that would ensure the club would run like a well-oiled machine. You may not know all of their names but their contribution to my Dream Team cannot be under-estimated.

For example, where would a football team be without a top-class medic and physiotherapist? Especially a side playing in Scotland where the tackles come flying in thick and fast to this day. The pace of the game means that, if anybody did a scientific study, it would probably show that the injury rates north of the border are higher than most other countries. Because of that you need a physio and a club doctor you can rely on. My first pick for my Dream Team backroom staff is Alan Rae, a man who went about his job quietly but who made a huge contribution to Hearts. He had a National Health background and was a clever guy who got involved in everything he could at Tynecastle and didn't just deal with injuries.

Alan, who had grown up in Dumfries, qualified as a physio in 1966, and worked for years at the Royal Infirmary in Edinburgh. He also ran his own chartered physiotherapy practice. It was Sandy Jardine who brought him to the club in 1982 and he was an important and highly respected figure at Tynecastle.

Alan used to tell us prevention was always better than cure. By that he meant we had to warm up properly and look after ourselves. He was always open to new ideas and he accepted a suggestion put forward by Alex MacDonald that the players have a bath before every game. We had one before we did our stretching and the idea was that having a bath would encourage circulation from the stomach area to move to the extremities so that the limbs were full of blood even before we started to jog.

Alan used to feel that part of the reason Hearts were promoted to the top division was because the defensive core of the side in the lower league – Henry Smith, Sandy Jardine and Roddy MacDonald – hardly missed a game. A lot of that was down to how they looked after themselves and how he cared for them.

Alan didn't have much money to work with at times at Hearts when they were going through financial troubles, but he did his best. He tried to help us without giving us lots of pain-killing injections and sometimes I was told a strapping was all I would need to get through ninety minutes on a Saturday. Can I tell you, sometimes I woke up on Sunday morning wishing I had pushed harder for an injection because of the pain in my legs, but I am sure Alan was right not to give me lots of injections because he had my welfare at heart.

He was a stickler for detail and demanded professionalism from everyone inside the club, from the youth players to the most seasoned pros. His love of Heart of Midlothian Football Club made him more than just the club physio. For example, he hated mess and never wanted stuff left lying about. Everything had to be tidied away. These wee things were marks of his profession-alism. A lot of clubs have kit men, men who do various jobs round the stadium. Alan, because he cared about Hearts and was a total professional, filled all these jobs without realising it. He would only leave Tynecastle, where we all used to be based all the time, remember, because there was no academy, when his room and the area round it was in pristine condition.

His treatment room was in the bowels of the stadium and you would go past the home dressing room and face to go down the tunnel, turn left and it was at the end of the corridor. Because of that he would walk past every other room on his way to his own office every day. He would go past the referee's room, the washing and drying room, the changing rooms. He could see everything when he came in every morning and would see everything as he left last thing at night. If he went for a coffee and saw something lying about as he returned to his room, he would say that was not the standard that he wanted and get an apprentice to tidy it up.

He had a really dry sense of humour and used to make me laugh a lot, even when the joke was at my expense. I remember once we were playing against Raith Rovers and I was on the dugout side in the first half, straight in front of Alan and the management team and, to be honest, hadn't done much. I was playing wide right in the second half on the far side of the pitch and unfortunately my fortunes had not improved. A train went past the stadium, maybe ten minutes into the second half. Fifteen minutes later Alan turned to Alex MacDonald and said, 'Gaffer, did Gary Mackay get on that train because I haven't seen him on the park lately!'

I never required Alan's services as a physio very much but I liked going into his room because he was a learned man, full of knowledge. Also he liked fit players coming into his room as it kept the morale up of players who were injured. Over the period I was there some top players spent a lot of time in Alan's room recovering from serious injuries. I am talking about guys like Craig Levein and Stevie Frail, both of whom he helped a lot.

Alan was not alone in giving top-class medical health. One of the unsung heroes for me at Tynecastle was the club doctor W. Dewar Melvin who came on board in 1980. It was reassuring to know that someone of his expertise was around the club, especially on match days. Only in 2004 when he moved to the youth academy in Riccarton did the facilities he have at his disposal improve, but he always gave us top-class medical care whenever we required, regardless of where he was and how tough the conditions were he had to work in.

Another two vital parts of my Dream Team backroom staff are my first-team coaches, George McNeill and Bert Logan, both of whom had been top-class professional sprinters and also had played senior football. In George's case, he was a world-class sprinter, winning events like the 1970 Powderhall Sprint and also the prestigious Stawell Easter Gift Handicap Sprint in Australia in 1981. He had played football for Hibs and Stirling Albion, while Bert had been at Motherwell.

George was good enough to have won a medal in the Olympic 100 metres, I have no doubt, but because he had signed professional forms for Hibs, he wasn't allowed. That's because, in his day, athletics was allegedly fully amateur. Everybody knows it was more 'shamateurism' as runners were being paid and it was scandalous that George was banned from running for his country.

George kept himself in such great shape that when he was sprint coach at Hearts he was still winning titles and took the British Veteran Athletics 100 metre and 200 metre crowns.

It was Pilmar Smith's idea in the first place to bring them in, as he wanted to increase the level of professionalism at the club. Pilmar had sponsored George to run on the professional circuit when he was a bookmaker and they were good friends. Bert and George had a long-standing friendship and they fell into the changing-room humour at Hearts. Both felt when they came in that the players had just scratched the surface in terms of improving their fitness and their speed.

George used to say we all had powerful legs but no core strength and we needed to improve our stomach muscles. To that end we used to have to do fifty abdominal exercises and twenty press-ups in a row as a matter of course at every training session. Hard as it may be to believe, but back when I played some players would go on holiday for the whole of the summer. Not just for a few weeks but for five or six and they would return to pre-season training out of shape. Some guys would return 10lbs heavier than when they left to go on their holidays, as they would sit around the pool eating rubbish and not doing enough exercise. There was not the same level of professionalism back then.

During the first summer they were at the club both George, and especially Bert, made themselves available three days a week at Meadowbank Stadium for any players who wanted to do a bit extra training. When I went down there was a specialised training regime they had brought in for us to try, and I hated it. It was designed to make you more explosive from a standing start and was also meant to give you more power in your spring when you jumped for a ball.

As well as sprinting there was a gruelling circuit made up of burpees, press-ups, chin-ups, dips, trunk-curls. You name it, George and Bert put us through it. The whole programme was incredibly tough and I was so ba' heided back then that I walked out in a huff when I could not stand it any longer. I wasn't going to muck up my summer holidays by doing all these exercises long before the start of the season, I told myself.

As it turned out, other players who were down there and had finished the programme under Bert and George had really good seasons, players like John Colquhoun and Craig Levein. I identified that, as did Bert and George, who took great pleasure in telling me I had made a mistake acting like a prima donna and had missed some important pre-season training sessions that would have done me the world of good. Suffice to say, I made sure I never missed out on these pre-season training sessions at Meadowbank ever again.

Bert and George also used some techniques used by boxers to help us. For instance, we did circuits with a speedball – which is the wee ball that hangs from the ceiling for boxers to hit repeatedly and quickly to help their hand-to-eye co-ordination. With the *Rocky* theme blaring out in the background, we were a lot like boxers preparing for a big fight.

It takes a long time to get the speedball right and I struggled to hit it regularly to begin with, but I decided to persevere. Every Friday I would go up to the gym on my own and do six and a half minutes on it flat out and I felt it improved greatly my hand-to-eye co-ordination. Craig Levein was fantastic on the speedball, the best of any of us, and he turned into a great puncher, as Graeme Hogg found out. I always maintain that the way Craig laid Graeme out when they had their on-the-field punch-up was down to his ability with his fists that he developed on the speedball. There is no doubt about that because he was so quick when he hit him Graeme had no chance. Muhammad Ali at his peak couldn't have put together a better punching combination than Craig did that day.

Craig's general fitness improved under Bert and George, as did mine, and I have a lot to thank them for, looking back, as they improved my all-round fitness. They used to claim I was never strong in the tackle till they arrived. They claimed they made me stronger, especially in my upper body and nobody ever shoved me about on the pitch after they had finished working with me, and I can't really argue with that.

Socially they were great fun and they were also the conduit between the dressing room and the management team. For part of the time they were there both Alex MacDonald, who was the manager and liked to keep himself fit, and Sandy Jardine, who was his assistant and still playing, took part in some of the sprint training that was taken by George and Bert. Because George and

Bert were hammering us in training, it meant Alex and Sandy weren't in our firing line at the end of each session for pushing us so much. If we were moaning about doing back-to-back sprints, it was them who got it in the neck but they used to just laugh it off. Deep down we knew they were the best in the business and doing us all a favour by pushing us to the limit. As well as training, they would do massages for us to keep us in shape. Nothing was too much trouble.

Bert was still there when Hearts won the Scottish Cup on that famous day back in 1998, although George wasn't, as he had joined Livingston where he had built up a friendship with Davy Hay and Jim Leishman. The longevity of Bert and George in football circles shows their importance and quality. I bet a lot of sides would want them in their Dream Team backroom staff, both for their ability to hone a player's body, improve their all-round fitness and also bring some laughter to training sessions.

The lifeblood of any club is their young players, and my youth coach has to be Sandy Clark, who played a major part in the development of some of the most promising players at Tynecastle. His Hearts team won the BP Youth Cup back in 1993 when they beat Rangers at Ibrox, and he also coached the team that won the Reserve League and the Reserve League Cup final with a win over Dundee United.

I still believe Sandy could play a big role at Hearts to this day, as he is such a top-quality youth coach. He can see a top player at a young age a mile off and is brilliant at developing them. Also there is no better person to learn how to play football from than Sandy Clark.

Let's face it, if you are going to be a postman the guy you learn from is the guy who takes you out on his round. If you are going to be a sportswriter you ask for work experience on the sports desk at a newspaper. If you want someone to tell you which young players have got what it takes to make the grade, ask

Sandy Clark. Ask Gary Locke, Allan Johnston, Paul Ritchie, Grant Murray, David Murie, Mark Bradley, Gary Naysmith – they will all say that Sandy Clark was a huge influence on their careers. The way he dealt with young players was fantastic from the minute they walked through the door at Tynecastle. He also had a spell as Hearts manager but was not given a chance and sacked far too soon and that decision, in my opinion, was criminal, as I suggested elsewhere in the book.

They say if you bring through one or two players from the youths you are doing well. Nowadays, most top clubs have youth academies and the best training facilities. Imagine how much great work Sandy would do in these circumstances. Sandy brought on the promising young players at Hearts at the public playing fields at Saughton Park. They had to pick up dog crap before they trained on the pitch. It is a no-brainer for me. Sandy would be a top youth coach nowadays if he was given the chance, absolutely no question. I sincerely believe he would have a role to play at youth level for Hearts. You can have the best facilities in the world for the youths – and Hearts have great facilities at Riccarton – but if you don't have the best people at the top working with the youths, you will never get the best out of them. Sandy would be a lot better than the set-up they have in place just now.

Remember as well the guys Sandy brought through didn't come into a bad Hearts team. They made their mark when we had a decent side, which shows the quality they must have possessed thanks to him. Players like Robbo, Dave Bowman and myself came into the Hearts team a bit by default because they didn't have a great side at the time we were coming through the ranks. We were flung in at the deep end into a mediocre team. The team Sandy's crop of young players came into included players like Pasquale Bruno and David Weir. It was a tough team to get into. Sandy was instrumental in bringing them through so they did not look out of place.

To this day I love working with boys' club players, seven- or eight-year-olds because it is very fulfilling and also maybe because they don't talk back to you. Sandy took teenagers and everyone who has kids that age knows they can be a bit headstrong and not easy to keep under control. You need a strong coach to deal with them. That is why Sandy was perfect. They wouldn't talk back or give any lip to Sandy Clark.

Alex MacDonald, when he was Hearts manager, would get frustrated working with a group of headstrong teenage boys. Sandy Clark would not. He had great patience and could get his ideas across very well. He was a top-class teacher. I was not surprised that Sandy went on to become an excellent first-team coach at Dunfermline and Aberdeen, where he continued to improve their young strikers. I always felt if I had an input at Hearts Football Club nowadays I would go out my way to get Sandy back in charge of all youth development.

You would need a man who could bring players into Hearts for Sandy to work at youth level and a great choice to do that job would be John Binnie, who was reserve team manager and scout when I was at Tynecastle. He was a young lad at Rangers when Alex and Sandy Jardine were there and he learned a lot at Ibrox that helped him after he hung up his boots. He was one of their first appointments at Tynecastle because he was trustworthy, had a knowledge of the game, was great with footballers of all ages and did not suffer fools gladly. He had a good eye for pinpointing weaknesses in the opposition and had been working with Falkirk before he joined us. He compiled dossiers on teams we were going to play and he was seldom wrong in his assessments. He had a knowledge of the game about him second to none.

If John Binnie said to Alex MacDonald he did not think a player was ready to go into the first team Alex would accept his recommendation, regardless of how good that player was. The other side of the coin, and I talk of this elsewhere in the book, is when John tipped off Alex about the quality Alan McLaren had shown in the reserves and recommended he fast-track him into the first team. Alex took his advice and we all know how great a call that turned out to be.

John used to take the reserves and groups of sixteen-year-olds for training at Tynecastle on a Monday and Thursday night and he had such a good eye for a player there was virtually no chance of a good youngster slipping through the net at Tynecastle. I would like to think John could scout at youth level for up-and-coming players for my Dream Team and bring them along for Sandy to work with.

Willie Montgomery is another behind-the-scenes star who deserves a special mention. Never heard of him? That's because he was another of the unsung heroes at Tynecastle where he was groundsman. Come rain or shine he would be out there making sure the pitch was in perfect condition. Remember, in his day we trained on it at times as well so he always had his work cut out to ensure it was in decent condition, but he never failed to make sure it was. It is important to have upbeat people around the football club and Willie fitted into that category. He was a great bloke.

My backroom Dream Team would not be complete without two men who helped bring the big match atmosphere to Tynecastle. Scott Wilson is a name well known to radio listeners in the east of Scotland and also to every Hearts fan who has heard him on the microphone before big matches. The role of match day announcer in getting the crowd up for the game is very important and nobody does it better than Scott. Both Scott and his brother Tom, who tragically died much too young, were huge Hearts fans and you can tell that from the passion in his voice when he takes the mike at Tynecastle.

After Scott had finished naming the starting elevens he would hand over to Mark Donaldson, who would be the man I would want to commentate when my Hearts Dream Team was in action. I used to be his analyst when Mark used to host Hearts World on match days and it was great fun. Our broadcasts over the internet received feedback from all over the world and the emails flew in from as far afield as Australia, Japan and the USA during the game. I think those listening loved the fact Mark and I came to the commentaries from a Hearts perspective. Broadcasters like the BBC could not be as biased as we were and we loved every minute of being able to tie our colours to the mast from the first minute to the last.

Perhaps the finest bit of commentary I ever heard Mark give was when Hearts played Hibs at Tynecastle on 2 January 2003. It was an incredible game, with Hibs going two goals up after twenty minutes. Steven Pressley and Mark de Vries managed to get us level before an insane last few minutes. Hibs went 4-2 up with two late goals in regulation time before the late, late show by Graham Weir had Mark and me in seventh heaven. In the fourth and final minute of injury time he scored twice to secure Hearts an incredible draw, which we never saw coming which added to the drama of the occasion. I don't know how the roof of the commentary booth didn't explode as Mark was incredibly, and understandably, loud when Graham's late goals went in. He stayed professional enough to describe them hitting the back of the net but the emotion in his voice in those final few exciting minutes sent a tingle down my spine. When the final whistle went both Mark and I lost the plot and were screaming like a couple of teenage girls at a Robbie Williams concert. You had to get us down off the ceiling that day and there were several other times when Mark's commentaries captured the moment of a Hearts win superbly well. I am not surprised to see that he has carved himself out a great career commentating on matches for ESPN from his base near New York as he showed he was a world-class broadcaster from his days with Hearts World.

So there you have a backroom line-up that would do great things for Hearts. Sandy Clark would pinpoint the best young talent and along with John Binnie train the youths, George McNeill and Bert Logan would put us all through our paces and the medical team of W. Melvin Dewar and physio Allan Rae would keep us in tip-top condition. Willie Montgomery would make sure the pitch was in great condition and on match days Scott Wilson would whip the crowd up into a frenzy before kick-off when Mark Donaldson would take over the commentary and make even the most dull nil-nil draw sound interesting.

All the men I have picked had enthusiasm, drive and a real love of Hearts. How they would all get on remains to be seen, but they are all confident people that I like to think would work well together for the good of the club. Everybody knows that the most important people at a football club are the players but it is important to pick the right team off the field as well. I think I have picked the best men to help my Hearts Dream Team who would run out of the tunnel at Tynecastle be the best they could be.

6

GOALKEEPING GREATS

Hearts have always been blessed by having some top-class goalkeepers. Through good times and bad you could always guarantee we would have a man between the sticks that wouldn't let the team down. Because of the quality I had to choose from, picking my Dream Team goalkeeper was one of the toughest decisions I had to make. Even from my time at Hearts and since I retired there have been some fantastic goalkeepers. Antti Niemi, Craig Gordon, Henry Smith and Gilles Rousset are just four of the men I have either played with or watched. These guys would have walked into any team.

Take Craig Gordon for example. He is a goalkeeper who on his day is one of the best in the world. I first saw him play when he was a youngster with Tynecastle Boys Club. It was their coach, Dougie Dalgleish, who tipped me off about him and although I'm not a goalkeeping expert, even I realised straight away here was someone who was very special. He hadn't grown to his full height when I saw him play but he was agile. I believe Tynecastle Boys Club got a substantial amount of money for helping him in his formative years when he moved from Hearts to Sunderland for £9 million in 2007 and that was only right and proper given the grounding he got from the staff there when he was growing up.

Sometimes in football you need someone in your corner supporting you and there is a story regarding Craig that illustrates exactly that. Remarkable as it may seem, there were two or three at Hearts who were not convinced he was going to be big enough or good enough to make the grade. Billy Brown, who was Hearts assistant manager at the time, speaks about a game at Musselburgh Juniors when he watched him in action. Billy said his handling was spot on and he had a real physical presence about him and he was astonished that some at the club still had their doubts. Craig was sixteen at the time and Billy fought tooth and nail to bring him into the professional set-up in the first place and then keep him at Tynecastle because he knew Craig had a special talent. Sometimes you need to have someone in your corner and, knowing Billy, he would have really fought Craig's cause. After that there was nothing lucky about Craig's career and he made the people within Tynecastle who had doubted him to begin with look very foolish indeed. Sheer hard work and dedication brought him the just rewards his talent deserved.

He was well looked after in his early days as a professional and put out on loan at Cowdenbeath, which helped him a lot. When Craig returned to Tynecastle he was a better and much more experienced player. He made his debut for Hearts in a 1-1 draw with Livingston on 6 October 2002 and within the year he had replaced Tepi Moilanen as first-choice goalkeeper. Craig Levein nurtured his talent and showed great faith in him from first to last.

A key moment, in my opinion, in Craig Gordon's career came in a Scottish Cup game against Falkirk. I was working with Hearts TV at the time and Lawrence Broadie, who was the producer, said to me when I got up to the old ramshackle stand at the back of old Brockville that he feared for Craig, and you could understand why. If you were looking at going anywhere, outwith Celtic Park, Ibrox or Easter Road at that time, to play a tough, daunting Scottish Cup tie then Falkirk is the place you would not want to go. I don't know exactly why there has always been a bit of ill feeling from Falkirk fans towards Hearts but I always sensed that was the case. I am not saying that the Hearts fans do not feel the same way towards Falkirk, but I felt they had a real grudge towards us for some reason that I never managed to fathom. Against that background of animosity between the sides and the fact that old Brockville was an intimidating place to go meant it was a tough game for Craig to be thrown into. Now goalies are very rarely put into such an important match at a young age but putting twenty-year-old Craig into a game like that showed the confidence Craig Levein had in him.

To say Craig didn't have a great day way back on 25 January 2003 would be an understatement. Collin Samuel scored in three minutes and had a hat-trick within the first half hour. Owen Coyle also scored for Falkirk to give them a four-goal cushion at half time. Thankfully there was no more scoring, which was good news for Craig. The reason I bring that game up is because the score could have been a lot more if it had not been for him. He could have crumbled after losing four goals as, remember, he had played just a handful of first-team games up to that point. The fact was that he didn't and actually went from strength to strength and pulled off some great saves in the second half. His ability to bounce back from such a drubbing for Hearts showed his strength of character.

I think Craig Levein made a strong statement on the pitch that day at Falkirk, in that he was telling the world Craig Gordon was the type of player he had total faith in. He knew he was going to be Hearts' number one for as long as he wanted to be and he would not be dropped, even after a high-profile Scottish Cup defeat.

Now I would love to tell you my favourite Craig Gordon save, but to be honest, there were too many to pick from. If I was pushed there was one he made at Easter Road when he was going one way and twisted back the other to keep the ball out that will always live with me. There was another world-class stop, this time against Motherwell in August 2005, when he dived full length to turn away a David Clarkson shot that helped Hearts hold out for a 2-1 victory. You have to say that learning from someone with the experience of goalkeeping coach Jim Stewart must have been great for Craig. The benefits worked both ways because maybe the way he brought Craig Gordon on helped Jim get a move across to Rangers as their goalkeeping coach. All you want as a goalkeeper is the confidence that your specialist coach, in this case Jim, feels you have the raw ingredients to be a top-class player on the day when the pressure is on and backs you one hundred per cent. Jim always did that with Craig.

It was a tragedy that Scotland never qualified for a major championship when Craig was at his peak, which, in my opinion, was in the last few years at Hearts and his first season at Sunderland before he got injured. If he had been exposed to a World Cup or a European championship as a Scotland number one and had stayed injury-free he would be playing at one of the top clubs in Italy, Spain or an even bigger one in England than Sunderland. He is that talented. Craig always came across as an intelligent, well-brought-up young man who knew how to treat triumph and disaster the same. He had a very good family, which was important, and his father Davy in his younger days was a very good goalkeeper in his own right, so the footballing talent was clearly in the genes. Even when I watched him as a teenager you could tell he was a lad who was level-headed and who was always destined for great things.

Craig was unanimously worshipped by the Hearts fans while my next candidate split opinion. Despite that, Henry Smith totally deserves to be a candidate for my Dream Team. He played for us from 1981 to 1996 and was a loyal servant from start to finish. He had started out as a coalface miner in South Yorkshire before signing for just £2,000 from Leeds United, and what a bargain he turned out to be.

Henry was a really interesting character and when he first came into the changing room I wasn't entirely sure what to make of him to be honest. He walked in trying to look cool, wearing a long black trench coat, but it was the only trench coat I have ever seen that had a patch on it. Maybe someone had burned it with a cigarette but he had had to put a huge patch on the arm that ended any hope Henry had of giving the impression he was a cool dude. He was introduced to the players and although he was born near Lanark he had this sort of strange, broken English accent. Anybody who has been at a Hearts function or met Henry will know that he has an accent for whatever part of the world you are in. Do you remember Steve McClaren trying to speak English with a Dutch accent when he was managing in Holland? If you do, you'll know what I am talking about.

People talk about Graeme Souness having lost his Scottish accent and speaking like someone who was a born and bred Englishman. Henry was able to bring to life an accent whether he was in Germany, Spain or down at Whitley Bay for pre-season tour that he thought made him sound like a local. As you can guess, Henry, like all great goalkeepers, was a little bit eccentric at times and great fun to have around the club.

I felt a bit sorry for him because after so long at Hearts he had nothing to show for all his hard work but then again he wasn't the only one. You always need lots of confidence when you are a goalkeeper and Henry wasn't short of that, or at least that was the impression he gave you. For instance, if you were to ask Henry who I should have chosen to be my Dream Team goalkeeper he would have answered that it should have been him. That is no bad thing as having confidence is a vital part of a goalkeeper's make-up. Henry looked like he had lots of it but part of me thinks it was maybe a bit of a front because he did take a battering at times from the fans.

Some may have felt he blotted his copybook by dropping a couple of balls in the Scottish Cup semi-final against Celtic in

1988, but I like to think that Henry just made all the mistakes he would make in his career in just a few matches. Unfortunately they were the ones people remember. Yes, we were 1-0 up in that semi-final with three minutes to go and we lost 2-1, but that does not take away from the fact Henry was a top-class goalkeeper. You have to remember we may not have even got that far without him as he pulled off some great saves in the earlier rounds, especially in our 3-1 away win over Falkirk. I always felt it was significant he got his three Scotland caps – against Saudi Arabia in 1988, Northern Ireland in 1991 and Canada in 1992 – after his well-publicised mistakes against Celtic as it showed he had the inner strength required to shrug off such errors.

I prefer to dwell on some of Henry's saves that either won us matches or kept us in games. I remember way back in April 1986 we were playing Dundee United and Maurice Malpas hit a rasping shot from outside the box. Henry was unsighted and was going in the opposite direction but managed to twist around just enough tip the ball over the bar. It was so good that Dundee United manager Jim McLean compared it to Gordon Banks' save from Pelé at the 1970 World Cup. Praise indeed. Also, what about his penalty save from Brian Hamilton of Hibs, where he again showed great agility to keep the ball out? Perhaps the one I remember more than most was when he threw himself through the air to tip away a shot from Tommy Coyne of Celtic that was heading into the top corner.

Henry had an incredible work ethic and trained very hard and always wanted to be number one. He never wanted to be rested. Andy Bruce and Ian Westwater were both young goalies at the club and came with decent pedigrees but were not able to shift Henry. Andy ended up joining the police because he could not get a starting spot, while Ian left in similar frustration but went on to have a good career with Falkirk, Dundee and Dunfermline. The statistics show that in Henry's first nine seasons he missed only four league matches and was only dropped when Joe Jordan took over as manager. For me, Henry Smith deserves to be rated as among the greatest goalkeepers ever seen at Tynecastle. He will always be held in high esteem by people like me who played alongside him and hopefully by the fans as well, who appreciated his honest endeavours.

When Antti Niemi was at his peak I was managing at Airdrie so maybe didn't see much of him in the flesh but the mid-week games I did see and the Hearts matches I watched on television left me incredibly impressed. It was ironic that when he joined us some people thought he was on the way down as he had been at Rangers where he had hardly played, as Andy Goram kept him out of the team. He came to Tynecastle in 1999 and had three great years there during which time he played eighty-nine times. Things may have started badly for him as Hearts lost 3-0 to Hibs on his debut, but they finished on a high. His last game in Hearts colours was when he got his revenge over Hibs in a 5-1 win.

He was so good during his time at Tynecastle he won a move to Southampton and from there he went to Fulham. The fact he was Finland's number one international goalkeeper for nearly a decade shows the level of his consistency at the top level. I used to describe him as the modern day equivalent of Jim Cruickshank, who I will discuss later in this chapter. By that I mean Antti was not the biggest but he was absolutely world class on his day. Like Jim, he threw himself all over the place and was one of the most agile keepers I have ever seen. Antti looked like he had fun playing in goals, putting his body on the line. He was one who you would say had cat-like talent in the way he could move his feet quickly and dive all over the place.

Before I tell you the name of my Dream Team goalkeeper and the man who will be his understudy I have to mention the name of some players from yesteryear that also came into my considerations. I never saw Willie Duff play but the older members of my family tell me he was a top-class goalkeeper. Out of his ninety-six appearances for Hearts he managed twenty-seven shutouts from 1952 to 1957, with most of them in the two seasons from 1954 to 1956. When I was looking through the record books it showed he was signed for just £200. Not sure what, with inflation, that would be nowadays, but it sounds like a good deal to me. He was part of the Hearts team that beat Motherwell to win the Scottish League Cup in 1954 and in April 1956 was between the sticks when we beat Celtic to win the Scottish Cup. The only time he was beaten in that entire cup run was when Celtic scored a consolation goal in the final. At the end of that season he moved south to do his National Service and because of that joined Charlton Athletic.

Even before that there was Jimmy Brown who joined Hearts way back in June 1942 and stayed at Tynecastle until 1952. He joined us from Bayview Youth Club in Fife and by all accounts was one of the real characters at the football club. Style wise he was ahead of his time and wore bright coloured tops and a baseball cap every time he played. He also had to go through exactly the same pre-match ritual. He would run on and do a few chin-ups on the crossbar then touch one goalpost and then the other one. Jimmy also scored a penalty in a reserve match against Queen's Park in 1947 and always fancied his chances of scoring from the spot if he got the chance. Unfortunately for Jimmy, he dislocated his shoulder in February 1950 against Queen of the South and then two years later broke his collarbone. He got both injuries by being brave and coming out for cross balls and that was a major part of his excellent goalkeeping career, but those injuries restricted his appearances.

One man who had a great career, not just with Hearts, is Gordon Marshall. He joined us from Dalkeith Thistle in August 1956 and was with us until he joined Newcastle United seven years later. He made his debut as a seventeen-year-old in a 3-2 home win over Kilmarnock on 17 November 1956 and went on to play 338 games for Hearts with eighty-four shut-outs. Gordon was a Hearts fan as a boy and you imagine how he must have felt when he ran out of the tunnel alongside players he had idolised, such as Bobby Parker, Freddie Glidden and Johnny Cumming. Gordon remains one of the most decorated goalkeepers in the history of Hearts, winning two league championship medals and three Scottish League Cup medals.

Guys like Gordon, Willie Duff and Jimmy Brown all deserve to be considered for my Dream Team. Indeed I am sure a few older fans with more vivid memories of that era will feel one of them at the very least deserved a place on my Dream Team bench. I can understand why they may think that, but for me the man who I have chosen to be my reserve goalie is a gentleman of such standing it was a privilege to share a dressing room with him.

Based on my own experience playing in front of him and partly because he is one of the nicest individuals I have ever met in my life means I am putting Gilles Rousset on my Hearts Dream Team bench. Craig Gordon, Henry Smith, Antti Niemi, Willie Duff, Gordon Marshall and the rest of the Hearts goalkeeping greats would not be offended at being left out for Gilles. If you are going to have a bench with top-quality players you have to make sure that their noses are not too much out of joint by not playing. Gilles would have an acceptance of the situation if he felt I was being honest in my assessment that he wasn't the man to start in goals. That is the kind of lad Gilles was.

He was a fantastic guy who always had time for everybody at the football club. I remember vividly the first time I met him. I used to spend a lot of time in the away changing room before training in the morning, which was where the young guys such as Gary Locke, Paul Ritchie, Alan Johnston, Kevin Thomas and Grant Murray would all gather. The young goalies at the time were Myles Hogarth and Roddie McKenzie. You would go in there and have a cup of tea and a bit of a laugh. Then this 6 foot 8 inch huge man walked through the changing room door and had to duck down to get in as he was so big. With him were Wattie

Kidd and Paul Hegarty, who had brought him in to introduce him to everybody.

Our physio Alan Rae was also there, who took one look at him and said, 'Christ, we'll need a huge jersey to fit you.' Gilles just laughed as he had been in the same situation before. Not one of the clubs he had played for before in France could ever find a jersey that would fit him so he had them custom made and he brought them with him.

I introduced myself and I knew just looking at him, with his big smile, he was an absolute gentleman. His English wasn't great at the beginning but what made me laugh was the look on his face whenever Gary Locke, from Bonnyrigg, spoke. He could not understand a word he said and even when Gary tried to speak slowly for Gilles' sake it made no difference. It was very funny to watch.

He joined in late October 1995 when we were going through a bit of a bad spell under Jim Jefferies and after we lost 2-0 to Falkirk on his debut we fell to the foot of the SPL table. I remember soon after he joined, Jim told me to help him choose a sponsored club car and because of that Vicky, who I was married to at the time, and Nelly, who was Gilles' wife, became good friends.

Because of his good nature a lot of players went out of their way to help him. He had a common touch off the pitch but toughness on it. There was also a calm assurance about him as an individual. He hardly ever raised his voice and was very soft spoken and became a huge part of the football club. Gilles, his wife and family just immersed themselves in all things Heart of Midlothian, which for people like me, Donald Ford, Gary Locke, and Scott Crabbe came naturally because we were brought up supporting the club.

For someone like Gilles, who would have known nothing of Hearts when he arrived, it was different. Like so many players at so many clubs he could have just picked up his wages and not shown any interest into the history of Hearts but that was not his way. He was a clever man who wanted to feel part of the football club and used to read up a lot on its proud history.

Within the first few games he played I could see straight away his top-class goalkeeping qualities. He was assured and commanded his box with a quiet confidence and he gave me confidence watching him play. As part of the 1985-86 team I knew all about disappointment and Gilles also suffered such a fate in the first cup final we played in when we lost 5-1 to Rangers in the Scottish Cup final of 1996. It was a game to be forgotten as they had some of their big signings in their team like Brian Laudrup, who scored twice, and Gordon Durie, who got a hat-trick. At the risk of opening old wounds, Gilles will never forget letting the ball from Brian Laudrup squirm through his legs when we were 1-0 down to Rangers in that game. In the dressing room afterwards Gilles was inconsolable but the bottom line was that, although his one mistake didn't help our cause, we had come up against a rampant Rangers side that may have won without his error.

To be fair to Gilles, he was in fantastic form between the sticks all the way to the final that year. The game I remember more than most was when we just got the better of Kilmarnock at Rugby Park in the fourth round and he was immense. He caught every cross ball that came near him in the quarter-final against St Johnstone at McDiarmid Park and deserved all the praise that came his way that day. In the semi-final he also pulled off some great saves against Aberdeen, who we beat 2-1. It is testimony to the character of any footballer or anyone in life who shows the desire and determination to come back from adversity, and Gilles did that time and time again after his mistake against Rangers in that Scottish Cup final. I have never liked the phrase 'mental strength', as I don't think that is what gets you over setbacks in football. Based on my own experience, I think it is having a bit of humility and a realisation that the only way of getting over a disappointment is to work hard. That is exactly what Gilles had throughout his Hearts career. That ability to never let his head drop allowed him to still be around for the highlight of his Hearts career.

On 16 May 1998 he was in the team that won the Scottish Cup. I was in the stadium half an hour before kick-off and my seat was in the main stand at Celtic Park just a few rows from the front. I was so close that I shouted loudly to wish him all the best and he acknowledged me by giving me the thumbs up. On the best day of his life he picked up the Man of the Match award and it was an indication of how highly regarded he was that Andy Goram went out of his way to congratulate him on his performance at the end of the match. The way Gilles was that day is the way I will always remember him. He had a big smile on his face and he gave me a big hug when we met. I was delighted for him.

As well as being a great goalkeeper for the club, he was also one of the nicest guys there too from the start to the end of his career in the capital. It was nice therefore, that his performance in the Scottish Cup final of 1998 meant he was able to be forever remembered for the good things he did at Tynecastle rather for any mistakes. Looking back on his time at Tynecastle brings a smile to my face as he kept us in so many games against teams that were technically better than us. None more so than Red Star Belgrade in 1996. When we played them in Belgrade it was a real backs-to-the-wall performance. John Colquhoun played the lone striker role and he worked his bollocks off that night. You always knew you would get that from John but you also knew at the other end of the pitch our penalty box was being controlled by someone with a massive presence who would not let us down. Gilles put in a supreme performance that night against one of Europe's top sides, and he was instrumental in us being able to come away with a commendable 0-0 draw.

I admire Gilles even more for things I found out about later in my career. For example, at the height of his great form for Hearts he had an opportunity to go to Sunderland when Peter Reid was manager and he would have trebled or maybe even quadrupled his salary. That was not in the public domain but he was not interested in a move, regardless of the money. His family were settled in Edinburgh; he loved Hearts and wanted to stay at the club. That loyalty, allied to all his other qualities, made him an incredible man who demanded respect both on and off the park. When Gilles knew the quality of the man I have chosen as my Hearts Dream Team goalkeeper, I am sure he would be honoured to be his number two.

For all of the great goalkeepers Hearts had during the years the best, the most charismatic, the most iconic, has to be Jim Cruickshank. My Hearts Dream Team goalkeeper is a man who is a Tynecastle legend, especially for those of us privileged to have seen him play. When I was a young Hearts supporter I used to go behind the goals that we were shooting into because I had confidence we would not lose many goals at the other end with Jim between the sticks. He was a world-class player in a team that wasn't the best and that is a hard thing for any goalkeeper to be. Time and time again he showed his genius with some great saves that left the crowd gasping. I always felt safe as a youngster when Jim was in goals. I knew he would never throw any in or make any big mistakes.

He joined us from Queen's Park and spent nineteen years between the sticks at Tynecastle. He was such an unmistakable character with his big moustache. He looked very debonair, a bit like the man in the Milk Tray advert. It was Tommy Walker who signed him for Hearts in 1960 and he made his league debut that year as a nineteen-year-old against Ayr United at Somerset Park but it was a good two years before he took over from Gordon Marshall.

From the moment he made his breakthrough he was near impossible to shift. He played 610 times for Hearts in total if you count friendlies. Out of his 394 competitive league matches he kept an incredible 102 clean sheets, which, remember, was in a very average Hearts team. My family were huge Jim Cruickshank fans and while researching this book they reminded me of a penalty save he made from Joe Davis of Hibs in the New Year's Day derby game of 1967. He didn't just save Davis' penalty, he also saved not one but two shots on the rebound. Jim had a reputation as a great saver of penalties and even stopped one at Tynecastle taken by Celtic's Tommy Gemmell, who had one of the hardest shots in British football at the time.

In one match over the festive period that my family were at they tell me he put in one of his greatest displays ever. Celtic eventually won 3-2 but it would have been 13-2 if it had not been for Cruickie. He should have represented Scotland more and I always thought the fact he played in a poor Hearts team counted against him. The fact he won just six caps over eleven years was a disgrace, as he deserved many more. I know guys like Ronnie Simpson were around at the time but Jim was as good as if not better than him. Would he have played more times for Scotland if he had been playing for either of the Old Firm? I am sure that would have been the case.

His international career began in 1964 in a 2-2 draw against West Germany, the year before Hearts lost the Scottish League Championship on goal average to Kilmarnock, who beat us 2-0 on the final day of the season at Tynecastle. Jim had no chance with either of the two goals that gave Kilmarnock victory and clinched them the championship. After being in a similar situation when we lost the title to Celtic after losing to Dundee on the final day of the season, I know how low Jim must have felt. Sadly Jim never won a domestic honour and lost in two Scottish Cup finals and also finished on the losing side in the Anglo-Scottish Texaco Cup Final in 1971 when Hearts lost to Wolverhampton Wanderers over two legs.

Jim was never the biggest – he stood around 5 feet 11 inches tall – but you could have fooled me. To me as a boy he was an absolute giant because of the way he imposed himself in the penalty area. He was a man who had an aura about him that not many football players have, let alone goalkeepers. He was an absolute superstar in my book. I wasn't alone. All the Hearts supporters at that time really identified with him. It was a troubled time and we were becoming a bit of a yo-yo club going up and down between divisions and one of the few constants was the great form of Jim Cruickshank. I always felt he was a man of the people, a player who never forgot his roots. As an excited teenager I used to get to Tynecastle as early as possible and sometimes I would see Jim getting off the bus, walking down McLeod Street on his way to the stadium. You could never imagine that happening nowadays. Today's footballers would be straight into the car park in their top of the range cars. It was like Jim was one of our own. From a supporter's perspective that endeared him to you but over and above that his abilities as a goalkeeper made me always put him on a pedestal.

I first saw Hearts in action in the Scottish Cup final of 1967-68 when Jim was in goals. I was taken there by my grandfather on my mum's side, called Jimmy Munro, and my grannie Lilly. Luckily it was my granddad Jimmy who indoctrinated me into Hearts first but it was a close thing as all my dad's family were Hibs supporters. We may have lost to Dunfermline 3-1 at Hampden that day but as far as I remember Jim was blameless. In saying that, looking back, he was always blameless in my eyes. He could do no wrong.

I was always impressed by the fact that he always looked so cool under pressure. He wasn't shy in coming forward and the times I was behind his goal I could hear him moan big time at the players he felt were not pulling their weight. One of the players he used to get stuck into was Jim Jefferies, who went on to be my gaffer. If I knew then how Jim Jefferies was going to make my life hell in a similar way when I was a player I would have appreciated Jim Cruickshank having a pop or two at him all the more. In fact, even now thinking about Cruickie giving Jim Jefferies a bollocking for a misplaced pass or two brings a big smile to my face.

He played seventeen years at Tynecastle and I used to watch him whenever I could. I saw him make so many world-class saves in the flesh it is difficult which ones to mention. He had a double save against Celtic that lives with me when he looked like he was double jointed as he changed direction in mid-air to keep out a shot. Near the end of his time at Tynecastle Hearts drew 2-2 against Hibs on 13 April 1977 and I don't think I have seen a better goalkeeping display. I don't know if he ever did gymnastics in his youth as he looked to me he was so agile he could have been a world-class acrobat with the way he could twist himself about.

I did not see Russian goalkeeper Lev Yashin play but if you are a certain age you know that he was always hailed as one of the greatest goalkeepers in the world at the time. There is a Hearts song that will live forever about Jim Cruickshank being better than him and I would certainly not argue with that sentiment. As a young laddie I used to sing the song at the top of my voice. Lev Yashin may have been world famous but in my eyes Jim Cruickshank had that same level of fame. To the tune of the old hit song 'Ay Ay Ay Ay', we all sang, 'We all agree, Cruickshank is better than Yashin; Donald Ford is better than Eusebio, and the Hibees are in for a thrashing.' Brilliant stuff.

I had the good fortune of meeting Jim just the once and I must admit I was a bit nervous about coming face to face with one of my idols. I had an ambassadorial role at the time with Hearts and, along with club historians David Smith and David Speed and Lawrence Broadie, we were helping to set up a Hearts Hall of Fame. For all of us it was a no-brainer. Jim Cruickshank should be among the first group to be inducted. The problem was that he had only been back at Tynecastle once since he retired after a disagreement with the club over his testimonial match. Time had not healed Jim's anger but I was hoping I could talk him round to be inducted into the Hall of Fame and for him to attend the dinner. I volunteered to go up to Jim's house to try to win him around and when I knocked on the door I was met by his wife, Rosalind, who was a really lovely person. She was absolutely charming and explained he had just nipped out for a paper and would be back soon. Just at that moment Jim got out his car, recognised me, realised it was something to do with Hearts, and then – and I remember it to this day – put his hand up and said no. That was even before he had any idea of what I wanted to talk about. To be fair to Jim and Rosalind, they still invited me into their house and were superb with me. I chatted with Jim but it became evident early on that he had moved on in his life.

He chatted with me about my own footballing experiences and was receptive to what I was doing in terms of trying to set up a Hall of Fame. Going back to a Hearts function, even if it was to be inducted into the Hall of Fame, wasn't something he felt comfortable with unfortunately. I was really disappointed because, first and foremost, as a Hearts fan I had a huge appreciation of the role Jim Cruickshank had played in the history of Hearts Football Club. I tried to explain that to him but as he stood up at the end of our conversation in his living room he politely said in his own eloquent way he had moved on. I told him I would be genuinely thrilled and would have felt privileged if I could have helped induct Jim Cruickshank into the Hearts Hall of Fame where I felt he truly belonged. It would be lovely. I tried to put that across to him one last time but he just said it was not the right time.

That saddens me to this day. Having since passed away, Jim was never inducted into the Hall of Fame, which was a tragedy because, for me, he was an absolute shoo-in. Would Jim have ever changed his mind through time? Sadly we will now never know.

What we do know is that Jim Cruickshank and his goalkeeping expertise will always be remembered by Hearts supporters of all generations. He was an all-time great and it is an honour for me to name him as my Hearts Dream Team goalkeeper.

7

FANTASTIC FULL-BACKS

In my career I played alongside some of the best full-backs you could wish to find. Some pushed forward at the earliest opportunity; others would get a nosebleed if they crossed the half-way line. Either way they fulfilled the role of unsung hero time and time again. Let's face it, playing full-back probably isn't going to get you headlines. They best go about their business in an efficient manner and don't look for plaudits. Consistency is one of the most important factors required and the group of men I considered for my Dream Team right-back and left-back slots hardly ever put a foot wrong.

The first player I considered was a man who went on to be capped for Scotland under Walter Smith, and had a great long throw and a fantastic footballing brain. Robbie Neilson was a vital player for Hearts under Craig Levein, as he had the engine required to get up and down the right side of the pitch. If your team does not have enough quality going forward you need the defenders pushing on to support the midfield and front men, and that is exactly what Robbie did time and time again when he was at Tynecastle. Defensively very few players got the better of him. What I loved about him is that he went about his business in an understated way and never let you down.

Now I should maybe declare an interest here as I was on Robbie's testimonial committee. But then again he has never even bought me a drink for all the work I did on his behalf, so maybe I shouldn't even be considering him for my Dream Team! Seriously though, there are some players who you know without a shadow of doubt are deserving of a testimonial and Robbie fell into that category. We were initially talking about taking on a big English team at Tynecastle in May 2008 but I suggested we try and get a mix of old Hearts players, mostly but not all from the 1998 Scottish Cup-winning team like Stephane Adam and Gilles Rousset, to take on the one that won the trophy in 2006, one who I would order not to try too hard to give us oldies a chance. He loved the idea and an indication of what the fans thought of Robbie came from the fact there were 8,000 inside Tynecastle to pay tribute to him, and what an atmosphere they created on what was a very special day for him. He even scored a penalty in a 4-3 win.

Among the many things I liked about Robbie is that he was always open to learning new ideas. For instance, when he was on loan at Queen of the South from Hearts early in his career I went to see him play against Clyde on a miserable winter's night. It was a game not for the faint-hearted and late in the second half Andy Millen and Robbie went into a tackle together near the touchline. Andy was a hard bit of stuff and he took his studs virtually all the way up Robbie's thigh towards his private parts. I wasn't Robbie's agent and was there watching Eddie Malone of Clyde with the view of taking him onto my books. After the tackle Robbie lay on the ground receiving treatment and lesser men would have taken the easy option and come off but Robbie was a strong character and he soldiered on.

That night after watching Robbie get up, give Andy Milne a glare and then get back to work I knew he would turn out to be a good pro. He was made of the right stuff. I was delighted and not terribly surprised when he made it into the Hearts team where he performed consistently. If he was out injured for a game he would come back and be the normal Mr Reliable he always was.

He learned a lot from Craig Levein, who was his manager at the time. If you are going to learn from defenders you are never going to learn from a better man than Craig.

On the other side of the pitch I was also spoiled for choice with the first man I want to consider for the left-back role being a Greek who came bearing gifts to Tynecastle. Takis Fyssas was a calm and composed defender who was a wonderful, wonderful guy off the field. He was a rock-solid player who complemented the flair George Burley had brought in to play in front of him in midfield. He was not the biggest but he was athletic. He was someone young players could learn from. I don't doubt Lee Wallace learned a lot from watching Takis Fyssas when he was a young lad. It is a huge education for young players to watch and improve their game by watching older pros like Takis in training. When Bobby Moncur was Hearts manager he taught me the value of watching people who have more experience of playing in my position and I learned a lot from the way older pros handled themselves.

Takis was a real rock in the Hearts team, especially that night in May 2006 when they defeated Aberdeen to beat Rangers to second place in the league and therefore make it into the European Champions' League qualification rounds. His salary would have been big when he was at Hearts because they had to pay him lots to get him to come to Tynecastle in the first place. It was well known he had other offers on the table from English and German clubs which befitted a player who was outstanding for Greece when they won the 2004 European Championship. But I would argue it was right and proper to pay him big money to come to Hearts as he was value for money and paid them back with a string of top-class performances.

Back on the right side of defence Alan Maybury was another typical Craig Levein-type defender. I watched Alan on a regular basis and, like Takis, he was a defender who liked to get forward. He could look after himself in a manner you respect as a fellow professional. He was experienced enough to know the right time to give an opponent a dunt. He knew you didn't give him a fly push twenty yards from your goal; you maybe do it on the half-way line when the ref isn't looking. It's wee subtle things like that you only learn from playing the game.

Jim Brown and Dave Clunie are players I want to talk about together. Jim may have committed the ultimate sin by crossing the divide and signing for Hibs but he was a top man when he was at Tynecastle. Both played a lot of games in the 1970s and both were decent on the ball and top class, no-nonsense defenders. Dave stood out because of his really blonde hair. If you have ever seen him recently you will notice it has been replaced by grey hair, but he still looks in great nick. Jim has aged slightly differently – and quicker – compared to his big mate Dave. They were both more comfortable at right full-back but could also easily play on the other side of the park if required. They may have been rivals for first-team places but they clearly put that aside as they are good friends to this day.

I used to see them a lot at Tynecastle and the pair were a great double act and loved a wee night out. Jim played in more high-profile games than Dave and was in the side when Hearts famously beat Lokomotiv Leipzig in the first round of the European Cup Winners' Cup in 1976-77 before going out to Hamburg. Although neither of them was the most physical defensively they were comfortable on the ball and they were guys I was brought up watching and who always gave their all for Hearts.

One man I did play alongside was George Cowie, who is a good pal of mine but in his playing days he was, and there is no easy way to say this, absolutely nuts. He was brilliant fun and a real character in the dressing room. For instance, we used to have a Christmas night out and it used to be compulsory fancy dress. There was a draw, which meant you would get a list of all the outfits available and what you wore was picked out a hat. Then I think it was Dave MacPherson and Craig Levein and a few others who wanted to choose their own outfits so we ended up picking our own things.

On one of the first-ever Christmas nights out George's outfit had us all in stitches. He came into the pub fully clothed and I remember it well because we used to have our Christmas party at my mum and dad's hostelry just off Lothian Road in Morrison Street. He went into the bathroom and came out totally naked, apart from a red balaclava. We were all bemused. What the hell had he come as, we asked?

'I have come as a matchstick,' was George's reply. To be fair he did then put on a pair of red underpants but he was still walking about the pub for a long time in nothing else than a red balaclava and a pair of red pants pretending to be a matchstick. He did pull the balaclava back occasionally to drink a pint but he stayed dressed, or should that be undressed, like that all night. That was just one example of George's crazy sense of humour.

Our changing room was very important during the 1980s and there were a lot of big characters in it. George was integral to the upbeat mood because he was someone who, although he didn't play regularly, never let his head drop. He never moaned at the time but later on in life being dropped on one important occasion was something he had a bit of lingering resentment about. What bothered George was that he was devastated at not playing against Dundee in that final game of the 1985-86 season at Dens Park.

As I said, he was an integral part of our squad and the week before we played that last infamous league game he started against Clydebank and played a great ball to me from which I scored the winning goal to keep our league challenge alive. Walter Kidd was suspended for that match at Tynecastle and the previous two games, which had given George his big chance. George had hoped he would have kept his place in the big game against Dundee but instead Alex MacDonald put Walter straight back in. He felt he had come into the side, had done well in the three matches in which he had replaced Walter and we had won against Clydebank thanks to a goal he had laid on, yet he was cast aside when it mattered. You could see why he would be disappointed at that. Anybody would. To this day I can understand his pain but, in all honesty, if I were manager I would have tried to find a place for Walter Kidd in that team to play Dundee. With Craig Levein being out and others struggling with viruses, George felt he should have been in the starting eleven but he didn't even make the bench, which was a real shame. He did make it onto the bench the following week for the Scottish Cup final against Aberdeen but again that ended in disappointment and we lost 3-0 at Hampden. He now lives in Australia with his family and is still involved in the game over there. He remains a class act and a great laugh.

Many fans of a younger vintage than me will remember Stevie Frail as the Hearts caretaker manager at a turbulent time for the club. Others of my generation remember the man who had the nickname of 'Shaggy' as a top-class full-back, who could also play on the right side of midfield, who if he had not been hit by injury would have been a top-class player. Remember, Stevie is the guy who scored a couple of goals that helped keep Hearts in the Premier League in the 1993-94 season and who was one of the fittest, most clever players in the side in the mid-1990s.

His first important goal was a twenty-yard pile-driver that earned a 2-2 draw against Celtic at Parkhead in the sixth-last game of the season when we were battling it out with Raith Rovers, Dundee and St Johnstone to escape relegation. His second was the opener in a 2-0 home win over Dundee United in the second-last game of the season that took us out of the relegation dogfight and left Raith Rovers and Dundee to go down.

He was signed by Sandy Clark for £130,000 in March 1994 from Dundee but a year later he picked up a horrific knee ligament injury in an away match against Dundee United that was a huge setback for him. It is hard to explain how he must have felt that day because he would have known his career was in jeopardy. He was maybe never the same player after the injury. When you fight to get back to full fitness then realise you are not at the level you were before, it must be heart breaking. Stevie would have played for Scotland no question if he had not been injured that day. It was sad to see his Hearts career end after four years when he moved to Tranmere Rovers, and I am sure if he had not been injured so much he would have played a lot more than the fifty-eight times that he actually did for the club.

He was a great lad and is now forging a good coaching career at Celtic, the team that was always his first love. He maybe will try to deny that when he reads this but I know for a fact that, although he has a big feeling for Hearts, it was the team from Parkhead that he was brought up supporting. That is nothing to be ashamed of because Stevie's commitment to Hearts could never be questioned. Even when he took charge of the team, along with Hearts sporting director Anatoly Korobochka in March 2007 when Valdas Ivanauskas departed, he did things with dignity. It was a tough time for Hearts but through it all he was a vital link between the club and the fans. He even took over on his own in January 2008, but Stevie was under no illusions he would get the job permanently. It is an indication of his coaching ability that within a year he had been snapped up by Celtic where he is currently coaching their Under-19 team. In my view Stevie is a fantastic coach and don't be surprised if he turns up managing another top SPL club one day.

What can I say about Jim Jefferies the player? I will look at his management qualities in another chapter but here was a man who at times made my life hell when he was manager of Hearts but who also made it hell when I used to watch him from the Tynecastle terraces. Then again, he wasn't the only one who maybe didn't hit the heights during the era in which he played.

I was lucky because out of the Hearts' first team squad I was old enough to say I saw Jim playing so I knew how bad a player he was. Sorry, Jim! You may ask, if he was such a bad player why am I considering him as a Dream Team full-back candidate? All joking aside, Jim is there for his loyalty to the cause, his love of the club and for me he personified what being a Hearts fan who plays for the club is about.

He wasn't the best by a long, long way but he was living the dream as I did. He would have died for the jersey. I would want such men considered for my Dream Team. In fact, I think Jim is one of the few players who got hotter after he retired. Now you see a lot of managers take part in training and Jim's party piece was flicking the ball up for you to run onto and shoot. That was our usual exercise on a Friday in the couple of years I played under him at Hearts. Actually, Jim's touch in training all these years later was a lot better than I remember it as a player. At times when he played it was really bad and I am sure I must have booed him a few times, or at least I wish I had, considering how tough a time I sometimes got on the training pitch.

In his day Jim would have probably been described as an imposing defender and he was a great servant of Hearts and a Jambo through and through. His family were fans of the club and he used to go on about how great players like Davie Holt used to be and how much an honour it was for him to play left-back for Hearts like one of his idols.

I played a couple of reserve games with Jim before he hung up his boots and it was an experience. I was making my break-through and maybe I'm not being fair to him by saying he wasn't that great as he was on the way down and I was on the way up. To be fair to Jim, he will always remain a Hearts legend but even he must admit it will be because of what he achieved as manager, rather than what he achieved as a player. He played 227 times for Hearts from 1967 to 1981 with the highlight, if that can be used for a defeat, being part of the Hearts team that lost the 1976

Scottish Cup final to Rangers. He was captain for a time and part of a 4-2-4 system at Hearts with Rab Prentice down the left and Kenny Aird down the right, which although they never won anything played some great football.

The next man mentioned is someone who came very close to making my Dream Team. Now I know Alan McLaren was known as a centre-back when he went to Rangers but I first saw him as a right-back at Hearts and have fitted him into my Dream Team considerations in that position. He was catapulted by Alex MacDonald into the spotlight after he made his debut for Hearts in a 0-0 away draw against Dundee United in the final game of the 1987-88 season, aged just sixteen. Everybody sat up and took notice when Alex tipped Alan for the top. What happened was, early the following season, a newspaperman asked Alex how good he was and he said he was good enough to go on to captain Scotland. That was out of character for Alex because he never said how great his players were. He liked to keep your feet on the ground.

An indication of how we all hung on Alex's every word comes from the fact that if Alex MacDonald had told me my shoes were on the wrong feet, even if they weren't, I would have believed him. Hearing him so full of praise for a young player made me sit up and take notice. Alex had great faith in Alan and consistently used him in the first team despite his tender years. The minute I set eyes on Alan I also knew he was something special. To me the art of defending is maybe even more of an art than attacking. You have to anticipate the reaction of your goalkeeper, you have to make sure you get in front of people and if a cross comes into the box you have to realise how to react before the attacker. Alan just had an awareness of the right areas to be in. He could mark players tight and not give them a kick.

He used to remind me of Jimmy Sandison's immortal line when asked what he thought about his own man-marking performance against the great Herbert Prohaska of Austria

Vienna during a European tie. The assembled press men must have thought all their Christmases had come at once when Jimmy answered, 'I am bringing him back in my suitcase as I haven't let him out of my sight all the time I've been in Vienna.' Jimmy's performance that night was special, but nothing compared with the one given by Alan when asked to man-mark the great Italian star Roberto Baggio for Scotland. Is there any Hearts player, or someone connected with the club, who has been asked to man-mark someone of such incredible talent? I don't think so.

I remember watching Alan in action against Baggio that night on 18 November 1992 and it blew me away, Scotland drew 0-0 in the World Cup qualifying match and Baggio hardly got a kick. Alan had moved to Rangers in October 1994 in a £2 million part-exchange deal with Dave McPherson going in the other direction. He was forced to retire from football in 1999, aged just twenty-eight, due to injury. He won twenty-four Scotland caps from 1992 to 1995 and would have definitely got a lot more if he had stayed fit.

Alan still struts his stuff for the Hearts old boys and how he does it carrying that amount of lard about is beyond me. He always had a bit of natural colour about his face and always went a bit red when he was running. That colouring when he was a teenager maybe made him a bit of a shy, unassuming lad when he broke through into the Hearts first team. Players are unforgiving and he got the nickname 'Tomato Pus' but he took that in good part and unfortunately for him it stuck.

Alan was versatile and could play right-back, centre-back as he proved at Rangers or as a man-marker. He had an ability to defend very well and his concentration was spot on, and even for a young lad when he started out at Hearts he showed a maturity beyond his years.

I have tried not to let personal friendships cloud my Dream Team judgement and the next man came into my consideration through merit. Now I regret very little from my professional career but I do regret not keeping Kenny Black on as my assistant when I was manager at Airdrie. He was still there as a left-back when I got the manager's job and I should not have let him go. He knows that I regret that decision but probably not as much as I regret some of the nights out we had together when we were both at Hearts. He was my best man at my wedding and we went down to Sheffield for his wedding when he married Toni. I'm not sure if I have ever recovered.

Kenny and I go back a long way. We were in the same age group at boys' club level and played together for Scotland at Under-18 level. He was always a top player and went straight to Ibrox to join Rangers when he left school. He never cracked it there and joined us from Motherwell in the summer of 1984 for a bargain £30,000. The fact that Hearts sold him on five years later for £350,000 tells you all you need to know about his ability.

What made Kenny stand out from the crowd was his fitness. Even now, as he heads towards his fiftieth birthday, I would back him to beat anyone his age in a sprint. Kenny was frighteningly fit. He had a great engine and was a far better football player than people give him credit for. He would always swivel around to make sure he kicked with his left foot because his right one was just for standing on but what a left foot he had. He could play left-back or left midfield and was equally important in either role.

A couple of years ago we went down to Berwick Rangers for a testimonial for Grant McNichol and Kenny scored a couple of great goals with his left foot. Kenny was forty-seven at the time and he was doing all the running, leaving a lot of the younger guys for dead. For his first goal he chipped one over the goalkeeper's head from twenty yards and it was just exquisite. That was what he was capable of, even in his advancing years.

He always enjoyed life but he was one of those lucky buggers who could burn the candle at both ends without showing it and that used to crack me up. If I was even just late to my bed I would be grouchy and have low energy levels and sometimes that would be after just a late night with Kenny when I was not drinking. Kenny would have a few bevvies and come in the next morning and be right as rain. That came from that natural fitness I mentioned and a natural desire to work hard to work off any excess alcohol.

He had a wonderful positive attitude and was a very sociable individual. He liked a wee bet and he introduced me to the dog racing at Powderhall, which was not a good idea as the bookies made a few bob from me through the years after that. If he had a fault in the eyes of Alex MacDonald it was that he was too keen to be everybody's pal. Once, at a behind-closed-doors bonding session when lots of wine was drunk, some honest truths were spoken. Alex had opened up about what he thought were all our faults. Some of us couldn't defend; some were rotten trainers; others had the wrong attitude. Nobody was spared but he couldn't find a thing to criticise Kenny for other than he was far too chummy with the opposition at the final whistle.

Kenny would always stand up for you, either on or off the pitch, and it was that quality that made him such a popular guy. A prime example of that came when Kenny and I went to meet Jimmy Sandison and Malcolm Murray for a drink in town after a defeat. The *Edinburgh Evening News* used to do a late-night sports paper called the *Pink* which, at one point, published readers' comments on the performances of Hearts players the previous week.

We went out one night and ended up with more drink in us than we should have after being at the dog racing. Now back then our judgement at times was pretty bad even when sober, never mind after a few sherbets. Kenny, Jimmy, Malcolm and I were in the Market Bar near Waverley Station and some of the things printed about Malky in the *Pink* were not very complimentary. It was not like nowadays when people post things anonymously on the internet. The name and address of the person who had made the derogatory comments about Malky were there for all to see in the *Evening News*. Kenny, Jimmy and I did not want to let things go so we used the public phone in the pub and phoned directory inquiries to get the number of the gent who had been disrespectful of Malky. We were not big enough or brave enough to tell him who we were but Kenny said he thought it was disgusting what the *Evening News* reader had said about Malky and he gave him a piece of his mind.

Now I know criticising someone for saying something negative about a footballer is a bit like the pot calling the kettle black in my case, as I have been critical of certain individuals at Hearts since I retired in the media. But at the time I was part of the Hearts playing squad so if one of us was criticised he deserved a right of reply and Kenny was the man who would always stand up for the rights of the players. Kenny more than anyone gave the poor chap who had criticised Malky a piece of his mind before Jimmy and I also had a go before slamming the phone down on him.

Even when Kenny left the club we stayed in touch. He had been playing so well he got a big-money move to Portsmouth in 1989 and Jimmy Sandison and I went down to watch him play against Bradford. Bradford has a good ethnic mix with a big black and Asian community. Kenny didn't know we were coming to watch him so when he ran out for the warm-up I shouted, 'Blacky' because that was his nickname and how we knew him. We gave no thought to the ethnicity of the fans around us, many of whom turned round thinking the ignorant Scots had racially abused them, which was never our intention. I had to apologise and explain Blacky was just a friendly name for their new signing, Kenny Black. Thankfully the fans saw the funny side.

There are several nights out that Kenny and I had that were memorable, mostly after drink was taken. For example, we were on the Isle of Man for a pre-season tour and when we returned to our hotel after more than a few drinks we heard music coming from the basement. Down there we found a disc jockey just starting up and not a single punter in with him. Blacky asked for a few requests and as the beers had been flowing between the pair of us we dared each other to strip. At Blacky's request the disc jockey put on 'The Stripper' and off came our tops, then our shoes, then our trousers. The Y-fronts were about to go next when Sandy Jardine walked in and said, 'I hope the pair of you haven't been drinking.' Even Sandy realised how funny a line that was. As if we would have stripped down to our underpants if we hadn't been drinking! D'oh! Thankfully we just managed to put our clothes back on before a family of four turned up to check out the disco. Luckily they had just missed two near nude, milk-bottle-coloured Scots strutting their stuff on the dance floor by seconds.

I'm beginning to think Kenny enjoys dropping his trousers because I also remember going through to a nightclub in Stirling and he welcomed me by handing me a glass of champagne with his trousers round his ankles. As well as being a joker and great, great fun I always knew Kenny would stay in the game as he always had great footballing qualities and was a clever guy. I have included him in my Dream Team discussions as a left-back but he could easily have slotted in to the left midfield as well. It was great that Craig Levein brought him into the Scotland coaching set-up in the summer of 2010 and an equally good move when Stuart McCall named him as his assistant at Mother-well, as he is a bright football man who can put his points across eloquently, which is vital for a coach.

David Holt was a left-back my granddad watched and used to rave about. When I met Davie in the Tynecastle hospitality suites he turned out to be a great bloke with some fantastic stories. He was not a big man but a real gentleman who was part of a successful Hearts team. A lot of Hearts fans of that era will remember him as a top-class player. It was the likes of Willie Bauld and John Cumming who got all the glory in the early 1960s but Davy was part of that great side. He was also part of the Great Britain football squad that played in the 1960 summer Olympics. Over nine years from 1960 he played 231 games before he left to join Partick Thistle before retiring a year later.

Tam McKenzie was another left-back from a previous generation who was a great servant of the club who he played for from 1942 until 1957. One reason he is included in my deliberations is the fact that the older members of my family always used to say that he had Gordon Smith, when he played for Hibs, in his pocket in every derby match. It goes without saying that was a tough thing to do.

Tam went on to captain Hearts in the 1949-50 season and was a man who led by example. He was a cool customer and was always smartly turned out with his short, Brylcreemed hair and impeccable suits. He won the Scottish League in 1957-58, the Scottish Cup in 1955-56 and the Scottish League Cup the season before and was one of the most successful players in the history of the club. He went south to manage English non-league side March Town in 1960 but was tragically killed in a car crash in 1967.

Another top defender from the 1960s was Willie Polland who was a right-back who could also cover in the central defence if required. He joined the club at the same time as striker Willie Wallace and spent six good years at Tynecastle after moving there in 1961 from Raith Rovers. He was a member of the Scottish League Cup-winning side of 1962-63 and an important part of the side.

Moving forward to my time as a player we always were blessed with athletic full-backs like Brian Whittaker who could get up and down the pitch. I have spoken about Kenny Black already and Brian was a player in a similar mould in that he could support the midfield and the attack. Brian had great energy levels and on his day was a top player. He was at Partick Thistle then went to Celtic and although it did not happen for him at Parkhead he came to Hearts for £250,000 in 1984 and he was brilliant. He had a great attitude and he returned to Tynecastle as reserve coach in 1993. I also worked with him on the commercial side of the club. It was a tragedy that his life was suddenly cut short in a car crash.

The next man who deserves an honourable mention in my Dream Team discussions is Bobby Parker, who I only really knew when he became a director then chairman of the club, and who I have mentioned elsewhere in the book. He was a Hearts man and knew the tradition of the club. Attending Supporters Club functions and Remembrance Day services at the War Memorial were hugely important to him. He also knew how important the supporters were to the football club. He could guide people such as Pilmar Smith, although Pilmar knew a bit more than other directors about the football set-up. He gave out a lot of good advice, such as telling the directors not to pass judgement too quickly on new players. He would tell Wallace Mercer that regardless of how much or how little money he spent on a new player he should always give him six months to settle in at Tynecastle.

He was a smart old fox and because he had been a top player he brought that knowledge of how players wanted to be treated at a football club. For example, he knew that if a player had a first child how important it was for him not to have his sleeping patterns affected before big games. The wives and girlfriends may not have been too happy with Bobby's advice to all us players when we became new fathers but, at the risk of sounding selfish, it made perfect sense.

He watched me play a few times when I was starting out and his opinion was much appreciated by us younger boys. He stayed at Drumbrae and was in touch with the fans all the time after he retired and was a regular at Tynecastle. He was a lovely man and a big part of the success at Hearts during my grandfather's day. My granddad says you maybe did not notice Bobby for long periods but that was just because he was going quietly about his job. He was originally a centre-half, and then moved to the wing-back position before making the right-back spot his own. He was famed for his crunching tackles and the power of his penalty kicks. He was captain of the side for long periods, although injury kept him out of the 1956 Scottish Cup final. He was at the club as a player from April 1947 till the summer of 1958 and during that time was a huge inspiration on the playing side.

Jim Townsend could play full-back or midfield and was someone I admired because he got himself into the Hearts team and gave his all. The same goes for Chris Shevlane, although he was more at home playing at right-back than he ever was pushing forward. There was not so much money around back then so the fact that people like Jim and Chris could play in two positions was important for a club like Hearts.

I had a long, hard look at the defensive make-up of my Dream Team before choosing two full-backs who would grace any side anywhere in the world. At right-back it has to be Walter Kidd. Zico. Bald Eagle. Call him what you will. The longevity of his career, his reliability, his leadership qualities are vital. He was a competitive animal, even on the training ground, and was the perfect example for the younger players. Until Alex MacDonald took over as manager a lot of the young players did not know what the term 'professional footballer' meant. People were selling cans of Coke and Mars bars at lunchtime for profit to other players and I witnessed that myself time and time again.

Wattie was a fledgling professional when this was going on and had been at Newtongrange Star before he joined Hearts. He could have easily been a follower rather than someone, through the fullness of time, who was followed because of the example he set. Wattie could have taken the wrong turn in the road because he was part of that group who bought Mars bars and Coke to begin with. The guy who sold them, Jim Docherty, was a great lad and I think he made 10p for every can of Coke and every

Mars bar he sold, and that was before you went back to training in the afternoon. That was what some players had for lunch.

Wattie also liked his fish and chips and would go to a Gorgie Road chippie after training and have his pint of milk and fish supper for his tea on the way home. Clearly he had to change his eating habits but when it came to being afforded the opportunity to learn from better people in a more professional environment, Wattie grabbed that chance and cut out the junk food.

He did not like doing a lot of running at training and even after he cut out the crap he still did not eat a lot of vegetables. He was built like a brick shitehouse and could easily have put on extra weight if he was not careful, which would not have done his career any good. Fitness was judged on recovery time under Alex MacDonald when George McNeill and Bert Logan were there as fitness coaches. Wattie didn't recover that quickly early in his career because he had a lack of iron due to an unbalanced diet. What Wattie had in his favour was that he had a natural talent and he listened to Alex, George and Bert when they told him he had to eat better. The three of them soon got rid of the Mars bar and can of Coke lunch mentality that horrified them when they all first arrived at Tynecastle.

That was good news for Wattie, who became a better player under Alex as time went on. He always had lots of talent but it was Alex who brought the best out of him and drove him on to better things. His fitness levels improved with the iron tablets he was ordered to take and the extra vegetables he was eating meant he recovered better from a night out than he used to do.

What I remember most about Wattie was that he worked like a bear in every game he played. We might be three goals down but he would never stop trying. He was a great example to everybody. He had natural defensive qualities but had to work hard on his skill levels to keep them up to standard. He didn't use his left foot very often but there was reliability about his right foot. Also his timing in the tackle was superb and he never gave away that many stupid free-kicks. There were a lot of right-backs who would have found it hard against world-class players around at the time such as Peter Weir and Davie Cooper, and of course he did struggle on occasion, but overall he knew how to handle the best wingers in the business.

There are moments of Wattie's career that always come to mind. For instance, his great cross that allowed Mike Galloway to score against Austria Vienna, his top-notch display against Bayern Munich, his umpteenth great game against Hibs. Wattie was a solid defender and maybe he did get a nosebleed at times when he crossed the half-way line but that didn't bother us as we knew he would do his defensive duties well. In saying that, sometimes he would take you by surprise. He had this tendency to go on mazy runs, sometimes ones that started and ended in his own half and for that the Hearts supporters christened him 'Zico'. As a player if you are going to be given a nickname, even if it is a bit tongue in check, Zico is not a bad one to get. I still call him Zico, as does Jimmy Sandison and Scott Crabbe.

For Wattie, or Zico if you like, to captain the club shows he came a long way from a young player who used to eat nothing but junk food. It was a massive achievement and honour for him to wear the captain's armband. He always led by example as captain and although he was not overly communicative you knew what you would get from him. He would never back down from anybody. He had a resolve about him and was hugely important in our group.

Part of my reason for going with Walter Kidd as my Dream Team right-back is because if I played in front of him I knew what I would be getting. I knew the licence I had and the licence other players had to go forward as he would always be there to cover. If John Colquhoun lost the ball out wide he would know that Zico would be in behind him to sweep up.

He had a great career and another good one at Airdrie when he captained them to two cup finals and went on to be Eamonn

Bannon's assistant at Falkirk. The fact that Alex Totten, a great football man, who had never came across Wattie until that moment, kept him on when he took over as manager at Brockville gives an indication of his character and what other top football people think about him. When his contract with the club was at its end, he was offered a one-year contract extension to stay at Falkirk. However, I got him a three-year contract as my assistant at Airdrie, and he took it. Little did we expect, though, that eight months later we would go into administration. He said he would have got more staying at Falkirk and he warmly shakes me by the throat over that to this day.

I was thinking of the best way to sum up Wattie and I thought I would mention the man marks he used to get in newspapers as an indication of his consistency. Of course you always wanted a ten-out-of-ten, rather than a seven-out-of-ten, but Wattie was a seven-out-of-ten every single week as he was so consistent. I can count on one hand the number of bad games he had for Hearts. The only time he lost it was in the Scottish Cup final defeat of 1986 to Aberdeen, when he got sent off for throwing the ball at an opponent in protest at me being booked. That was his way of showing his frustration as we had just lost the league title on the last day of the season and he knew he wasn't getting any younger and that would be his last chance of winning some silverware at Tynecastle.

I am not making an excuse for Wattie because he was daft to get sent off but things just boiled up for him that day. He spent fourteen years at Hearts in total and also worked with the reserve team under Sandy Clark. He was awarded a testimonial match against Everton in October 1987 and he thoroughly deserved that honour.

On the other side of my defence I have chosen one of Scotland's best left-backs of all time. Tosh McKinlay is the opposite of Walter in that he would get a panic attack if he had to stay too long in his own half. He was an overlapping full-back who worked his socks off throughout a match. My Dream Team needs someone getting wide on at least one side of the park and Tosh could do that. He made his debut in December 1988 against Rangers at Tynecastle, which was Robbo's first game back after his short spell at Newcastle United. Tosh used to always tell me that the minute he walked into Tynecastle he loved the place to bits.

He was there when Hearts beat the likes of Bologna and Atlético Madrid but it was the match against Bayern Munich that he used to always go on about. He maintains to this day that the German side, for all the experience they had in their team, were intimidated by the crowd and the tightness of the Tynecastle pitch.

Although his qualities going forward were never in question sometimes people did question his defensive qualities but I feel that was totally wrong as he improved in that area as his career went on. Occasionally teams would put a big man on Tosh and I remember Aberdeen used to do that a lot. They used to put Dutchman Willem van der Ark on him to try and out-jump and out-muscle him in the wide-left area but Tosh stuck at his task and had an inner determination and hardness, which meant he never gave the big man a kick. I know he could also play left wing-back but in terms of my Dream Team I feel he would slot into one position back much better.

Tosh is a player I would spend money to go and see and I did exactly that when I went to watch him play for Scotland in the World Cup in France in 1998. He had moved to Celtic by this time but he had made his name at Hearts before that. In fact, I was absolutely gobsmacked he did not get capped during his time at Tynecastle because he was magnificent for us. Hearts player Jimmy Murray was the first player to score for Scotland at the World Cup and players like Craig Levein had very good Scotland careers but I still felt there was a bit of Heart of Midlothian inside Tosh when he played for Scotland in France

'98. Celtic fans may not want to agree with that but he learned a lot at Tynecastle and his time there was vital in his development as a player.

I know I have handed him my Dream Team number three jersey but under Joe Jordan he was a left wing-back and I was a right wing-back. We had a close friendship anyway and it became closer because we both found it a bit of a Groundhog Day-type position playing at wing-back. It was great to play there when we were on top of the game but when we were at Ibrox or Celtic Park it was difficult because we were covering that whole flank and more often than not spent a lot of time defending. Neither of us loved the role very much but Tosh, with his greater fitness levels, had the ability to cover and get up and down the park much better than me. Not that I told anybody that at the time.

Now I am not saying there was a huge drinking culture at Hearts but for Tosh to be teetotal made him the exception rather than the rule at Tynecastle back in my day. I have never seen him drunk. It didn't make team nights out easy for him and a couple of times Mike Galloway would throw away his car keys. Tosh had the last laugh because he went on to have a longer career than most of us and especially the guys who would maybe take the mickey out of the fact he didn't drink, which looking back, was pretty pathetic behaviour.

Tosh retains a soft spot for Hearts despite being a Celtic man and I will always be thankful to him for the way he found drinking facilities in a Rutherglen pub for the fifty mad Hearts fans who were on the buses we ran to the Scottish Cup final in 1998. Tosh had his Hearts scarf on the day the team won the cup and nobody was cheering louder than him. He always had a dry sense of humour and interestingly he is now a brilliant after-dinner speaker and that surprised me a bit because back when he played he was not that outgoing, unless he was in company he was very comfortable in. I can assure you he has a host of great stories about his times at Hearts, Celtic and Scotland.

I still talk to Tosh and he never ever changes. He is a snappy dresser and is great company. Nobody I know in football has a bad word to say about him. He was a class player and has retained that class off the pitch to this day. With Tosh at left-back and Zico on the right side of defence, I would not expect many members of the opposition to get past the pair of them.

8

CENTRE OF ATTENTION

Getting the right combination in the centre of defence is vital to any side because that partnership is the rock on which any successful team is built. I was lucky enough to have had some great central defenders at Tynecastle when I played but, to be fair, there have been some other crackers before and since. That was why it was not an easy task to pick my middle two as I had lots of great players to choose from but it was all about finding that perfect match.

Some of the centre-backs I considered were great readers of the game who made defending look effortless. Others were tough guys who would take a broken nose rather than let a striker get the better of them. In the old days maybe central defenders were more physical as refs would let them get away with more. Nowadays any aggressive behaviour is clamped down on which forces the middle two to use their brains more than their brawn.

Perhaps the perfect example of the modern day central defender is David Weir. He was one of the calmest and most mature players I have played alongside and a real clever guy on and off the park. Maybe it was because he came to football a bit later than most after taking up the offer of a football scholarship in the States but either way he was an intelligent man who falls into the category of a player who could read the game and make defending look effortless.

To be a success you need to either have natural football ability or be a very intelligent, hardworking person who makes the most of his attributes. David was one of the few players lucky enough to have both. Out of all his talents I felt the fact he was brainy enough to read situations and second-guess his opposite number made him stand out from the crowd. Don't get me wrong. David could do the basics well when required as well. Ultimately he knew he was a defender and his main aim was to keep the other team out. If he had to put the ball into the stand he would put it there.

When you look at David's time in football it is the ultimate case of career progression. He was not picked up in Scotland as a young boy but that did not put him off to the extent he went to the States on a football scholarship at the University of Evansville from 1986 to 1990. He came back and spent four seasons at Falkirk where he played 134 times before moving to Hearts where he made his debut in the opening games of the 1996-97 season. He had joined for just £180,000, with David Hagen and Craig Nelson heading to Falkirk. Jim Jefferies had got him ahead of Alex Miller of Hibs, who had wanted to bring him to Easter Road, and he was a hugely important signing.

We were lucky to get Davie, as Alex Miller wanted him to play wide right in a five-man defence at Easter Road. They had offered him £650 a week in his first year, then £750, then £850. Then he went to Hearts and spoke to Jim. His contract offer was £750 a week, then £850, then £950, but even though those terms were a bit better he always knew Davie had felt a better vibe during negotiations with Hearts.

I remember when he first arrived he was in the young team that started to beat us old boys – me, Neil Pointon, John Robertson, Dave McPherson and Gilles Rousset – with embarrassing regularity in bounce games at training. At that moment I knew that maybe some of us in the veteran category were nearing the end of our time. There were some real strong personalities in the Hearts dressing room around that time and Davie, like a lot of the newcomers, took time to find his feet.

I remember him telling me a great story against himself about his first Christmas night out at Hearts. He had been practising singing along to 'Wonderwall' by Oasis in his car coming into training so he could sing it at karaoke, as he was scared he would make a fool of himself. Can I just say, after murdering so many songs at karaoke through the years Davie had nothing to worry about but as a new player at Tynecastle at the time he didn't know that. My dreadful attempts to sing 'Things', the Bobby Darin hit song from the 1950s, were legendary but all for the wrong reasons. Craig Levein was usually the master of ceremonies on our nights out and drew the names out of a hat to decide who would sing next as he sat there with his tequila and orange juice.

We had been through about twenty-two dreadful versions of every song under the sun, as you couldn't sing the same song twice. The last two left in the hat were Davie and Colin Cameron. I have never seen anybody's face drop as much as Davie's did when Colin got up and sang 'Wonderwall' by Oasis. Davie didn't have a back-up song and although I can't remember what he sang, he absolutely murdered it. Suffice to say he always had a song in reserve for future Christmas nights out.

We played in the same team that drew 0-0 away to Red Star Belgrade in the European Cup Winners' Cup on 8 August 1996 and he scored his first goal in his third match for Hearts, which came in a 3-2 home win over Kilmarnock just a week later. He started thirty-four games for Hearts that season – fourteen more than me – and it was no surprise to me that he won his first Scotland cap that season against Wales as he was always international class. In all, David played 116 games for the club and of course was part of the famous 1998 Scottish Cup-winning side.

I remember being at that match and Davie giving me a bit of a scare – and tens of thousands of Hearts fans – right on the full time whistle. Ally McCoist had broken through and Davie brought him down on the edge of the box. Willie Young was the referee and when he blew his whistle my heart stopped. I thought it was outside the box but wasn't sure if Willie agreed. Thankfully Willie just gave a free-kick, which left Davie relieved, me cheering and McCoist banging the ground in disgust. I would have loved to be part of that Scottish Cup-winning team and an indication of how they became overnight heroes came when Davie was walking back to the Caledonian Hotel from a huge party at Tynecastle. A police car sped up behind him and an officer said, 'Mr Weir, we can't have you walking tonight, son.' They bundled Davie into the back of a police car and dropped him at the door of the Caledonian Hotel.

I was saddened but not surprised that he left Tynecastle midway through the following season when he was bought by Everton for £250,000. He went on to be club captain under two different managers – Walter Smith and David Moyes – during his eight-year spell at the Merseyside club. When he arrived at Rangers under Walter Smith in 2007 he was a revelation and also became captain at Ibrox two years later in place of Barry Ferguson. He won a host of silverware with Rangers and the fact that he was still playing past his fortieth birthday showed how well he had looked after himself through the years.

Off the pitch he is up there among the nicest guys in football, while on it he was an incredibly consistent performer with a ruthless streak. Certainly he was one of the most important characters in the Hearts dressing room near the end of my time at Tynecastle. To clock up sixty-nine Scotland caps, which made him the sixth most capped player in Scottish history behind Kenny Dalglish, Jim Leighton, Alex McLeish, Paul McStay and Tom Boyd, is another example of his worth. The fact that on 24 August 2010 he was recalled to the Scotland squad at the age of forty for the Euro 2012 qualifying matches against Lithuania and Liechtenstein to become the oldest-ever Scottish internationalist tells its own tale. I can't see any outfield player ever beating that international record and in a way I hope nobody ever does because David Weir is a worthy man to hold that honour.

Another strong character, possibly even stronger than David in his own way, is Steven Pressley. He was a real leader and an individual who bought into, and made everybody else buy into, George Burley's vision for Hearts that could have led to the team winning the Scottish League title. For that, along with many other things, I have and always will have massive respect for Steven who had some great years at Tynecastle.

For a while he had been one of those players who had jumped about a few Scottish clubs and one in England without making much of an impression until later in his career. He went from Rangers to Coventry City to Dundee United to Hearts in 1998 on a Bosman where it all kicked off for him before he got his final big move to Celtic. I accept that he played for bigger clubs in terms of support at Celtic and Rangers, but even Steven will surely have to admit he played his best football at Hearts. He had a commanding presence and he was a great professional. To be captain of a team with guys with huge experience from all over the world like Takis Fyssas from Greece and Roman Bednar from the Czech Republic was a tough task. Also remember you also had seasoned Scottish professionals in the Hearts dressing room at the time like Paul Hartley, while young stars like Craig Gordon were starting to make their mark.

It was a big task, particularly with the problems Hearts had at the time, but Steven was up to it. I am not surprised that his managerial career is going on a similar trajectory to Craig Levein, as he has similar characteristics. To begin with, both are very single-minded and driven. In a way, Steven would just push you out of the way if he did not think you were helping the cause and I don't think there is anything wrong with that. If that attitude gets you to where you want to go and means some people get dropped along the way then so be it.

During the players' revolt, if these are the right words, against Vladimir Romanov, Steven was statesmanlike and an absolute rock. For Romanov to suggest he was also going to sell players if they didn't beat Dunfermline was ridiculous in the extreme and in my view Steven, Craig Gordon and Paul Hartley were correct to take a stand. As the club captain Steven was very eloquent in the way he put the points across and I can empathise with him as well as Craig and Paul.

Steven and his two team-mates had a go because they were concerned about how Hearts were being run. It was a brave stance, as Steven would have known that Romanov would try and get his own back on the 'Riccarton Three'. He was always going to be first in the firing line and less than three weeks after he had led the players' revolt he was stripped of the captaincy and left the club for Celtic in early December 2006. The history books will show that Steven, Paul and Craig helped Hearts put together a great run in the league and also helped them win the Scottish Cup. In my view, it was a huge error by Mr Romanov to get rid of Steven, but after he stood up to be counted against him it was always on the cards.

During his time at Tynecastle he had captained the team to famous European wins over top sides like Bordeaux, VfB Stuttgart and Basel. He helped Hearts split the Old Firm and finish second in the league in the 2005-06 season and in the Scottish Cup final of that year he took the first kick in the shoot-out as Hearts beat Gretna 4-2 on penalties. The fact that Steven is part of the Hearts Hall of Fame shows the status that he quite rightly enjoyed at Tynecastle.

The only time that Steven tarnished his reputation in the eyes of myself as a big Hearts fan was when he celebrated a bit too much when he scored against us when he played for Celtic. It was a bit too extravagant for me. Will Steven ever admit to that?

He probably wouldn't, but deep down I would like to think he realises it was maybe over the top and he should not have reacted in such a way because of the great rapport he had with the Hearts fans. By the same token, that does not change my positive thoughts of him, as he was a really important figure in the history of Heart of Midlothian Football Club. In that memorable 2005-06 season when Hearts finished second in the league and won the Scottish Cup he was all you would want as a captain.

Sometimes when I have a spare moment and want to go back in time and relive some good memories I watch re-runs on DVD of when Hearts beat Hibs, which happened a few times when I played. On one occasion in the same game at Easter Road I was fortunate enough to score for Hearts but also had the misfortune to score for Hibs. Let me draw a veil over my own-goal and tell you about my one for Hearts. After sticking the ball in the net I ran across to the old enclosure at Easter Road where our fans were. If you look closely at the DVD you can see among the crowd a teenage boy celebrating wildly. That thirteen-year-old was Paul Ritchie. He was always a dyed-in-the-wool Hearts fan, born in Kirkcaldy, and came into the club as a youngster and was another who was developed by Sandy Clark.

He was strong and quick, could be a bit erratic in his use of the ball but you would want him in your team. He went to Rangers and Manchester City but got a lot of injuries, which was a crying shame. Paul was driven by a desire to be a good player and maybe he did not gain as many Scotland caps as he should have but he is a player I admired greatly. For me, he was a great example of a Hearts fan who joined the club and was developed by the Tynecastle coaching staff and made even better.

He joined the club in 1992 and six years later was part of the Hearts team that won the Scottish Cup. His transfer from Hearts was looked upon, if you remember, as a kind of victory for Sir David Murray over Chris Robinson, who was Hearts chairman at the time. Hearts didn't want him to go to Ibrox so they sent him on a short-term loan deal to Bolton Wanderers where he appeared in both an FA and League Cup semi-final before he finally joined Rangers on a Bosman in June 2000.

Bizarrely, after lobbying so hard to get him, Dick Advocaat, who was the Rangers manager, sold him to Manchester City for a fee of £500,000 without Paul even playing a competitive first-team match, which must have been hugely embarrassing for such a proud young man. Paul then played for several other clubs, including Dundee United, and the last time I heard from him he was an assistant coach at MLS Vancouver Whitecaps. I hope things work out for him there, as Paul was a true Jambo who played the best football of his career at Tynecastle.

Out of all my central defender candidates I feel Paul is the one amongst all others that maybe never really fulfilled his full potential. He was a great player but I believe he could have been world class. He had that great footballing brain and his skill level was high. I am not criticising his career, far from it, because he did a lot better than me and most other players but the injuries and the timing of his moves between clubs made him an unlucky man who didn't find the success he deserved.

My next candidate for my Dream Team is a man who was a real character and a player I would have loved to have seen playing at his peak as a footballer. Pasquale Bruno was a guy who could charm the birds out of the trees at one moment and leave you completely exasperated the next. He was also an incredibly hard tackler. Not for nothing was he nicknamed 'The Animal'.

It is worth me giving you a quick potted history of his career because he played at the top level in Italy and was one of their finest players when they were spoiled for choice. He used to joke – at least I hope he was joking – when he said he never knew how a man of his talent ended up at Hearts among players like me.

Pasquale started out with his hometown club Lecce before moving to the little-known Italian team called Comon before he joined Juventus in 1983. Six years later he won the UEFA Cup with the Bianconeri after they beat Fiorentina in the 1989-90 final and a Coppa Italia winner's medal in the same season. In my world it would take a strong man to move from Hearts to Hibs considering the pelters he would get from the fans for making the jump across to the enemy. Imagine the strength of character that Pasquale needed to show when he moved to Juve's fierce rivals Torino where he won another Coppa Italia medal in 1993. Pasquale then joined Fiorentina who he helped win the Serie B title before he moved to Lecce again.

It was in the summer of 1995 he joined us but he was still a fantastic player. I would have loved to have seen Pasquale at his peak because when he arrived at Tynecastle he was still in great form and because of that had an arrogance about him all of his own. He had legendary status at the club because of his impressive football pedigree and also because he was one of the few Italians up until then to ever play for Hearts. He was a great physical specimen, even as he was getting older. He was also a total professional who brought his good habits to Hearts. He watched what he ate, trained hard and was a model pro for the young players to learn from. As I said, he had that wee degree of arrogance that comes from being a man who played for Juventus at the very top level at a time when Italian football ruled the world.

He probably felt he was better than anyone else in the Hearts changing room at the time, and he probably was! He wasn't a nasty man but he could fight his corner both on and off the pitch. He had good English and could give as good as he got in any verbal jousting. If anybody had a go at him, even over the way he dressed, he wasn't slow in reacting.

Pasquale could have been an honorary Scotsman because he knew how to keep a pound in his pocket. For that two-year period he was at Hearts he stayed in a suite in the Caledonian Hotel, courtesy of the club, and they gave him a credit card to buy his meals in top restaurants like Bar Roma in the west end of Edinburgh. As everybody knows everything about everybody else in football dressing rooms, we were all in awe of his ability to sweet-talk the club into letting him stay in the Caledonian Hotel and eat at Bar Roma, for what we thought would be just the first three months of his time at Hearts. After that we thought when he brought his family across he would be moving into a house. He didn't. He asked the Hearts board if he could have two adjoining suites at the Caledonian and the club paid for that too. And he was still eating free at Bar Roma.

I went in there after we defeated Dundee 3-1 in the semi-final of the Scottish League Cup at Easter Road. I remember Darren Beckford played really well that night and got a goal with Stéphane Paille and Colin Cameron also getting on the score sheet. I went in to Bar Roma with my family and as we were leaving, Pasquale, Dave McPherson and two friends of Dave's came in. I said hello on the way out and thought nothing more about our brief encounter.

We were in at eleven o'clock for training the next morning and Davie, a cool and calm individual, was seething when he arrived. I asked him what was wrong. He said, 'That Italian bugger! At the end of our meal last night he took £25 off each of the three of us, put in nothing himself and then signed for the bill on the Hearts club account.' In other words, Hearts had paid the bill and Pasquale had fleeced three people, one of whom was his team-mate, of £25 each. He had left with a full stomach for free and £75 in his pocket.

When Dave told everybody that story Pasquale got absolute pelters but he just shrugged his shoulders. His attitude was that some guys joined him for dinner and he was such an entertaining superstar they should pay him for that pleasure! It wasn't nasty;

it was just the way he was. He believed that. In his eyes he was the top man.

He was part of the banter in the changing room but felt he was a class apart and, to be honest, as I said earlier, in many ways he was. His family was lovely and he was a great guy but he was a different character compared to other foreign players at the club around that time, like Stephane Adam and Gilles Rousset. He was more guarded and I don't think I really got to know him.

Against Red Star Belgrade in the European Cup Winners' Cup in Belgrade he was immaculate on a night when we got the run around but came away with a creditable draw. I understood that night why he had won European medals in the past as he marshalled the defence superbly. He was asked to man-mark Dejan Stanković, Red Star's playmaker, and I remember Pasquale turning to Jim Jefferies and saying, 'I understand, Jimmy; you want your best player to mark their best player.'

If you need an indication as to how great a player Stanković became, can I say he left Red Star Belgrade to join Lazio for £7.5 million in 1998. They may have had Pavel Nedved, Juan Sebastián Verón as well as Roberto Mancini, who went on to be Manchester City manager, in their midfield but Stanković was always the first name on the team-sheet. He then went to play for Inter Milan and in a glittering career captained Serbia in the 2010 World Cup finals.

Stanković may have been marked tightly a lot during his career but I don't think anybody could ever have done such a good job as Pasquale. He started to get under his skin even during the warm-up and never stopped. Before the game had even started he was running beside him and shouting things at him. Once the game started he never let him out of his sight for the ninety minutes. It was like playing ten-a-side as Pasquale only marked Stanković, who couldn't get away from Pasquale.

Although there was no doubting Pasquale's talent, time waits for no man and just after the two Cup finals when we were beaten, both he and I started to realise our legs were going a bit. I thought in the 4-3 game against Rangers in the Scottish League Cup final at Celtic Park when we played three at the back he was a bit slow and culpable for a few mistakes in our defence. He left us in the summer of 1996 to join Wigan but only played one game before retiring and moving back to Italy, where no doubt he is still enjoying life.

Many players like Pasquale shone brightly but only for a short time at Hearts but few stayed the course like the majestic Alan Anderson. By the time Alan arrived at the club the glory years had started to diminish and it had all become a bit of a struggle, but the one man who was rock solid during that time was big Alan. He was magnificent. You knew that when he put that jersey on and went on that pitch he was going to give everything for Hearts. Any time I met him I could tell he was proud of his association with the club, and quite rightly so. He deserves to be called a Hearts legend.

He used to have a bar called The Pivot and one of the Hearts supporters' buses used to run from there. He also had a business near Aberdeen and a lot of supporters used to stop at his pub up there as well on the way to Pittodrie. I know I am not getting any younger and if I was to look at myself in fifteen years' time I would like to think I could attend Hearts Supporters functions with my head held high in the same way as Alan still does.

He was signed by Tommy Walker in 1963 and stayed with the club up until he retired in 1976 at the age of thirty-six. He was part of the team that finished runners-up in the league in 1964-65 and was in the Scottish Cup final team that lost to Dunfermline in 1968. Alan used to talk about how important a role Jock Wallace played in his physical development when he was assistant to John Harvey. Alan, who was a great physical specimen at the best of times, told me that after being put through his paces by Jock on Gullane Sands he felt strong enough to take on King Kong.

I didn't score too many goals but I really loved celebrating them with the likes of my good mates Kenny Black and John Robertson.

Hearts have been blessed with some world-class goalkeepers through the years but none came close in my book to matching the late, great Jim Cruickshank.

A more consistent defender than Walter Kidd you could not meet. Zico was a real fans' favourite who gave his all for the club.

Craig Levein was an athletic, world-class central defender whose career was cruelly cut short by injury. In this picture he gets the better of Scott Nisbet of Rangers, with Brian Whittaker and his centre-back partner Dave McPherson providing the cover.

Sandy Jardine may have had a glittering career at Rangers before he signed for Hearts, but the influence he had from the minute he walked in the door at Tynecastle cannot be under-estimated.

As an attacking left-back, Tosh McKinlay had no equals. Here he gets the better of Willie Miller of Hibs before setting off on one of his customary runs into the opposition half.

Lifting two Scottish Cup medals for Hearts makes Rudi Skacel a club legend. His two goals against Hibs in the famous 5-1 Scottish Cup win of 2012 will always be remembered.

Steve Fulton had the honour of being captain in the 1998 Scottish Cup final win over Rangers, and after celebrating in style at Parkhead he then led the club on a lap of honour around Tynecastle when they returned to Edinburgh.

Many of my family believe the Hearts team of the 1950s when Tommy Walker was manager was the greatest in the history of the club. With the legendary Dave Mackay as captain of the winning 1958 Scottish League Cup side, in this picture you can understand why.

Freddie Glidden (left) was the captain and Dave Mackay (right) his midfield general in the 3-1 1956 Scottish Cup final win over Celtic, where two goals from Ian Crawford and one from the legendary Alfie Conn brought the trophy back to Tynecastle after a fifty-year wait.

When Willie Bauld visited Balgreen Primary School when I was a pupil, I got him to autograph a picture my family had kept of him from his playing days. It remains amongst my most treasured possessions to this day.

I couldn't have been more delighted for John Robertson when he lifted the 1998 Scottish Cup as it set the seal on his magnificent Tynecastle career.

Robbo was the greatest goal scorer I ever played alongside, and here he acknowledges the fans after yet another of his goals against Hibs.

Donald Ford was one of the most intelligent footballers of his generation who scored vital goals for Hearts throughout his long career at Tynecastle. He also had a great turn of speed which even left his team-mates such as Ernie Winchester (left) and Kevin Hegarty (right) struggling to keep up.

My biggest regret in football was not helping Alex MacDonald bring the silverware to Tynecastle that his hard work at the club deserved.

© ERIC MCCOWAT

Wallace Mercer's (centre) best decision was appointing Alex MacDonald as Hearts manager and Sandy Jardine as his assistant.

COURTESY OF IAIN MERCER

Wallace Mercer was a charismatic, flamboyant Hearts chairman who transformed the club and laid the foundations for future success. He was great fun to be around, as you can see from the day he jumped into the team bath in his expensive suit to celebrate us qualifying for Europe.

The highlight of Steven Pressley's time at Tynecastle was captaining the side to the 2006 Scottish Cup after a nail-biting penalty shoot-out against Gretna.

John Cumming was a real Hearts hero, while Jimmy Wardhaugh was part of the legendary Terrible Trio alongside Willie Bauld and Alfie Conn.

Jim Jefferies (right) and his assistant Billy Brown were the men who brought the Scottish Cup to Tynecastle following the 2-1 win over Rangers back in 1998.

David Bowman (front row, second left) was one of the youngest players to ever turn out for Hearts after he caught the eye playing for Scotland age-grade teams. Here he is alongside yours truly and some other top Under-18 talent such as Paul McStay, Eric Black, Brian Rice, Neale Cooper, Kenny Black and Gordon Marshall at a tournament in France. Not a bad team, don't you think?

When I first arrived at Tynecastle I was part of a five-a-side squad that included (from the top) John Robertson, Pat Byrne, Derek Strickland, Stuart Gauld, goalkeeper John Brough and myself that played in various tournaments across the Lothians.

Sometimes one player captures your imagination as a youngster and in my case it was Ralph Callachan. I used to have his poster up on my wall in a Hearts strip but tore it down the minute he signed for Hibs!

What intrigued me about Alan was that he was a Leith boy who chose to support Hearts ahead of Hibs. When the trains were running back in the 1950s his dad used to take him and his brother to Leith Caledonian Station and they would get the train to Dalry on their way to Tynecastle. He fulfilled his dream of becoming Hearts captain but I am told he could also have become player-manager of Hearts in 1976. He felt he was too young to replace Bobby Seith and the job went to John Hagart.

One young man who I felt made a great impact on Hearts over a short period of time and was like a modern-day equivalent of Alan Anderson was Christophe Berra. Now can I say at the outset I represented Christophe in his early years, although I did not do the deal that saw him move to Wolverhampton Wanderers, which maybe left a wee bitter taste in my mouth, and I think Christophe will understand why. That doesn't take away from the fact that I still rated him as a player, good enough to come into consideration for my Dream Team.

He was spotted playing in a game for Edina Hibs Boys Club at Campbell Park in Edinburgh at the age of sixteen and came into the Hearts when Bert Logan and I were still doing some of the summer training. He came down to Meadowbank when we were doing sprints and he was incredibly fast. Bert wasn't there that first day and the first thing I did when I got home was phone him to say we had a real speed merchant and real find on our hands.

In the modern game pace is a huge asset, although I never liked to think that way when I played because I didn't have any. Christophe was an incredible athlete and I remember one day he had done nine 220 metre sprints with small gaps in between and he ran his guts out for the duration. Just before the final one he asked for permission to leave, which was very unlike him because he was always there to the bitter end. When we asked why he had to go he said it was because he had his PE Practical Exam to take at school the following day. Now to run nine 220 metres at the pace he was doing them at and then go in the next day to do his PE Practical exam gave me an inside knowledge of his dedication, physical ability and recovery rate. I knew at that moment he was a driven individual and his successful career since then has proven that.

There is a scarcity in football of quick, left-sided, good-in-the-air central defenders. His use of the ball still needs to be improved but he is working on that and he already has a lot more international caps than I ever got. I admire him a lot and other centre-backs will envy him because at international level with Scotland he is working with Craig Levein, one of the greatest defenders of his generation, while at club level at Wolverhampton Wanderers he had Mick McCarthy, who was a hard-nosed central defender in his day to work with before he was sacked.

Talking of hard-nosed central defenders, don't be deceived by Dave McPherson if you ever meet him. Quite rightly you will come to the conclusion he is a super, big, gentle bloke. During his playing days on the pitch he was very different and was a real tough, aggressive no-nonsense defender. Indeed, what discussion about the greatest central defenders in the history of Hearts would be complete without reference to Dave?

The pair of us go back a long way and we were part of the Scotland squad that played in the FIFA Youth Championship in Mexico way back in 1983. What a squad that was. Paul McStay, Pat Nevin, Brian Rice, Eric Black and Jim McInally, to name but a few. I still can't quite understand how we managed to lose in the quarter-finals to Poland. Our paths crossed again when big Slim went from Rangers to Hearts then back to Rangers then finally back to Hearts again in that last part-exchange deal that saw Alan McLaren go to Ibrox in October 1994 as part of an overall £2 million transfer package.

Dave was one of the few who survived all the personnel changes made by Jim Jefferies and Billy Brown and he went on to win the Scottish Cup and had a fabulous career at the top level. Also a lot of people forget that he was a versatile player and slotted in at right-back – although he would prefer the phrase right wing-back because he got up and down the pitch a lot – when he lifted the Scottish Cup in 1998.

He played in a World Cup and European Championship for Scotland and when you see where Scottish football is just now he could turn out to be one of the few in history to play in both tournaments for his country. Slim surprised the fans, and maybe himself at times, with his football skills. Some of the mazy runs he went on during matches were incredible. He would meander into the midfield and go past players and you wondered what the hell was going on.

He is a lovely bloke who, as I said, was a gentle big guy off the pitch but he did not suffer fools gladly. As his career progressed, he got even harder and wasn't scared to make his mouth go on the pitch. He brought on players like Gary Naysmith and Paul Ritchie by encouraging and berating them in equal measure. At times he may have looked ungainly because he was so big but nobody can question what he achieved in his career.

Big Slim is still great company and had lots of great stories that used to make me laugh out loud. One of the funniest – partly because I can picture the scene – was when he was partnered with Gilles Rousset during a golf outing we had in Majorca. Both Dave and Gilles are big blokes but the Frenchman had neglected to tell Dave he had hardly played golf, if at all, in his life up till that point. He stepped onto the first tee, took an almighty swing and the ball smacked sideways into a tee box and shot thirty yards behind him, with Gilles shouting like a French Victor Meldrew, 'I don't believe it.'

Near the end of one of Dave's longest ever rounds of golf, as Gilles was taking double figures at some holes, the big goalkeeper lost control of his golf buggy and ran it straight over the eighteenth green in front of the furious members watching from the clubhouse. At the end he kept saying he had never worn golf shoes before and kept complaining about his 'bleesters'. Dave being Dave kept his cool but I am sure he could have throttled big Gilles when they came off the eighteenth green. As a player Dave was one of the best during his two spells at the club from 1987 to 1992 and again from 1994 to 1998 and a man who nearly made my Dream Team.

It was Gordon Strachan who, more than anyone, has made people aware of the importance of having players who help cultivate a good team spirit and he re-emphasised his point a few times when he was manager at Celtic. Grant Murray, when he was at Hearts, helped create that dressing room team spirit that is so vital for any successful club. He won a Scottish Cup Winners' medal in 1998 and was an important part of the side. When Jim Jefferies got an injury in a vital defensive area and they needed to stiffen up the team they would move Grant to where he was needed. He had a huge appetite for the game and could fit in anywhere along the back line. Whenever I watched Grant he gave me a master-class in how to defend. He could read the game superbly and you could bet your bottom dollar that if the ball came back off the goalkeeper, he would be the first to deal with the rebound and clear the ball to safety as he had lightning reflexes. He worked like a beast to keep himself fit and in the gym he trained harder than most people I ever played with or watched, as he wanted to be as good as he could be.

Some people may ask why Grant comes into my thinking for my Hearts Dream Team as he wasn't a huge star at the club. All I can say is that you need dependable guys in your side and if you were looking to ask someone to do a job on the field and not let you down, then Grant would be your man. He was versatile, which maybe worked against him a bit, but the fact he was still playing in the 2011-12 season at the age of thirty-seven tells you all you need to know about him. He looked after himself and worked hard to give himself that longevity in football. He may not have been blessed with the most natural ability but he made the best of every minute he had in the game, and I was not surprised to see him go into management with Raith Rovers at the start of the 2012-13 season.

When Andy Webster came into the centre of the Hearts defence he looked immense. He was a great defender and it was a real bonus that the club signed him in the first place, as there were one or two other teams sniffing around him when he was at Arbroath. He came into Tynecastle and had a steep learning curve under Steven Pressley, who helped him develop as a player and as a man. He had great defensive knowledge but also a nasty streak that he would camouflage quite well, which as a defender you have to do because you will come up against nasty front players who will try and kick you now and again behind the back of the referee.

Although he was a natural top-class defender and a clever player, he was unlucky in many ways. For instance, it would be hard for Andy to carry the negative press that came from the way he left Hearts first time round. It was a ground-breaking moment and there was an extra focus on him because of that. Just to refresh your memory, Andy made football transfer history when he was the first player to invoke a loophole in Article 17 of new FIFA transfer regulations that brought it into line with European law. This enabled him to cancel his contract with Hearts in the third year of a four-year deal, with the proviso that he join a club in a foreign country and that sufficient notice be given to his former employers.

Andy's controversial move to Wigan Athletic was ratified by FIFA on 4 September 2006, seemingly creating a legal precedent for the conduct of international football transfers. Just when Andy thought he was settling in well in English football, the whole thing kicked off again. There were legal wranglings with a subsequent FIFA investigation ruling that Andy had cancelled his Hearts contract without just cause and ordered him to pay

Hearts compensation and suspended him for two games with his new club, Wigan.

It was a mess and must have taken its toll on Andy and it did sour his relationship with the Hearts fans. In the end the supporters did forgive Andy to the extent that in 2011, five years after he left the club, he rejoined us. He repaid them with superb performances in his second spell, most notably in the Scottish Cup 2-1 semi-final win over Celtic at Hampden on 15 April 2012, when he never gave Georgias Samaras or Gary Hooper a kick. I know Hooper scored with a header but he was offside when he put the ball in.

In the Scottish Cup final win over Hibs the following month Andy was equally immense. The Hibs attackers were never given a look in and Andy showed his class from first whistle to last. His confidence in his own ability rubbed off on the rest of the Hearts defence that day and he was the rock on which the famous win was built.

I think any manager would tell you that if Andy puts together a run of games he would be in the Scotland squad every time. In fact, I have a sneaking suspicion that if he stays fit at Hearts he will pull on an international jersey on a regular basis in the years to come. He didn't have the happiest time when he played in the Scotland team that was beaten 5-1 by the USA in Florida a few weeks after Hearts' 2012 Scottish Cup win, but I firmly believe the best has yet to come from Andy Webster.

Roddy MacDonald joined us in 1981 after nine years at Celtic, but despite leaving his boyhood heroes he still put in a great shift for us. He was an old fashioned centre-back who attacked the ball and maybe needed people around him with a bit more composure to make up for his uncompromising approach to the game. He taught me a lot about how to look after myself in the gym as a young player and he was a real tough guy.

When I was an apprentice he was the first person to drop a medicine ball time and time again from ten inches onto his stomach, when he had his feet six inches in the air. He did that forty times in a row. Try that yourself if you can. If you can do it forty times you are a better man, or woman, than me. He did that exercise because, and I don't know if it was an Old Firm thing, but like Alex MacDonald before him Roddy thought the core area was massively important in your physical wellbeing. That was your main engine and you had to keep it in excellent working order. Although Roddy was a big gentle giant off the park, on it he was hard as nails. He was an important part of the team under Alex MacDonald and Sandy Jardine and he brought a high level of professionalism to the football club.

The next two men who I feel deserve a mention are players from yesteryear that my grandfather used to mention to me when I was young. Bobby Dougan was a big part of the Hearts team in the late 1940s and early 1950s after he joined from the Scottish Junior Cup holders, Shawfield, in September 1946. What my grandfather used to tell me about him was that he was no ordinary centre-half. He was a two-footed ball player who could dribble the ball out of defence as easy as he could simply hoof it clear. Back then most centre-backs were big, strong men put in to do the job of stopping the opposition centre-forward. For Hearts to have a guy who stood at nearly six feet tall and who could actually play the ball on the floor made him extra special, which is why I considered him for my Dream Team. He apparently never panicked and was an intelligent footballer which, let's face it, not all central defenders are!

Bobby was a mainstay in the Hearts team from October 1948 to September 1951, until an ankle injury kept him out of action for a whole year. He left us in December 1954 to join Kilmarnock for £4,300 but his eight years at Tynecastle made a huge impact on the older generations of the Mackay family.

The man who replaced him was another huge star to the Mackay clan. Freddie Glidden is a name that deserves legendary status at Hearts, as he captained the club to the 1956 Scottish Cup win. He was a real fun character and even the way he joined Hearts made me smile. He was working for the government in St Andrew's House and got a phone call asking him to go to reception as there was a Mr Fraser waiting to see him. That was the name of his local minister in Stoneyburn and he could not for the life of him think what his local minister wanted to see him for. He thought maybe someone had died or something bad had happened.

The opposite turned out to be true and the Mr Fraser in question was the Hearts chief scout who wanted him to go to Tynecastle immediately to meet manager Davie McLean who wanted to sign him. Freddie breathed a sigh of relief but always used to say divine intervention had a part to play in him joining Hearts. His time at Tynecastle started in 1946 but he was immediately farmed out for two years to Newtongrange Star where he played at right-half in the same team as an up-and-coming Willie Bauld.

He was working for the West Lothian Water Department by the time he made his breakthrough into the Hearts second team in 1948. He remained part-time and used to train on a Tuesday and a Thursday evening and got £6 a week. He made his debut at inside-right in a 4-3 win over Queen of the South in the league in November 1951. It was when Bobby Dougan got injured that he moved back into defence. It was a masterstroke as he won a full house of Scottish domestic trophies. He won the Scottish League in 1957-58, as well as the Scottish Cup in 1955-56. On top of that he twice won the Scottish League Cup, in 1954-55 and again in 1958-59.

Freddie was fantastic in the air and was an inspirational leader who had an incredible presence both on and off the pitch. I met him a few times in hospitality at Tynecastle on match days and socially at other club events, and he was a strong personality. I remember discussing football with him and he had definite opinions. Things got a bit heated and he never once backed down in our discussions. As a leader you need to be strong and knowing Freddie and the way he stood his ground with me in our football discussions he must have been an incredibly strong captain when he was a younger man. He would have led by example out on the pitch.

One of the favourite stories he told me was surrounding the 1956 Scottish Cup final win. Every player got £100 a man and by the time Freddie got his tax taken off he had £66 3s 4d for lifting the trophy in front of 134,000 fans at Hampden. He used to say it wasn't very much but he never complained because wearing the Hearts jersey mattered more than the money back then.

After the win in Glasgow the Hearts team bus made a detour first via Blackburn, where Freddie stayed, and then to Stoney-burn, where his mum and dad came to their garden gate to give him a big cheer. It then went to Livingston where Tommy Walker had been brought up to allow him to show the trophy to his folks. At the Maybury roundabout they all got on an open-top bus on the way to the North British Hotel. As he was captain he was at the front of the bus with the trophy, and he described it as one of the proudest moments of his life. And how did he celebrate victory that night? Freddie said he was never a big drinker and only a few glasses of sherry passed his lips.

What he also used to constantly tell me was that the game was cleaner in his day. Yes, Hearts had some tough tacklers but he didn't remember having his jersey pulled once. He said he would have probably got sent off for retaliation if he had been playing nowadays.

It seems the dressing room wind-ups were on the go even in Freddie's day because even as club captain he seems to be have been on the end of a few. One of the best he told me about was when Tam McKenzie, who was a full-back, was rooming with him on a tour to South Africa. The pair of them were out buying fruit and Freddie bought a pineapple. He put it in his room to eat later but when he was out Tam cut the top off it and spooned out all the insides. He then put an apple inside to give it a bit of weight before putting the top back on. When he went to eat his pineapple Freddie got the shock of his life to find an apple inside his tropical fruit.

As a former successful Hearts captain, Freddie was pushing hard to be in my Hearts Dream Team starting eleven but after long deliberation my two choices are men who I think would fit together superbly well at the centre of defence.

Sandy Jardine, at his prime with Rangers, was easily one of the greatest defenders in the world. The fact he was full-time at Ibrox from 1965 up until he joined us as a player and assistant manager in 1982 shows his consistency at the top level over a long period. Sandy's pace was dwindling a bit by the time he arrived at Tynecastle, but he was still a class act. I have paired him for that reason with Craig Levein who had an athleticism about him that was unmatched in any player I played with. I am sure Craig could run round behind Sandy and clear up anything that he missed. Both of them had good football brains, could pass the ball and kept cool under pressure, which is vital for central defenders.

Sandy won the Scottish Football Writers Player of the Year in 1986, at the age of thirty-eight. To pick up such an accolade so late in his career is an incredible achievement. It did not happen by chance. It happened because Sandy lived his life to make sure that on the Wednesday or the Saturday when he played he was one hundred per cent fit and ready for the challenge ahead. He had class and calmness and an assurance about him that was higher than any other player I knew. Although he always pushed me hard at training and during games, I could always relate to Sandy. He came from the same sort of background as me and went to Balgreen Primary School and Tynecastle Secondary School, just like me.

I remember him coming in to Balgreen Primary when he was doing a trophy presentation to our school team. To a young, star-struck, would-be footballer, it was an amazing moment for me. Sandy had an aura about him and I could hardly speak when I was introduced to him. When I was supposedly an equal to him as a player at Hearts I still felt he had that aura, and to begin with, it was hard for me to think I was an equal of such a great man.

I accept he is associated more with Rangers and was at his peak when he won all those trophies at Ibrox. I realise that and take all that on board, but what Sandy brought to the Hearts team and the influence he had on players like me cannot be underestimated. It must have been hard for Sandy, who had won thirty-eight Scotland caps and the European Cup Winners' Cup among his haul of trophies at Rangers, to play with lesser players at Hearts, and I say that with the utmost respect to all Hearts players, including myself. I accept we got the tail end of Sandy's career but what a tail end it was.

As for Craig Levein, well, a better centre-half you will never find in Scottish football looking back or forward. Now, after being given the honour of picking my Hearts Dream Team, I was never going to leave Craig out just because I had a falling out with him. I am not saying he would put me in his Dream Team but I'm not bearing a grudge with Craig when it comes to my admiration for him as a player.

A lot is made of my relationship with Craig and I have to say it is just one of those things that happens in football. There is never going to be a changing room when everybody gets on with everybody. You have closer friendships, people you have more of a respect for and things evolve from there. Others you keep your distance from, and it was a bit like that with Craig and me.

Looking back maybe part of the reason for a bit of friction between Craig and me was the fact that he was very single-minded and opinionated. Very much like me. When we played together Craig, as a defender, was closer to Sandy Jardine at management level than Alex MacDonald, while I was closer to Alex being a midfielder. As I said earlier Sandy was really hard·

with me when I played and it was like good cop–bad cop for me when he was co-manager with Alex. Sandy was on my back to make me play better and keep up high standards. He certainly managed to keep me on my toes, while he probably could see a lot of Craig in himself in terms of both of them being top-class defenders and helped him a lot in many ways on and off the park.

Our fall-out still does not take away my respect for him as a footballer. Craig for me, barring injury, would have played for one of the top clubs not just in Britain but in Europe. I could have seen him one day turn out for one of the top Spanish clubs, as he had a great football brain that would have been perfectly suited for European football. His pace was one of his biggest attributes. He was like a top thoroughbred racehorse coming into the final furlong. He was a smooth runner and physically was in great nick. He had learned his trade at Cowdenbeath and had paid his dues and when he arrived at Hearts in November 1983 for £30,000, he was an absolute bargain. He played in a World Cup for his country and you cannot do much more than that apart from winning domestic trophies.

As for the incident with Graeme Hogg, when he had a fight with him on the pitch, well, I don't know the reason why it happened, and it came as a big shock. It should not have happened but it did. I think that even after that incident there was no way Craig Levein would have been forced out of Tynecastle. Absolutely no way. He was much too important a player for us and it would have been irresponsible for the manager at the time not to keep him.

It has been well documented that Craig missed that infamous final league game against Dundee at the end of the 1985-86 season because he was under the weather. Would we have won the Scottish League title that fateful day at Dens Park if Craig had not been sick and unable to play? Absolutely. He could have made that big a difference, as he was that great and important a player. I was gutted that he was too ill to play, as the team against Dundee would have been so much better balanced with Craig in it and we wouldn't have lost any goals. Roddy MacDonald came in for Craig at Dens Park, and I am not being disrespectful to Roddy, but they had different styles. I am sure Craig would have been an influential, calming figure and led us to victory.

Out of everybody in the Hearts dressing room it does not surprise me one little bit that Craig went on to be the most successful of any of us from a managerial point of view. His drive was always there and in football, as in life, you need to have a great intelligence, have a good knowledge and be strong enough to know how to put that knowledge across to others. Craig knows how to do that very well.

From a Hearts point of view what can't be forgotten is the great service Craig gave the club. Being at the one team from 1983 till 1995 is a great shift in any language. There are so many games Craig excelled in it is hard to pick the best of the bunch. Among my Craig Levein highlights were the European tie against Bayern Munich in 1989 when he was outstanding and also the way he wrote himself into the history books by scoring the last goal in front of The Shed before it was pulled down to make way for the Wheatfield Stand. Off the pitch, like all born winners, Craig was a really competitive character and I don't remember him losing many bets when the squad played head tennis for money on the Friday before matches.

Craig could have gone on playing if he hadn't picked up a bad injury against Dunfermline in a League Cup tie on 30 August 1995. I was playing in that 2-1 home win and knew immediately something was wrong. It turns out he popped the same knee that he had had operations on in the past. It was testament to Craig's willpower that he had previously fought his way back to fitness after similar bad injuries, but this time it sadly was not to be. Craig went through rehabilitation but the knee never got back to being solid and stable enough for him to return to the standard he was used to out on the pitch. It was a crying shame to lose him but what a servant he had been.

For me, having Sandy and Craig together at the centre of my Dream Team defence would mean the opposition strikers would hardly get a kick. The pair of them, at their peak, were world-class and in the current transfer market they would be valued in the tens of millions of pounds. Out of all my selections, naming Sandy and Craig as my Dream Team central defensive partnership was one of my easier choices.

9

AT THE HEART OF HEARTS

The midfield area is one I obviously know very well after playing there my whole career. I thought it would be arrogant in the extreme to pick myself for my Hearts Dream Team, so you won't find my name anywhere in this chapter. Also as it is my Dream Team I would enjoy a lot more looking on and marvelling at the midfield I have chosen as they out-run, out-tackle and out-think any opposition they come up against.

The first man who came into my reckoning was someone I expect some of you may find a surprising candidate. Derek Ferguson came from Rangers in 1990 and was the record signing at £150,000 for the club at that particular time. He was signed by Alex MacDonald but it was Joe Jordan who got the best out of Fergie, who went on to play for Sunderland under Terry Butcher. It was Fergie who put in one of the two best individual performances in defeat I have ever seen by a player in a Hearts jersey. Neil McCann was the other in the Scottish League Cup final at Parkhead when we were beaten 4-3 by Rangers in 1996.

I am sure what motivated Derek's performance, which came against Rangers three years earlier, was to show Graeme Souness what he had lost when he let him leave Ibrox. We were leading 1-0 through a rare goal from Allan Preston in a Scottish Cup semi-final tie on 3 April 1993, and Derek was running the show.

He covered every blade of grass on the Parkhead pitch – Hampden was being renovated at the time – but the rest of us didn't reach the same standard. We were beaten 2-1 but that loss was not down to Derek, who was absolutely fantastic from start to finish. At the final whistle I felt more sorry for him than anybody else. Derek must have felt hellish, as he had given his all and had been the best man on the park and still finished on the losing side.

His great play as a central midfield man punted me out to be a wing-back but I could have no complaints as he had fabulous, fabulous ability. He had a great first touch, great passing skills and a great engine on him. He had a very good spell at Hearts and I remember us going through a period during Joe Jordan's first full season when Derek was injured. George Wright came in and we went through nine games undefeated but such was the importance of Derek that he was brought straight back into the team when he was fit. That was harsh on George but you could understand why Derek was always the number one midfield pick when he was fit.

If he had started at Hearts and then moved to Rangers, rather than the other way round, he would have been hailed as a superstar. Maybe he was in the wrong place at the wrong time with Rangers because Souness had money to spend and decided to let him go because guys like Ray Wilkins and Paul Gascoigne were coming in. Rangers' loss was our gain and although he maybe did not get as many goals as he would have liked, he was an incredible talent. Looking back, Derek Ferguson had the ability to make himself a permanent Scotland internationalist but for whatever reason it did not happen for him and he only won a couple of caps, which puzzles me to this day.

Davie Laing is a man I met a few times at various functions such as Willie Bauld Memorial Dinners and who wore the number six jersey for Hearts with pride. He used to say that his twelve years at Tynecastle were the highlight of his life, never mind his football career. He didn't win any silverware at

Tynecastle but said it was a privilege to be involved in the first game at Hearts when Alfie Conn, Willie Bauld and Jimmy Wardhaugh played together. They beat East Fife 6-1 at Tynecastle in 1948 and Davie could give me chapter and verse as to what happened. David used to laugh that people always remembered Willie got a hat-trick and Alfie got two but they kept forgetting he scored the other from the penalty spot.

He also used to tell me the Terrible Trio were such a potent attacking threat because they complemented each other's style of play. Alfie could run up and down the park and put in the tackles and could be relied upon to do the basics well. Willie did very little running but was always in the right place when it came to scoring goals. Jimmy was a much more natural player and played off instinct. He would never fit into any style of play and had to be given freedom to roam around the forward line.

He also told me that, although he had played for Bath City and went on to play for our rivals Hibs, Clyde and Gillingham, he never felt more a part of a football family than when he was at Hearts. He was part of the fabric of the football club when he was there and loved every moment of his time at Tynecastle. His late wife Betty and Jimmy Wardhaugh's wife Anne helped in the canteen on match days and helped set up what you would call nowadays a players' lounge.

My grandfather used to say how reliable a player Davie was to Hearts. He was a team player and, although there was nothing flashy about him, he was part of a successful team at Tynecastle and one of their unsung heroes. He joined us in 1942 straight from school but ended up playing for Bath City to begin with during his time in the Royal Navy during the Second World War. Although he didn't play in the Hearts team that won the 1954 League Cup due to injury, it was his goal in an earlier game that helped them on their way there. My grandfather always used to remember that goal because it was so special. It came in the group stages when Hearts needed to beat Celtic at home to

135

qualify. More than 40,000 people were inside Tynecastle to see the match which was level until David slotted home a penalty to give Hearts a 3-2 win.

The next man who came into my consideration is a player I could not ignore. Lots of well-known and respected long-term Hearts watchers, including Mike Aitken, the former chief football writer of *The Scotsman*, firmly believe that Willie Hamilton was the most talented man to ever turn out for Hearts. In preparing this book, Mike told me that the legendary Jock Stein, who managed Willie at Hibs, told him that he was the greatest player he had ever seen. Mike recalls talking to Jock in a Reykjavik hotel on a Scotland trip when he said that only Jimmy Johnstone and Jim Baxter came close to matching Willie for talent. Stein used to say to people to think of Kenny Dalglish at his peak and they would have a rough comparison of how great a player Willie was.

Also during that era, that hugely respected broadcaster and football historian Bob Crampsey claimed Willie was the most visionary player he had ever seen. He wore the number ten jersey and was what we would call nowadays an attacking midfielder who would play in the hole behind the front two. However, it seems, like Johnstone and Baxter, two men who liked a drink, alcohol also proved to be his undoing. There are stories of how he used to nip away from Tynecastle for drinking sessions at the social club at the Longstone Bus Depot. He tried the patience of the coaching staff time and time again by either not turning up for training or getting there late smelling like a brewery.

He joined Hearts from Middlesbrough for just £2,500 in June 1962 and he scored a great goal on his debut in a 2-0 win over Dundee. He played a major role in the 1-0 win over Kilmarnock in the Scottish League Cup final of that year, setting up the winning goal for Norrie Davidson after a run down the right and a perfect cutback that Norrie ran in to score from. But his drinking disrupted his season and after playing in a 3-1 win over Forfar on 12 January 1963, he started to miss lots of training sessions and was suspended for two weeks for his absence.

The patience of manager Tommy Walker finally snapped and he was shown the door. That was fair enough and something that Tommy was entitled to do, but as a Hearts fan looking back I find it hard to understand why he was sold to our rivals Hibs, albeit for a profit as he went for £6,000. Even so, it was a strange decision indeed as after Walter Galbraith stepped down as Hibs manager it was Jock Stein, when he took over at Easter Road, who brought the best out of Willie. He shone brightly, but not for very long at Hearts, but in that short period did enough to convince many respected commentators and fellow professionals he should be hailed as one of the true greats of Tynecastle.

One man who, in my opinion, doesn't reach those heights but does have a place in the history of Hearts is Frenchman Julien Brellier, who found his form and lots of confidence at Tynecastle. Julien probably knew very little about the club before he joined it but he embraced Hearts and its traditions. He was a huge part of the Hearts side that came out the traps so quickly early in the season under George Burley and would, in my opinion, have won the league if Burley had not been sacked. He played the holding midfield role as well as anyone I have ever seen play it for Hearts.

If you play 4-3-3 or 4-5-1, that person in front of the back four is hugely important. Brellier was magnificent in that position. Out of all the players that were lost after George Burley was sacked he was the one I felt was the most difficult to replace. He was sensational for Hearts in the short period he was there.

Stefano Salvatori will always be remembered as part of the Hearts team that won the 1998 Scottish Cup and he was magnificent when he was at Tynecastle. Initially Jim Jefferies and Billy Brown had brought in Paul Smith, who was a lifelong Hearts supporter, to challenge me for my position, as Jim and Billy liked to have two players fighting it out for every place in the team.

Paul had been at Dunfermline and Falkirk and was someone I lost my place to for a while but then I pushed myself on and got back into the team. When Paul drifted out of the picture they signed Stefano, who arrived in 1996, and to be honest in my advancing years, in football terms his challenge was one I simply could not overcome.

Hearts were still treating their players well when Stefano arrived at the club, and like Pasquale Bruno before him he was allowed to stay in the Caledonian Hotel with the club picking up the bill. The big Italian got to know the owners of Indigo Yard and Bar Roma very well, as he was always in both establishments when he had a moment.

On the pitch he had good athleticism and had that Italian discipline which had taught him how important it was to retain possession. He was a real team player and he would win the ball and give it to players who were more creative than he was.

Around that time Jim Jefferies was getting rid of the players who, in his eyes, would be dead wood, and I was one of them. The only two from my age group who made it to the 1998 Scottish Cup final were Dave McPherson and wee Robbo. That was just the way Jim and Billy were. They liked to change faces and a lot of times it worked, and it certainly did with Stefano, who was an important signing for the football club.

Perhaps the hardest call for me was who to pick to play on the right side of midfield. One man who came very close was Paul Hartley, who in the end just missed out, although I know he played more centrally for Hearts a lot of the time. I can remember Paul being introduced to the Hearts crowd after he signed at the same time as Dennis Wyness back in 2003. Paul did not get anything like the reception that Dennis got. Undoubtedly the fact that Hibs were among his previous clubs cooled the fans towards him. Despite that, he kept his head down and with the help of the coaching staff led by Craig Levein became a top, top player.

For someone who up until then had been a run-of-the-mill player, what he did at Hearts was nothing short of sensational. No disrespect to Hamilton, St Johnstone or even Hibs, but he got the opportunity at a bigger club to do well and made the most of it. Even after Craig Levein left and George Burley came in Paul still managed to retain his place. He did that through his vigour, his drive and his ability to get in behind defenders and link in with the front players. He had boundless energy and got goals.

Obviously the one big memory most Hearts fans have of Paul is him being part of the 2006 Scottish Cup-winning team that beat Gretna on penalties in the final. But what I will also always remember is that he scored a hat-trick against Hibs in the semi-final. For me, that is equally as memorable as being part of the Scottish Cup-winning team. You may not agree with that, but look at the background to Paul's hat-trick at Hampden Park that day. He had previously played for Hibs, a team that didn't care too much that he left Easter Road in the first place. He came to Tynecastle and the fans didn't take to him straight away because of his association with our rivals, which meant he took longer to win them over. But due to his own self-belief he became a fans' favourite and scoring a hat-trick against Hibs that day at Hampden in the Scottish Cup semi-final must have been a fantastic moment for him. I would have loved to have done that! It was the first hat-trick of his career. What a time to break his duck. For the record, I played more times for Hearts against Hibs than any player in history. Fifty-five times I took the field against them and lost just eight. For me that 4-0 win at Hampden at the time eclipsed any of them as it was payback time as far as I was concerned. For years and years I took lots of stick for the 7-0 defeat in January 1973. Beating Hibs in the semi-final of the Scottish Cup blew that result out the water but obviously that has since been bettered with the famous 5-1 Scottish Cup win over our less-than-noisy neighbours at Hampden in 2012.

I felt Hearts helped Paul's career as much as Paul helped Hearts. Celtic and Rangers are always looked upon as the big clubs but I don't think some players realised how big a club Hearts really are, both on and off the pitch. Playing for a big club like Hearts inspired Paul to great things. Through the years Hearts fans have always had iconic figures to look up to and, to a certain generation of supporters, Paul will be among those iconic figures. He will certainly always be remembered and welcomed at Tynecastle by the fans.

Because Paul's career flourished at Hearts he got a move to Celtic and also had a spell down in England with Bristol City before playing at the top level for Aberdeen before hanging up his boots. I feel it was his time at Hearts that extended his playing career. He was at a crossroads when he first arrived at Tynecastle but with the encouragement of the coaching staff and the warmth he felt from the fans, he left the club a much better player than when he arrived.

There are some players that fans remember playing in different positions, but for me I learned more watching Drew Busby playing in a midfield role for Hearts than I did watching him as a striker, which is why I have included him in this Dream Team category rather than name him as one of my striking candidates. I know he made his name as a fantastic striker when he played with Airdrie alongside Drew Jarvie and I remember him scoring a lot of goals against Hearts, but when I watched my club as a boy he played more games in the middle of the park and that is where I feel qualified to judge his talent.

I loved playing with Wattie Kidd, Brian Hamilton. Kenny Black, Neil Berry, guys that I could rely upon, and I would have loved to have played with Drew Busby for that reason. It would have been a dream come true, as he was a real warrior out on the park who I am sure would have looked after the younger, more inexperienced players in the Hearts team. He had been round the block when he joined us in May 1973 after spending time at

Coventry City, Third Lanark and Airdrie. In fact, one of his claims to fame was that he scored Third Lanark's last goal before they went out of business. He had been signed to partner Donald Ford up front and he was a real rumbustious front man who could use his muscle to get the better of defenders.

When I started watching Hearts he was playing more in midfield and I remember how his tough tackling made him the perfect man to break down the opposition attack. Drew was a gentleman off the pitch, a quiet man who I met a few times at functions at Tynecastle and thoroughly enjoyed his company. I think he remains a bit embarrassed at the esteem in which he is held by Hearts supporters to this day. That is more than thirty-five years ago but there still are people who remember Drew, who they called the 'Buzz-bomb', with great affection. He was a shining light during some very dark days for Hearts.

You don't sing a song about individual players at a club unless they are held in high regard and Drew had one in his honour. We spoke earlier in the book about the song about Jim Cruickshank and will talk later about one in honour of Bobby Prentice. There was also a song made up by the Hearts fans about Drew that showed how much he was loved. I used to sing it at games and it went along the lines of, if I remember correctly, 'His name is Drew Busby, he is the talk of the north. He comes from Tynecastle just over the Forth. He drinks all your whisky and Newcastle Brown, the Gorgie boys are in town.' That song was about how he was perceived by the fans. He was a hard man on the pitch and the fans liked to think of him acting in the same way off it. I don't even know if Drew liked whisky or Newcastle Brown but he was certainly a man's man.

I don't think I ever saw anyone win a physical battle against Drew over ninety minutes. He could really look after himself. If that meant being nasty then so be it. If he got laid into there would be no cry-baby stuff from him. If somebody tried to take Drew out off the ball he would not retaliate. He would give them a stare, bide his time and get them back when he was ready.

The only time I saw Drew get caught by the ref was at Easter Road in the late 1970s when he got sent off. I have stepped out of line there myself and got my marching orders, but when Drew went off he was still scowling and already plotting revenge. The Hibs players knew it wasn't a good idea to get Drew Busby angry and he scored two goals against them in a Hearts win next time the derby was played.

The goals of his I remember most include the one he got when Hearts beat Hibs 4-1 in 1973 and he also got a famous one against Lokomotiv Leipzig in the 5-1 win three years later. Drew used to say that his favourite ever match was one against Kilmarnock because it showed Tynecastle and the Hearts fans in their true light. The legendary Willie Bauld had turned up after being away from the place for decades and because of that the stadium was buzzing and the crowd was on their feet for the whole game. The fact he scored in front of Willie Bauld made Drew's day.

Drew was also a confident enough person to tell stories against himself, and after scoring twelve penalties out of twelve for Hearts, it proved unlucky thirteen against Dundee United in the League Cup quarter-final at Tynecastle on 16 November 1977. He had scored Hearts' only goal in a 3-1 defeat at Tannadice, and Walter Kidd and Drew had scored in a 2-0 win at Tynecastle in the return leg that meant the sides finished level, which forced the tie into extra-time and then penalties. With the scores level in the penalty shoot-out, up came Drew to take the fourth kick for Hearts but he slipped and the ball didn't even reach the goal. He laughs when he tells that story, which had a happy ending, as Hearts won 4-3 on penalties in the end.

The late Willie Ormond described Drew as the most under-rated player at Hearts because of the way he could play in midfield or up front and could score goals from either position.

Willie worked with hundreds of top players and his praise of Drew sums up how great a player he was.

The Austrian Thomas Flogel was at Hearts for five years and he had great qualities on and off the pitch. Thomas was fit and technically outstanding with a great touch with either foot and he got about the pitch with ease. He could fit in at full-back but I felt he was better in midfield. He was a great representative of Hearts and was a good guy who made his name at the club. A part of the 1998 Scottish Cup-winning team and the fact he won thirty-seven caps for Austria gives an indication of his pedigree.

When Dave Bowman made his Hearts debut he was the youngest player to play in the Premier League, which was no surprise as he was physically strong and a huge talent even at just sixteen. What a lot of people don't know is that he had severe back problems as a youngster and had had a couple of operations on his spine. When you think of a young man having to endure long operations like that, then playing in the Hearts first team, then getting a move to Coventry at twenty-one which was only pushed through to save the club because they needed the money, it shows his strength of character and how quickly he had to mature as a footballer and a man.

Bow and I go way back and we played together at Salvesen Boys Club, Edinburgh Primary Schools and also Edinburgh Secondary Schools. We also faced each other when he played for Portobello High School against me from Tynecastle High School. From the age of ten our football paths crossed and we became good pals. As teenagers we used to go together to Pittenweem to his grandparents' or to Dunbar to my grandparents' for weekend breaks, where we always used to end up playing football somewhere or other.

When he moved to Coventry from Hearts I remember going down to see him make his debut and we ate in the restaurant owned by Rusty Lee, who was a famous female television chef on TV AM in the 1980s. Bow got to know her well and they were alike in that both were crackers and great fun. Bow lives life to the full and has great enthusiasm and did a lot of crazy, but not hurtful things, while at Hearts. I have seen Bow lifting a bowl of rice and pouring it over somebody's head. He also used to nail players' shoes to the floorboards at Tynecastle for a laugh. He just had a streak of fun and madness in him. I even heard a story that he and Jim McInally once lifted a dog into the bath of former Dundee United manager Jim McLean after training at Tannadice just before he was due to jump in. Why he did it and whose dog it was and how he got it into the changing room I do not know. For all his crazy ways he was hugely respected at Tynecastle and I am sure he is doing a great job working with the youths at Dundee United and passing on the vast experience that he has to them.

At Hearts Bow would usually play on the right and I would play central in the early years but, to be honest, we did not play that much together because it would be too risky having two inexperienced guys in midfield at the same time. It is a man's game and having two teenagers would not work, despite the fact both of us knew each other's game and played with lots of confidence. Bow played alongside the likes of Derek Addison and Pat Byrne at the time he made his breakthrough. He was a big player for Hearts and one that deserved consideration for my Dream Team.

My all-time hero as a Hearts fan growing up was Ralph Callachan and he remains one of the top players ever for me at Tynecastle. I accept a lot of people may not agree but you could not question his natural talent. There is a picture of Ralph in the Tynecastle Boys Club clubrooms at Balgreen Primary School even now and I still bow to it every time I go in. He did commit the cardinal sin, and he knows I feel that way, by moving to Hibs, but before that he had gone to Newcastle United and brought in much needed finance for Hearts. He played at a time when the team was in a bit of a transformation but he was a quality footballer. He could see a pass, he had composure, could use both feet and was an all-round classy player.

I remember going to the re-opening of Mad Hatters, the nightclub in Edinburgh's High Street, when I had just joined Hearts and Ralph was there and I was in awe of him as he was my hero. When we first played against each other I was equally star-struck and did something maybe not terribly professional. I played for Hearts against Hibs in the East of Scotland Shield and I got him to sign a bit of paper for me afterwards, which read, 'Best wishes, Gary, from Ralph Callachan'. I kept it in pristine condition for years because he was my hero. Can I just say, I have never asked for the autograph of an opposition player before or since.

Like me, Ralph didn't really have pace, but he could still go past people pretty easily and could score from midfield. I would go to Hearts games and just watch Ralph as he played in a similar position to me. I know going to watch one player out of eleven may not sound very healthy but I held him in such high esteem. Any time I meet Ralph nowadays I think of how important a part he played in my love of football through watching him. There are a lot of Hearts teams I used to watch that I could tell you seven or eight of the players at the very least. I could not tell you a lot of the players Ralph played alongside because, as I said earlier, I just used to go to watch him.

He was coming to the end of his career when I was starting out and the biggest game in which I played against my idol was the 3-2 win over Hibs on 3 September 1983 when I got hooked at half time. I was rotten that day and had used up a lot of nervous energy even before kick-off and can have no complaints about being taken off. It was my first real competitive derby, and did the fact that my idol was in the opposition line-up put me off my stride? Possibly. Actually, let's blame him for me being rotten.

I still bump into him at Hearts functions and he is a man who is a Peter Pan figure, who still looks like he did when he played.

Ralph will admit a lot of that is down to the fact he does not eat but just drinks. He likes a lager, does my pal Ralph. That is his recipe to stay trim. Drink, don't eat.

Tommy Walker gets a bigger mention elsewhere in the book for his time as manager but also deserves a mention for his ability on the park. He joined us in May 1932 from Linlithgow Rose and stayed up until September 1946 when he joined Chelsea for £8,000. He was an inside-forward who scored on his debut against Ayr United in the league and picked up crucial goals for club and country throughout the years. An indication of how great a player he was came from the fact he won his first Scotland cap at the age of just nineteen, just two years after he joined Hearts. Just under two years later he scored the goal that made him an all-time hero for the Tartan Army.

Taking penalties at the top level is tough enough at the best of times. Scotland were 1-0 down to England at Wembley when they were awarded a late penalty on 4 April 1936. Tommy was relatively inexperienced at international level but still volunteered to take it. Twice the strong wind blew the ball off the spot. At the third attempt he put it back on the spot and calmly scored. That took guts.

He was a huge hero at Hearts and although Arsenal offered £12,000 for him, which would have been a world record at the time, fan power won the day and a threatened boycott of Tynecastle forced the board to keep him. Tommy played alongside some great Hearts players like Barney Battles, Andy Anderson, Alex Massie and Dave McCulloch but, like me, never won any major honours despite his best efforts. The closest he got, just like me, was a second place league finish, in 1937-38. During the Second World War he played for the famous Army 'All-Stars' team before Chelsea signed him when hostilities ended. At Stamford Bridge he was part of a forward line that included Tommy Lawton and he scored twenty-four goals in 103 appearances during his two and a half years at the club.

The next man up came ever so close to making my Dream Team. Some who saw him play will be flabbergasted that he didn't. The first time I ever met John Cumming was when I sat next to him at a Prestonpans Hearts Supporters function. I was a young lad at the time and was totally star-struck. I had seen the famous pictures of John with the bandage round his head in the 1956 Scottish Cup final when he would not come off after picking up a big gash on his forehead, the result of a clash of heads with Willie Fernie of Celtic. John told me he was bleeding all over the place and used a sponge to mop up the damage, but there was no way he was going to come off. It was only after the game he had four stitches put in his head wound. No wonder the fans called him 'The Lionheart' and 'The Iron Man'.

He still looked after himself when I met him at that function in Prestonpans all these years later and was bright as a button. He was well into his seventies then and in great nick. Although he never promoted the stories himself, he was still doing his neighbours' gardens as well as his own at that age. He was a fit, fit man. We got talking about how tough pre-season training was and I briefly mentioned about players stiffening up after a day of hard running. John said he was disgusted at that and couldn't understand it. He felt players were privileged to train every day and should always be at the peak of their fitness and never be too tired after a session.

He told me that trains didn't run very regularly from Edinburgh to Carluke, where he lived, and one day, after he had done a full training session on Gullane Sands, he got back to Waverley Station to find he had missed his train by five minutes and faced an hour wait for the next one. Rather than hang about he ran home from Edinburgh to Carluke. Now that is at least thirty-six miles by my calculations and he ran that distance quite easily, he claimed. It may have been ten miles more than a marathon but next day he was back at Gullane Sands as fit as ever.

Maybe he was trying to inspire me as a young player to stick in and work hard by telling me that story but for whatever reason he brought it up, it certainly worked. You would not find a harder trainer in pre-season than me after I spoke to John that day.

I saw John at games as he was a Hearts season ticket holder and came along to lots of matches with his pal. He was a gem. An absolute legend. He gained a medal from each of the seven domestic honours Hearts picked up during the glory years. Two Scottish League Winners medals, one Scottish Cup badge and four Scottish League Cup medals is an incredible haul.

He played at left-wing to begin with before moving back to left-half, although he used to swear he even played in goal once in a reserve match when the first-choice keeper fell ill. In more than 600 appearances he was never booked once. The term 'hard but fair' could have been created to sum up John Cumming.

Eamonn Bannon had two spells at Hearts, the first starting in July 1976, broken by time at Chelsea and Dundee United, but still deserves to be included in my Dream Team discussions. He was an educated player who was physically strong and could cross with both feet. He had a great engine up and down the pitch, and he was a player who was sold to Chelsea for £215,000 in January 1979 to help save the club from financial ruin. As far as I am aware, he did not look for the move to Stamford Bridge but could not turn it down when it came his way.

When he did play for us he gave the team great balance in the wide-left area. You could play 4-3-3, you could play 4-4-2 and Eamonn would fit in. Because he knew the game well he could even fill in at full-back if need be. He was a clean striker of the ball and demanded high standards from himself and his team-mates.

Eamonn could create goals and had a great work ethic. The great thing with him is that he never went looking for individual praise and was one of the most unselfish midfielders I ever played with. He may have got just eight goals in just under 300 appearances but one is famous, as his penalty in the final game of the 1977-78 season away to Arbroath clinched promotion from the old Scottish League Division One. Hearts had to win that match to pip Dundee to promotion and to go up along with Morton, and it was Eamonn's goal that made it happen. After his time at Chelsea and Dundee United he returned to Hearts in May 1988, and the following season he played in thirty-one league games – the exact same ones I played in, so I feel well qualified to talk about his ability. That season in particular I saw first-hand what a clever football brain Eamonn had as he was in his thirties when he returned for his second spell at Tynecastle and knew he had to make the ball do the work. He managed to do that and I learned a lot from playing in the same midfield as him.

Alex MacDonald, who I have talked about in my management Dream Team category, is a man who also deserves consideration as a player. He hated getting beat at anything – be it head tennis, be it dominoes. It did not matter. That was not something he developed. That was a quality he had been born with. His game changed a bit at Hearts when he arrived in August 1980 because at Rangers he had been box to box, goals at the back post, but he was getting older and slowing down. At the point he came to us he used his experience, got on the ball, made passes and let the others do the running more than he maybe did when he was at Rangers. He still had that winning mentality and we all learned from him on the pitch.

In the first game before our great unbeaten run in 1985-86 of thirty-one games when he was manager, we both started on the bench against Clydebank but he put himself on and left me on the side-lines. At times I felt he was keeping me out of the team intentionally but that was just me being pig-headed. To be fair, Alex saw all his players as equals but of course if we deserved a tongue-lashing he gave us one. He had no favourites.

If the boot was on the other foot and he was playing badly, I must admit I wouldn't have a go at him, partly because he was my more experienced team-mate but more importantly because he was also my manager. I had too much respect for him and would have found it difficult to lay into him during a game. Giving the manager stick was not something that came easy to me.

Alex could play in any position across the midfield but he realised in the 1985-86 season it was time for him to take a step back from playing. Because he had instilled so many good qualities in the rest of his midfield, he knew there was great competition for places in that area and he wouldn't really be missed too much.

While Alex had a bit of finesse about him, Neil Berry was a top-notch ball winner. He was hard but also fair. He took a lot of dunts but he was not nasty. I never saw Neil topping anybody, as he was an honest guy who knew his capabilities. I was fortunate to play with a lot of great players, but the two that helped me get my Scotland caps were Neil and Kenny Black. Their qualities allowed me to play the linking role to the front players, which I did during the early part of my career and which got me noticed by the international hierarchy. Neil won the ball and kept it simple. He never tried anything flash, while Kenny would cover for me if I got caught up-field.

Neil had been at Bolton Wanderers as a young player and although he didn't make it down there, he had an inner mental strength that meant he made the grade in a good Hearts team when he joined in December 1984. Neil could play in defence or midfield, but in terms of my Dream Team I am considering him as a midfielder because if Walter Kidd ever came forward from the back then Neil would sit in. Neil was one of the most unselfish players I have ever known, and I am not the only one who will tell you that. John Colquhoun got a lot of passes from Neil that allowed him to do his stuff, so he was an integral part of the resurgent Hearts team during the mid-1980s.

I would like to think that for as long as Heart of Midlothian exists the name of Gary Locke will always be mentioned. He was a fan turned player who would have played and lifted the Scottish Cup in 1998 if injury had not ruled him out. A true Jambo, he was on the terraces watching the team long before he set foot on the pitch. Lockey typified what Jim Jefferies and Billy Brown were trying to do when they were appointed. They wanted to blood top-quality young players and Gary, who made his debut from the bench in an away defeat to St Johnstone, fitted the bill. A few of the fans used to call him 'Son of Mackay', as he was as fanatical about Hearts as I was. He had no agenda and was simply a Hearts man through and through. I always felt his ability was under-estimated. People didn't realise how good a touch he had and how good a passer of the ball he was. In the group of young players that came through under Sandy Clark, he was up there with the best of them.

Unfortunately he had a career marred by injury and he picked up a serious one in the 5-1 Scottish Cup final defeat in 1996 when he was carried off. Only four minutes had passed before he was writhing and clutching his right knee after an Ian Ferguson challenge. He continued for four more minutes but pain eventually overcame his pride and he left the field on a stretcher.

Losing our captain was a huge blow for us so early in the game but fortunately for Lockey he made a comeback six months later, which I always knew he would because he had incredible mental strength. Would he have had the mental strength to come back so quickly from such a horrific injury if he had been anywhere else but his beloved Hearts? I am not convinced. His desire to play for Hearts flowed through his veins and spurred him on to come back early from injury.

Lockey was hugely competitive and his enthusiasm for Hearts probably overtook him at times and that is maybe why he got injured so much as he would go in for every tackle as if his life depended on it. I am delighted he is still involved with Hearts in their backroom staff at the time of writing, and I hope he is there for a long time. I like to think Lockey, myself and Scott Crabbe wore our love for Hearts on our sleeve more than most players of our generation at Tynecastle. I was absolutely delighted for Lockey when he lifted the Scottish Cup again after the win over Hibs in 2012. It was a just reward for a man who is Hearts through and through.

Now when it came to setting up my Dream Team midfield I was about to play three in that area but changed my mind at the last minute. If I had gone down that route Colin Cameron would have fitted the bill on the right side. He was to Jim Jefferies and Billy Brown what Craig Levein was to Alex MacDonald and Sandy Jardine. By that I mean he was a figurehead, a man who made sure their instructions were carried out on the pitch.

Colin had achieved great success across in Fife with Raith Rovers at a young age and had been part of their side that famously beat Celtic 6-5 in the Scottish League Cup final penalty shoot-out in the 1994-95 season. Jimmy and Billy got him for a relatively small fee, with John Millar joining Raith Rovers as a make-weight. Colin improved as a player from the minute he walked through the doors at Tynecastle. That improvement led to him playing international football for Scotland and, like Paul Hartley, you can pinpoint the rise of his career to the moment he joined Hearts. Sometimes the club has that hugely positive effect on players, and it certainly did on Colin, as it also did on Paul.

He may not have been the biggest but he was a great athlete and that was becoming increasingly important in football at the time, especially for midfield players who had to get about the pitch more and more. Colin was able to ally his athleticism with a great football brain that helped him to control matches from the right side of midfield. He was also a proven goal scorer, which was an invaluable talent for any footballer. He was very competitive, had natural football ability and in every training session his standards never dropped.

When both of us played for Hearts, some of the players may have had a bad night and didn't fancy running first thing on a

Monday morning, but not Colin. He was a true professional who never stopped working. When we played in the same team in the mid-1990s, he was the one I would rely upon to get into the box. I would try and sit and control things in the middle of the park and Colin would be the buzz-bomb who would make great runs into dangerous positions. I am a great believer that you make your own luck, and sometimes Colin would get into the box and the ball would hit off him and into the path of others who would score because of his hard work.

On the pitch he had the heart of a lion and would throw himself in front of things when he defended. When Colin started playing for Hearts, he was a breath of fresh air in the midfield area because, let's face it, I wasn't getting any younger and neither were a lot of the midfield guys around that time, so he was vitally important to Hearts. He had nerves of steel which was vital in the most important game of his life. Taking a penalty is never easy. Putting the ball on the spot in the first few minutes of the Scottish Cup final against Rangers in 1998 was never going to be easy, but Colin dealt with the pressure superbly to score. Colin will be on my Dream Team bench after being replaced at the last minute by a man who will go down in history as one of the most favourite players ever to grace Tynecastle.

I don't know if Rudi Skacel was forced out of Hearts and had to go to Southampton and, if that was the case, then I apologise to him here and now, but I think him going there was the wrong move. He was revered at Hearts and quite rightly so. At least he moved to a side that would not be a threat to Hearts, unlike some of the other top Tynecastle players of his era, like Steven Pressley and Paul Hartley, who went to Celtic, but even so I feel his career suffered by going south. I played alongside Rudi in Robbie Neilson's testimonial and I didn't realise how physically strong Rudi was and how big a man he was. Also I don't think I have seen a football player with such a short back-lift striking the ball so sweetly. He took a few free-kicks in that game and his style on the ball was world class. He is no Lionel Messi, but he could strike a ball with his left foot just like him at times.

He was the best-ever signing by George Burley, although he sometimes could be posted missing in away games. When Hearts were on top there was always a fair chance that Rudi would hit the back of the net at some point. What a quality that is for a man who is not an out-and-out striker and who would support the front men from the wide areas or from the midfield. When he returned to the club for his second spell at Tynecastle, he picked up the great relationship he had with the Hearts fans and he will always be a popular figure.

The fact he scored in the 3-1 win over Hibs in the New Year's fixture of 2012 only enhanced his popularity. Then scoring the opening goal in the 2-1 Scottish Cup semi-final win over Celtic at Hampden on 15 April 2012 and then getting two goals in the 5-1 Scottish Cup final win over Hibs the following month made him an all-time Tynecastle great. Rudi may have made a huge contribution in the Scottish Cup final win over Gretna in 2006, but he made an even bigger one in both the run to the 2012 final and in the famous victory over Hibs.

He scored in the 2-2 home draw against St Mirren in the quarter-final then got the second goal in the 2-0 replay win across in Paisley. As I already mentioned, he scored one against Celtic in the semi-final and then two against Hibs, and for me was the most consistent Hearts player through the whole winning Scottish Cup run. Over his two stints at the club Rudi proved he is a match winner who will quite rightly be looked upon as immortal by Hearts fans from now until the end of time for winning two Scottish Cup medals, six years apart.

Throughout his time at Tynecastle the rapport he had with the supporters transmitted itself to the rest of the team and that feel-good factor is one I haven't witnessed since wee Robbo left the club. His time at Hearts has been nothing short of stunning. Also let's not forget that in my view he would have also been part of a Hearts league-winning side if George Burley had not been sacked.

Bringing Rudi into my midfield in place of Colin Cameron means I had to change my formation at the last minute to accommodate him from a 4-3-3 to a more unusual 4-2-1-3, as I mentioned earlier in the book. The reason I left Colin Cameron out at the last minute was that I wanted Rudi in my side at all costs. Colin is unlucky to drop to the bench, but I felt that the pair couldn't play in the same team, as they were both too attack-minded, and at the end of the day, I felt Rudi had more of a cutting edge and would have an important free role behind the front three. Also Rudi and Colin would be pushing forward much too much and my Dream Team defence would be exposed.

The next man I have chosen for my Dream Team – my most important pick of the lot – will occupy the central midfield role and be my captain. For all the great players who turned out for Hearts the one man who stands head and shoulders above the lot of them has to be Dave Mackay. I wasn't of the generation who had the joy of watching him play, but I heard so many great stories about him from my family and watched some of his performances on DVD, especially the ones he made when he moved south of the border.

I first met Dave at a Hearts Hall of Fame dinner and he was a lovely man. He had success at the club but had even more away from Tynecastle. Despite that he never lost his love of Hearts and the Hearts fans never lost their love for Dave Mackay. He was voted the number one player in the history of Heart of Midlothian, and I won't be arguing with that. Yes, we have had the likes of Willie Bauld, John Robertson, Alfie Conn, Jim Cruickshank, and Jimmy Wardhaugh, but Dave Mackay for me was and always will be the number one. Maybe I am saying that because he was a midfield player like me, but no one can doubt his world-class talent. We may have both shared the same surname and both played for Hearts but I was very much the poor relation compared to him.

He epitomised the success Hearts had in the late 1950s, early 1960s and was a real man's man. He had a drive about him and enthusiasm that he retained both on and off the park. He was a hard man with a real edge to his play, but more often than not he would only lose the rag if he had been antagonised. The only time the opposition saw his true wrath was if they stepped out of line. He was a model of controlled aggression at other times.

Dave was hard but fair. He was an amazing man and to come back from two leg breaks and to keep playing at the top level is testament to his will-power. Remember the healing processes and the medical profession wasn't what it is now when Dave played. Because he achieved success on both sides of the border, he has to be named not just a Hearts but also a Scotland all-time great. He is somebody who, if he had been playing now, would have picked up a huge salary and would be transferred for millions of pounds between clubs. He could have played for Barcelona, Real Madrid, Manchester United, you name it. Indeed, Sir Matt Busby said that he was the one man he needed to rebuild Manchester United after the Munich air crash, and he was gutted when he failed to get his signature.

I must admit there is a bit of emotion in my thinking in picking Dave to lead my Dream Team, but I am not completely letting my heart rule my head, as he deserves the honour. Through the years I have spoken to a lot of Hearts fans, including my grandfather, who would always rave about Dave. There is genuine warmth felt by a certain generation towards the great man. Pilmar Smith, the former Hearts director, would never speak to me again if I hadn't picked Dave in my Hearts Dream Team. He was one of the tens of thousands of Hearts fans who idolised him.

My Dream Team does have great leaders, like Craig Levein and Sandy Jardine, but I am sure they would not quibble about missing out as captain to such a figure as the real Mackay. What adds to Dave's standing in my Dream Team is that he was a huge Hearts fan who was brought up near Tynecastle. How many clubs can honestly say that arguably their greatest player was also a lifelong supporter as well? Not that many, I would suggest.

He was brought up in the Balgreen area of Edinburgh and went to his first Hearts match at the age of five. Tommy Walker signed him for £10 a week over the winter and £8 in the summer, with a £20 signing-on fee at the age of seventeen. He made his debut a week before his nineteenth birthday in a 2-1 home defeat to Clyde on 7 November 1953 and a great football career was off and running. He was made captain five years later in one of the greatest ever seasons seen at Tynecastle. In his first two games as skipper, Hearts beat Dundee 6-0 and then put seven past Airdrie before beating Hibs 3-1. Dave also managed to score a hat-trick in a 9-0 drubbing of Falkirk two weeks later.

Over the season they lost one game and that was against Clyde, and beat both sides of the Old Firm, home and away. They conceded twenty-nine goals and scored an incredible 132. Then he broke his foot and missed the last few games of that championship-winning season, but it was only right and proper that Dave lifted the Scottish League Trophy at the end of the 1957-58 campaign on behalf of the club. It was the first time in sixty-one years that the league flag had flown above Tynecastle and it was twenty-three-year-old captain Mackay who had helped make it happen. On 25 October 1958 he was captain when Hearts beat Partick Thistle to win the Scottish League Cup, but he was to leave Tynecastle five months later very much against his will.

It was good to know, through speaking to Dave, that he wanted to stay at his beloved Hearts even when the great Tottenham Hotspur first came calling. Tommy Walker knocked on his door one Sunday to say Bill Nicholson was coming to Edinburgh the following day to talk to him. For Dave, that was a bolt from the blue, especially when he found out Spurs couldn't top his wage of £20 a week but would provide him with free accommodation. He cost Spurs a record £32,000 – the highest price paid for a defender/midfielder back then – but it turned out to be a bargain.

To lose Dave at his prime was a huge blow to Hearts but I suppose a player of his world-class talent was always going to move on at some stage. It is a shame that the club had forced his sale but Dave never held that against them. He remained a huge Hearts fan and in my Dream Team he deserves his starting place and the captain's armband.

I had many top candidates to play on the left side of my Hearts midfield and the man I have chosen is someone who I felt was under-rated at times. Billy McNeill when he was Celtic coach said a young Stevie Fulton could go on to be as good as Roberto Baggio, which was huge praise indeed. It was hard to live up to that level of expectation, and although Stevie was never as good as Baggio he was among the best to grace Scottish football. Stevie was one of the most skilful players I ever met. He could put a ball on a sixpence in training from any distance. Guaranteed. His passing and his touch were brilliant. He was quick over two yards and slow over ten yards.

There used to be chants from the terraces about Stevie being a bit overweight and that he had eaten all the pies but he still could play. Yes, he had an appetite and I saw the eating machine at work many a time. Club secretary Les Porteous used to do the lunches for us up in the room which is now the John Robertson Suite. Stevie had not been with us for long and I was sitting at the table, one of the last people still in the dining room. Two of the young lads had left some of their lunch – I think it was chicken pasta. I had finished mine and so had Stevie, but when he saw the rest of the food on their plates he put both their leftovers on another plate and ate the lot. He saw me look on in amazement as he wolfed it down. He said he always did that at home and when his wife made food for the family he wouldn't let anything go to waste. So I'm thinking to myself that he has just eaten three plates of chicken pasta for lunch. If he went home and ate his own evening meal and any left-overs from the plates of his wife and three kids, then no wonder he was carrying a few extra pounds. He just had an appetite. When I asked him about it he said with a big smile on his face he just ate all the food at home so his wife didn't feel bad about her cooking.

Maybe he ate more than he should have, but ultimately he had a professional football career that people would be envious of. He didn't like running in training and to be fair made no secret of it, but he always gave it his best shot, although that meant he was more often than not at the back rather than at the front of the pack during sessions. I would compare Stevie to Andy Ritchie, who was one of the most talented and skilful players in Scottish football history but who many felt was lazy. Stevie was never lazy, but like Andy, because he had so much natural talent, he made what he did look effortless. There were some games he was deliberately left out, like our European Cup Winners' Cup game away to Red Star Belgrade when it was going to be all about running and defending, which was never Stevie's strong point. He was on the bench for that game back on 8 August 1996 when we drew 0-0 and never got on. To be honest, I can understand why, as that was not his type of game.

Steve wasn't a player who would ever be effective in a team that wanted to be destructive in a game. If you wanted to win a football match by being constructive, he was your man. I always felt he would have flourished in Spanish football, where he would have been given more time on the ball. Stevie was brought to Hearts by Jim Jefferies and Billy Brown and was quite rightly one of their favourites but you always needed the right balance around him to make him completely effective. You needed someone to sit and cover for him in a 4-3-3, to do the running and give support to the front players, as he was never the most mobile. On the positive side, he was always composed and could hold people off in the tackle and was inspirational in important matches. Also if you gave the ball to Stevie Fulton you knew Hearts would not lose it very often. If he got it in an area where he could hurt teams, he would create chances. To be Hearts captain when they won the Scottish Cup in 1998 was a fitting tribute to Stevie. The iconic image of him with the trophy, flanked by wee Robbo and Gary Locke, will live long in my memory.

So there you have it. Dave Mackay and Stevie Fulton sitting in front of the back four, although full-backs Walter Kidd and Tosh McKinlay had the engines on them to give them support when needed. Rudi Skacel would be handed a roaming role in front of them, linking up with the three out and out strikers I have picked. It is an incredibly attack-minded midfield but I have so much faith in my captain Dave Mackay to keep that midfield together, I am sure it would work.

10

STRIKING MASTER CLASS

'He's fat, he's round, he bounces off the ground' was the chant. It could have been about wee Robbo, but most of the time it was about Jimmy Bone. The Hearts fans were as likely to sing his praises with these words in the same way as the opposition would try to tease him with the same song. Either way it didn't bother Jimmy. Boney was one of the most hardened professionals I have ever met. Roddy MacDonald and Stewart McLaren were in a similar mould. They were all old school.

The first time I heard his name was when Partick Thistle beat Celtic in the Scottish League Cup final of 1971, which was a massive result that sent shockwaves through Scottish football. Twelve years later I was rubbing shoulders with him. There was no arrogance about Jimmy but there was an aura about him, probably because of his role in that famous Partick Thistle win over Celtic.

He came to us later in his career but he was still incredibly sharp. He had been with Hong Kong Rangers and Hibs wanted to take him on as a player/coach under Pat Stanton. Alex MacDonald offered him a playing role at Tynecastle and although he was thirty-four years old he decided to accept that offer instead. I am reliably informed Jimmy could have got more money from taking a coaching role at Hibs but he was never a big-bucks merchant. He wanted to play football, loved the game and fitted right in at Tynecastle.

Jimmy liked a wee drink and I remember when he first met up with his old pal Willie Johnston. Bud and Boney met up for the first time in years when we went on a pre-season tour of the Highlands the week after Jimmy had signed. To celebrate their re-established friendship they decided to go out for a drink or two in Inverness on their first night back together. Big mistake. As they waited for a taxi together to go to the pub, Alex MacDonald showed up and fined them a week's wages on the spot. That would be a week's wages that Boney had yet to receive.

He may not have got off to the best of starts after trying to go for a quick bevvy and being fined, but he easily earned his money in his first year at Tynecastle by putting in some great displays. Even in training the way he used his body to keep off defenders was a master class to the young boys in how to play up front.

In our first season back in the Premier League after being promoted it was Jimmy who got our first goal back in the top flight when he scored the winning goal away to St Johnstone in the first game of the 1983-84 campaign. On 3 September 1983 when we beat Hibs 3-2 at Tynecastle our strike force was Jimmy and Robbo. I can comment with authority on how well they played because, as I have mentioned elsewhere in the book, I was rank rotten that day and was taken off and replaced by Alex MacDonald. Robbo got a couple of goals but it was Jimmy who did the donkey work. He slaughtered them with the way he held the ball up, how he battered into the Hibs defenders. The fact he scored as well was thoroughly deserved as he had put in an incredible shift. As younger players, myself, Robbo, Dave Bowman, Ian Westwater, all these guys who were about the place started to realise we had people in our changing room like Jimmy who had achieved things in football. To watch and learn from him was a privilege.

Robbo was always going to be a top striker, but I am sure he learned a lot from Jimmy and other experienced folk around the club, like Sandy Clark. Jimmy instilled in Robbo and me something I would describe as the importance of ensuring you have a decent work–life balance. He made us realise that it was important to train hard, play hard on a Saturday but when it was time to have fun, like a Christmas night out, to let your hair down big time. Actually I am sure it was Jimmy and wee Willie Johnston who first came up with the idea the players should have a fancy dress Christmas party.

Most of the time I played with Jimmy was when we played a 4-3-3 formation. Robbo and I had a telepathic understanding because we had played together at various times from ten years old onwards and Jimmy was on the same wavelength as us because of his experience and ability to read what his team-mates were going to do. Jimmy had a great impact on Hearts and although I might not see him for a couple of years I still feel a lot of warmth towards Jimmy and hopefully that is reciprocated whenever we meet.

I mentioned Sandy Clark elsewhere in my book for his coaching and managerial roles at Hearts but first and foremost he deserves a mention for his time as a player at Tynecastle. He played for West Ham and Rangers, among others, and fitted like a glove into our team. He cost Hearts £35,000 and I remember the club was in such a poor financial position they paid Rangers off in fourteen instalments of £2,500.

If you looked for an identikit player to replace Jimmy Bone, who left in 1985, then Sandy was that and more. They had played together from October 1984 until Jimmy left five months later but as a younger man he was always going to be picked ahead of Jimmy as time went by. He had more running in him than Jimmy did and played exactly the same role in the team that Jimmy had done. He had great aerial ability, he was strong and could hold the ball up and wait for the midfielders.

There was nothing nasty about Sandy, but let's just say he could take care of himself. David Narey, Paul Hegarty at Dundee United and Gordon Rae at Hibs could all testify to that as Sandy gave tough guys like them some real hard times. Off the park or on it Sandy didn't suffer fools gladly. There was a line with Sandy where you could have a laugh but if you tried to take the mickey out of him too much he would rip your head off.

If I looked around my team from a midfield point of view and I knew I had Walter Kidd behind me and Neil Berry and Kenny Black beside me and Sandy Clark in front I would be full of confidence as there was never going to be a team that would bully us with that bunch of hard men in our side. Looking back, it was a great experience for me to be surrounded by so many great football players of their day, men who were also top guys like Sandy who had great humility about him despite his huge talent.

Although Alfie Conn was there long before my time, he deserves a special mention for his role at Hearts and came very close to making my Dream Team. I heard about him from relatives and have watched some very old footage I have seen of the team from around that time. Everybody at Hibs could run off the names of the Famous Five and I am sure every Hearts fan could do the same with the Terrible Trio of Conn, Bauld and Wardhaugh. I always wondered if Conn was named first for a reason. They say he was hugely, hugely talented and maybe even better than the other two. That thought is something I am sure will continue to spark debate among the generation who had the privilege of watching him play. He could score great goals and he was also a great creator of goals, as well as a Tynecastle all-time great. He was born in Prestonpans in East Lothian in 1926 and joined us from Inveresk Athletic in June 1944. He was a small, stocky player and some members of the older generation have likened him to wee Robbo. He made a scoring debut against Dumbarton on 14 October 1944 and by the end of his career he had scored 222 goals in 400 games.

The legend of the Terrible Trio started because they all played together regularly, beginning with their first game against East Fife on 9 October 1948, a date that comes up elsewhere in this book a few times because it was such a significant one for so many important players and for Hearts Football Club. In all, Conn, Willie Bauld and Jimmy Wardhaugh played together 242 times for Hearts between their introduction as a unit and their final reunion for George Dobbie's testimonial match on 31 October 1960. The trio scored 945 goals in total and in the thirty games in which all three scored, only one was drawn, which was a 3-3 draw with Rangers at Ibrox in 1954. Only Partick Thistle managed to beat Hearts when the Terrible Trio all scored.

When Hearts won the League Championship in some style in the 1957-58 season, scoring 132 goals in the process, Alfie played just nine times as he had an injury problem. Being part of that league-winning squad was his final contribution to the club with Raith Rovers paying Hearts £2,250 to take him to Stark's Park in September 1958. Newspaper reports I checked while researching this book kept saying that Alfie had 'a spirited style of play that would upset defences'. Nowadays they would just describe him as a tough guy who wound up the opposition. He didn't look the most athletic, as he was stocky in build, but looks were deceiving as he was a great runner and a box-to-box player who apparently had the fiercest shot of any of the Terrible Trio. Apparently he was great in the dressing room before matches in that he could gauge the mood superbly well. There is always an air of tension before big matches but Alfie could apparently lighten the atmosphere with a few well-timed practical jokes.

The second member of the Terrible Trio that came close to making my starting line-up was Jimmy Wardhaugh, who was the club's record league goal scorer for almost forty years until wee Robbo came along and beat his record of 206 in 1997. Overall Jimmy got an amazing 376 goals in 519 appearances in all competitions. He joined the club as an inside-left in 1946 but only really made his mark in the 1947-48 season after he had finished his National Service.

Jimmy had fantastic old-fashioned dribbling skills, which meant he scored more solo goals than the other members of the Terrible Trio. Because of that particular skill he was nick-named 'Twinkle Toes' by the fans. He could have left Hearts in 1952 but couldn't agree personal terms with Newcastle United, who had a bid of £26,000 accepted by the Hearts board. It was a stroke of luck that he remained at Tynecastle, considering the future success they had with him in the team. He scored the third goal in the 4-2 Scottish League Cup final win over Motherwell in 1954 which gave Hearts their first trophy for forty-eight years. He was also part of the side that beat Celtic to win the Scottish Cup.

An indication of the talent of Jimmy came from the fact that, with Conn and Bauld struggling with injury, he had to fit into a new-look front line that also included Jimmy Murray and Alex Young. He took the younger players under his wing and in the 1957-58 season Hearts scored a remarkable 132 goals in thirty-four games, as I mentioned earlier. Jimmy got thirty of them in twenty-eight games, while Jimmy Murray scored twenty-seven in thirty-three games. Not to be outdone, Alex Young got twenty-four goals in thirty-four games.

Jimmy retired in 1961 and started a new career in sports writing with the *Edinburgh Evening News* and the *Scottish Daily Express*. He worked as a publicity officer for the BBC and tragically died after watching a match between East Fife and Hearts in 1978. He was just forty-eight years old.

I mentioned Jimmy Murray and Alex Young a bit earlier, and both men were considered for my Dream Team on the basis of their exploits for the club in the late 1950s. Jimmy was a top-class inside-right who won the league twice and the Scottish League Cup when he was at Tynecastle. He also earned a place in the history books by scoring Scotland's first goal in the 1958 World Cup in Sweden. Alex Young was a real superstar of his day, with his blond hair and ability to score goals with his head or either foot. He won a Scottish Cup winners' medal at the age of just nineteen in 1955-56 and was an ever-present in the 1957-58 league team. In 1960 Alex moved south to play for Everton for £42,000, where he won the English league title and two FA Cups and where he gained legendary status.

Another man from that era that deserves a mention is left-winger Ian Crawford. Many of the younger readers may not have heard of Ian, but mention his name to a certain generation and watch their faces light up. By all accounts he was an incredible talent. My grandfather Jimmy and my uncle Bill were Hearts daft and they spoke about how great a player he was. He apparently had great attacking qualities and was part of a hugely successful team.

He picked up a full house of domestic honours, with Hearts winning the Scottish League title twice, in 1957-58 and in 1959-60. Along the way he won the Scottish Cup and the Scottish League Cup. Remarkably he was rejected by Hamilton and Hibs – how they must have regretted that decision – as a teenager. He was fast off the mark and his pinpoint crosses from the left led to countless Hearts goals. He became such an invaluable member of the Hearts team that the board successfully petitioned the authorities for him to be given special leave from the Cameron Highlanders where he was doing his National Service in the second half of the 1955-56 season. It proved a worthwhile decision, as Ian was a mainstay in the team that won the Scottish Cup that season, securing immortality with two goals in the final win over Celtic with Alfie Conn getting the other.

The other thing my family would always tell me about him was that he scored four goals against Cowdenbeath in the 1959 League Cup semi-final that Hearts won 9-3 in one of that side's greatest ever performances. Johnny Hamilton got a couple, with the others coming from Bobby Blackwood, Gordon Smith and George Thomson.

Wayne Foster, or 'Fozzie' as we used to call him, will hate, and I don't like using the word hate but there is no other word for it, being considered for my Dream Team on the back of one of the most famous goals in the history of Hearts. Fozzie just hates, and I mean *hates*, being remembered just for scoring a goal against Hibs in the Scottish Cup at Easter Road, but he shouldn't be so precious about it. Sandy Clark was the manager when Wayne scored the late winning goal on 20 February 1994. He has to be considered for my Dream Team for that alone whether he likes it or not. Anyone who gets a goal to beat the enemy on their own patch in the Scottish Cup will always have a special place in my heart!

Fozzie will tell you he did a lot of other great things for Hearts, which is absolutely true, and should not be given hero status just because of one goal. Come on, Fozzie, it is better being remembered for scoring a special goal against Hibs than not being remembered at all. All Hearts supporters of that era will agree with that. Unfortunately the one man who will not agree is the man we are talking about.

No Hearts fan will ever forget the iconic picture of him running to the Dunbar end of Easter Road and climbing up the fence after his winning goal. I still laugh and tease him to this day about his special moment. His shooting was so erratic back then I used to say he didn't know he had scored and was really climbing the fence to try and find out what part of the crowd his shot had landed in. To be fair, he showed great composure to beat Jim Leighton that day. He had come on for Robbo and with four minutes left scored his famous goal. It was his first goal in nearly three years and extended our unbeaten run over Hibs to twenty-one games.

When I watched Hearts in the early 1980s, Willie Gibson had taken over from the legendary Donald Ford as the main striker.

He arrived when Hearts were a yo-yo team going between leagues and it was a tough time for everybody, but Willie helped the cause with important goals. He was one of the few guys back then who had a great instinct for goals as he was a penalty box finisher who could sniff chances a mile off.

When I first joined Hearts and played reserve matches there were guys like Willie and Bobby Masterton, who came from Linlithgow Rose, who went out of their way to be helpful. I was always told that would not always be the case, as some of the older guys would see the younger guys as a threat to their places in the team, and maybe they had a point. All I can do is talk from personal experience and say that Willie was very helpful to me when I was starting out. Although I had just been there a short period of time before he moved on, I have a lot to thank him for in terms of helping me settle in at Tynecastle. My judgement of character is not always great but I got it right with Willie, who was a real diamond, both on and off the pitch.

He had joined Hearts in July 1971 and in his early days combined well with Drew Busby. With wingers like Donald Park, Kenny Aird and the majestic Bobby Prentice in the side, there were plenty of pinpoint crosses for him to try and get on the end of. And there were many highlights of Willie's time at Hearts. He scored hat-tricks against Celtic, vital goals against Hibs, but his most important, at least in my eyes, were his two goals in the 5-1 demolition of Lokomotiv Leipzig. He had a decade at Hearts before leaving to join Partick Thistle for £35,000 in July 1981 and left behind nothing but good memories.

The next man who I considered is another who crossed the divide and played for both Hearts and Hibs. Alan Gordon was a top player who I got to know when he was a radio pundit on Radio Forth and I was still turning out for Hearts. He was a football player of great talent who was another humble man. He was a very intelligent guy who was fantastic in the air and who could score goals. Eddie Turnbull famously said to Alan that his problem was that 'his brains were all in his heid'. They most certainly were, and if I was coming up with a University Challenge Dream Team he would be my first pick. He was a very clever bloke with a wide knowledge of every aspect of life.

The next man who my family used to rave about from before my time was Johnny Hamilton, who joined Hearts in April 1955. He was a speed merchant who could leave most defenders for dead. He was so fast that the cries from the Tynecastle terraces at the time were, 'Open the gates at the bottom, here comes Pigalle Wonder!', which was a reference to a top greyhound that used to always win at Powderhall at the time. He was twice a Scottish League and League Cup winner with Hearts before he moved south to join Watford, where he won the English Third Division championship.

Johnny was a fit wee man who was a real bundle of energy. He was a rascal of a winger who caused opposition defences all sorts of problems. He was part of the Hearts coaching team when he returned north from his time at Watford and combined that role with running his newspaper shop near the stadium and by all accounts was a real character.

I mention Roald Jensen and Rene Moller together because one of my first clear football memories, albeit distant ones, was the pair of them playing together. Roald, who was Norwegian, was the longer serving of the two. He was at Tynecastle from December 1964 until May 1971. Rene, who was Danish, was with us from 1968 until 1970. Roald was a wee right-winger who was fantastic to watch but incredibly inconsistent. In the Scottish Cup semi-final against Morton in the 1967-68 season he was by all accounts magnificent. He scored Hearts' only goal in the 1-1 draw in the first match and in the replay helped set up George Miller for our first goal before showing a cool head to stroke home the penalty that won the game.

There were great expectations on his shoulders going into the final against Dunfermline, which is one of the first full Hearts games I remember, as I attended the Hampden final at the age of just five years old. Unfortunately Roald didn't have a great game and neither did his team-mates, as we lost 3-1 which, as I have said elsewhere, sent a wee boy unhappily on his way back to Edinburgh. Despite that disappointment, Roald remains a real cult figure to me. There was an exciting feel to him, especially through my eyes, as he came from a foreign country that I thought was thousands of miles away.

In researching this book, I was saddened to be reminded that he died of a heart attack back in 1987 at the much too young age of forty-four, back in his native Norway. I also found out that in his will he left a note to the football authorities in Norway stating, 'Take care of the youngest, give them the opportunities and teach them to love this sport.' Can I just say, the way Roald played for Hearts the times I saw him made me love football.

Rene Moller was a different type of player who was an out-and-out striker who was difficult to stop and who stood out because of his blond locks. He made his debut in a 2-0 away defeat to Aberdeen on 10 February 1968 and he rampaged about the pitch for a couple of seasons after that. In a remarkable Scottish Cup second round match against Dundee United at Tannadice the following week, Hearts won 6-5. He scored two great goals in the win with Donald Ford, Eddie Thomson, George Miller and Jim Irvine getting the others. On his day Rene was top class. On others I thought he was awful and he had a love–hate relationship with the fans. Me? As a wee boy I always enjoyed watching him play because he was so unpredictable you never knew what he was going to do next. He left in 1970 and some say he took the huff before storming off back to Denmark, but whatever the reason why he quit the club, he was a man who left a big impression on me.

A man who stayed longer than just a couple of seasons and who I used to marvel at during his time at Tynecastle was Allan Johnston, who was one of the most exciting players to ever turn out for the club. He had a great career that took him from Hearts to Rennes to Sunderland to Rangers and then from Kilmarnock to Queen of the South. The fact he played at the top level for so many years never surprised me, as he was a fantastic player and a huge talent.

Allan was one of the most naturally gifted players I have ever seen and I wasn't surprised when he made his Hearts debut at the age of just nineteen against Airdrie at Tynecastle on 8 May 1993. I was playing that day and knew straight away the kid was special. He showed he could find the back of the net with a belter of a goal on his debut that earned us a 1-1 draw. In the fourth game of the following season he became a real Hearts hero when he controlled a cross from Gary Locke before volleying the ball into the back of the Hibs net to give us a 1-0 home win. I think it must have been after that game that his nickname 'Magic' was created, after the famous American basketball star.

For me, Allan had tremendous composure, could cross the ball with either foot and could glide past players as if they were not there. He did not have electric pace but he had the brains to get past people. The way he moved his hips meant he could put his opponent off balance then drift past them. When you have such natural talent you have to teach him other things on the training ground, and Sandy Clark, when he was in charge of the youths, helped make him a top player. Allan was one of Sandy's top stars in the youth team that won the Youth Cup by beating Rangers at Ibrox. Sandy toughened him up mentally and gave him a bit more drive and determination. He worked hard on his fitness and physicality and when Allan walked into the Hearts first team he was in great shape, and a lot of that was down to Sandy.

The day when he scored a hat-trick at Ibrox, when Robbo and I were on the bench, was probably the catalyst for Hearts winning the Scottish Cup in 1998. Even though there were defeats along the way that 3-0 victory on 20 January 1996 was a one-off result that gave everybody confidence, especially Allan. If you want people to sit up and take notice of you in Scottish football, what better way to do it than score three goals against Rangers at Ibrox. That was the defining moment in Allan's early career and showed his undoubted ability at the top level.

He had moved on before Hearts won the Scottish Cup in 1998 but he had been one of the men who had lit the blue touch-paper that led to the revival of the club that in turn led to the success in the Scottish Cup final over Rangers. Allan was always in great shape and I am sure he will still be kicking a ball around the park when he is sixty-five, seventy years old. He was such a natural footballer it was as if he had been born with a ball attached to his feet.

He put his heart and soul into every game and I remember after we lost the Scottish Cup final 5-1 to Rangers at Hampden on 18 May 1996. I was sitting next to him on the way back on the bus and he burst into tears. Part of the reason for that was that we had lost, the other reason was that he knew that would be his last game in a Hearts jersey and he was sorry to be leaving. He joined Rennes, then Sunderland then a host of other clubs that led to him winning eighteen Scotland caps along the way. As I said, he was always super fit so it was no surprise when I saw Allan still playing for Queen of the South at the age of thirty-eight and he was still being as magic as ever.

The next man up is someone who is one of the greatest characters I ever played alongside. Willie Johnston is also one of the nicest gents I have ever met. If you wanted someone to look after you, someone to sit you down and talk you through the pitfalls of the game, he had time in abundance for everybody to do just that. Wee Bud, as he was known, was brilliant with his team-mates. I have a lot of respect for guys I played alongside but out of everybody, and I mean everybody, Willie Johnson is the one I had most respect for.

He was a real character on and off the field and as entertaining a figure to have in a dressing room as you would expect. When he first arrived at Tynecastle in the 1982-83 season, he smoked like a chimney. Because of that he had a wee room to himself and he'd go there in the mornings before training for his fags and a cup of tea. When I could see him through the smoke clouds we used to chat away and I learned a lot in that room, although my lungs suffered like hell.

I have already talked in the book about players like Paul Hartley and Wayne Foster being linked with certain games and events. Whenever you say the name Willie Johnston people automatically think of the World Cup in Argentina in 1978 and the failed drugs test. I think that is totally unfair and a real shame, as he was a top-class player who had a distinguished career that should not be tarnished by that one isolated incident. He played for Rangers when they won the European Cup Winners' Cup and went down to play for West Bromwich Albion where he became a real cult hero. He had a superb football career, of that there is no question.

Yes he would fly off the handle at times and got himself needlessly sent off, but I don't think anybody would have wanted Willie to have lost that edge. If he had, I don't think his career would have been as successful as it was. He taught all us young players at Hearts to play on the edge and with no fear. The number of times we would be at Celtic Park and he would say, 'Just give me the ball.' The crowd, with him being an ex-Rangers player, would be booing him big time but that just spurred him on.

I remember one great day he had scored against Celtic at Tynecastle after coming off the bench. The minute he had walked on the pitch after coming on in the second half Roy Aitken had started the verbals, saying he was too old to be still playing football. In answer to Roy's taunts he put a glorious thirty-yarder into the top corner behind Peter Latchford. I was laughing my head off as he celebrated straight in front of Roy, who had a face like fizz as wee Bud danced round him. A great moment. For a young player like me, having this older guy asking for the ball in big matches even when our backs were to the wall was a huge lesson and taught me never to hide during games.

Scott Crabbe tells a great story about Willie from his early days at the club. When Willie was out training, Dave Bowman and Kenny Black, who were injured at the time, grabbed his trousers and cut them off at the knee before stapling them back together. When Willie discovered this when he returned to the changing room rather than get mad he decided to get even. He quickly sussed it had been Kenny and Dave who were the guilty parties, so when he returned from training he put on Dave's expensive leather jacket and Kenny's trousers and sat there in the bath wearing them and smoking a fag. He then got out, handed them the dripping wet clothes, got dressed, tore the staples off his trousers and walked out of Tynecastle onto Gorgie Road to get the train back to Kirkcaldy wearing his cut-down trousers and brogues. He didn't blink an eyelid. It was Bud's way of making the point that he was an experienced pro and nothing but nothing would bother him, especially a couple of young whippersnappers like Bow and Kenny trying to get the better of him.

It was Willie and Jimmy Bone who taught us how to work hard but also, as I mentioned earlier, how important it was to relax. For the management team of Alex MacDonald and Sandy Jardine, both Willie and Jimmy were the men in the changing room who taught the younger lads when it was okay to have a laugh and a joke and when they had to screw the nut.

For all the fun he generated, Willie had high personal standards and great discipline. Every day, come rain or shine, he would travel to and from Tynecastle with a shirt and tie on and with his beloved parka on top if it was cold. It was shirt and tie by order at Glasgow Rangers and he kept that discipline with Hearts and never once turned up at the stadium looking slovenly.

The day he left the club at the age of thirty-eight in 1985 five or six of us jumped in the big communal bath with different items of his clothing on. The only thing he didn't allow us to get wet was his beloved parka. He was really concerned someone might jump in the bath with it on and said if anyone did he would rip their heads off. Not surprisingly, nobody did. When Bud left Hearts he was badly missed, both on and off the field. We will never see his like again at Tynecastle.

I mentioned Scott Crabbe earlier, who was a good pal of Willie's, and this is a fitting time to mention how great a player he was for Hearts. He was a true Jambo who was shaking like a leaf when he made his debut against Clydebank at the age of just seventeen. The end of his time at Tynecastle was very emotional because very few people had realised he had signed for Dundee United when he played for us against Slavia Prague in 1992. He came off the bench and gave his all as he always did and only told us after the game he was on his way out of the club. He loved Hearts so much that when Joe Jordan was still speaking in the dressing room after the game Scott went into the old kit-room and was on his knees crying because he was leaving. Wallace Mercer spotted him in such an emotional state and the way he handled him was different class. He took Scott out to the centre circle of a deserted Tynecastle and had a quiet word with him. He told him in a sincere manner he had been a great Hearts servant and it had been a privilege for Wallace to work with him. That meant a lot to Scott.

A striker who deserves a mention although he played long before my time is Barney Battles, Jr., whose story has always fascinated me. He was a real legend although his name may not be known to younger Jambos. He was son of the former Celtic and Hearts defender of the same name who tragically died at the age of thirty after contracting pneumonia just before the birth of his son, Barney Junior. The cash taken from the stand at the 1905 Scotland against Ireland match at Celtic Park was given to the family by Celtic, which was a wonderful gesture.

Barney was born and raised in Edinburgh but when he was a teenager emigrated to the USA with his mum and sister. He played for Boston Soccer Club at the age of nineteen in the American Soccer League under former Rangers player Tommy Muirhead, who was the player–manager. He was an instant success, helping his team to win the 1925 Lewis Cup and the American Professional Soccer Championship.

Although he was born in Edinburgh, he played for the USA national side at outside-right in a 1-0 defeat to Canada. Just when football was taking hold in the USA there was a dispute between league officials that coincided with the Great Depression and rather than hang about, Barney returned to Scotland. He signed for Hearts for £9 a week in 1928 and the magic started to happen. He scored six times in his first two pre-season friendly matches. The guy with a bit of an American accent and a real swagger about him was a real draw, and in one friendly a crowd of 18,000 turned up to see him play. He scored on his competitive debut against Queen's Park then got a couple in his next game before netting a hat-trick in his third match. By the end of his first full season, 1928-29, he had scored a club record twenty-nine goals – although some say thirty-one – in twenty-eight league games as Hearts finished in fourth position.

Part of the reason I was so fascinated by his story was because of his record against Hibs. If Robbo was the Hammer of Hibs then Barney Battles must have been the sledge-hammer. In three derby matches during his first season he scored eleven times. He scored twice in a 5-1 win in the Wilson Cup, four times in another 5-1 victory in the Rosebery Charity Cup and five times in an 8-2 triumph in the Dunedin Cup. In 1930-31 he scored an incredible forty-four goals with hat-tricks in three consecutive matches in November. What made that season's total even more amazing was the fact he had missed seven games after he fell ill with appendicitis.

FIFA weren't so strict about nationality back in Battles' day and he won his first and only cap against Wales on 25 October 1930 when he scored Scotland's equalising goal in a 1-1 draw at Ibrox, but injury and the form of Celtic centre-forward Hughie Gallacher meant he never got a look in after that. He kept scoring goals for Hearts and against Cowdenbeath at Tynecastle during the 1933-34 season he was on fire. Hearts were 4-1 down with only twenty minutes left before the great man scored four himself to help his team to a 5-4 victory.

He finally retired from professional football in April 1936, aged only thirty, his last match being a 2-1 home defeat to Aberdeen. In total he had scored 218 goals in around 200 competitive games for Hearts. Even wee Robbo would be proud of that record. When he retired he became a sports journalist with the Glasgow *Evening Times* and then the *Edinburgh Evening Dispatch* and my family maintain they remember the great man turning up to watch games at Tynecastle during the 1970s.

Another far-travelled player is a man whose goal in the 1998 Scottish Cup final will forever earn him a place in the history of Hearts. Stephane Adam, like his fellow Frenchman Gilles Rousset, bought straight into the Hearts ethos and scored some important goals for the club. What a lot of people don't know is that he had a trial with Hibs and could have signed for them before Jim Jefferies nipped in to pinch him from under their noses. It was worth Jim's while to push the boat out financially for Stephane as that goal against Rangers in the Scottish Cup final was worth its weight in gold. The reaction to it was amazing and Stephane used to say that for days afterwards people would keep coming up to his house in Stockbridge asking to have their photograph taken with him. Others just rang the bell to thank him for helping give them the greatest days of their sporting life. Injuries stopped Stephane achieving even more success with Hearts but his little boy Arthur was born in Simpson's in September 1999 so you never know; another Adam could one day grace Tynecastle some-time in the future.

The next man up is a legend of Scottish football, and although he is associated with other clubs, most notably our rivals Hibs, I make no apologies for bringing him into my Dream Team considerations. Gordon Smith spent the predominant part of his career at Easter Road and was, of course, part of their Famous Five. I considered him because he did really well at Hearts as well and had two terrific years at Tynecastle. Also let's not forget he played superbly, not just for Hearts and Hibs, but also Dundee. Here is a man who shone at three, what some people would call, Scottish provincial clubs and brought them success. Is there any greater achievement in the history of Scottish football than winning a league medal at three different Scottish clubs as Gordon did? I am not sure there is.

The fact he played for Hibs does not bother me on this occasion. He was one of the greatest players of his generation. For the record, he won the Scottish League three times with Hibs, once with Hearts and again with Dundee. On top of that he won the Scottish League Cup with Hearts as well. Absolutely remark-able. He graced Scottish football for twenty-three years and was an outside-right who could drift past players and excite crowds wherever he played.

When I looked back over his career, it was interesting to read how Gordon ended up at Hearts. He was given a free transfer by Hibs after eighteen years because he had a lot of ankle problems and some at the club thought he was finished. Gordon set out to prove them wrong. He paid for an operation to sort his ankle, signed for Hearts and was such a huge draw an amazing 12,000 people turned out to watch him play his first reserve match at Tynecastle. In his first season at Tynecastle in 1959 he helped us win the league and Scottish League Cup after a 2-1 final win over Third Lanark. In the league he scored eleven goals and missed just five games, while in the League Cup he played seven times and scored twice.

Another player more associated with a club other than Hearts was Willie Wallace, but like Gordon Smith and Willie Johnston, I feel he has to be considered for my Dream Team. He played for Hearts for five years from 1961 before he went to Celtic where he was part of their 1967 European Cup-winning team. He was an inside forward that I heard so much about, again from my family.

Maybe he peaked at Celtic, and good luck to him for doing that, but let's not forget he got a move to Celtic because of his play with Hearts in the first place. The people who remember that era have told me Willie, who was known as 'Whispy', was a goal poacher who had taken over from his idol Willie Bauld in the Hearts forward line. From the 1962-63 season up until he left in 1966 he was the leading scorer at the club. He won a Scottish League Cup medal along the way. Some say he left under a cloud and took his foot off the gas when he knew that Celtic were looking to sign him, as he didn't want to risk injury. I am sure that is a myth but either way that does not detract from the fact that he was a top player for Hearts.

One of the greatest wide players ever seen at Tynecastle was Neil McCann. He was brought to Hearts by Jim Jefferies and Billy Brown in 1996 and was a fantastic talent. It was no surprise to me when Dick Advocaat came in for Neil, as he had great games for us against Rangers. In the 4-3 League Cup final defeat in 1996 he was up against Craig Moore and latterly Alex Cleland and he was outstanding. Of course we were all gutted that day but Neil had more cause than most, as he had ran his heart out and nearly won the game for us on his own. They started with Moore marking him then doubled up and put Cleland on him too but they could not stop him and he had more cause than any of us to be gutted after the defeat.

He was part of the 1998 Scottish Cup-winning team before he moved to Rangers but he rejoined Hearts in 2006 once his contract at Southampton expired. It was a shame a new generation of Hearts fans never saw Neil at his peak during that period, as he picked up a serious leg injury in his first match back at Tynecastle against Kilmarnock. He did try and come back yet again but on 25 August 2007 he picked up a double leg break against Celtic. Good on Neil for fighting back from such an injury, and he kept playing with Falkirk and Partick Thistle well into his thirties. He was a versatile player who could excel out wide and also play in a 4-4-2 alongside a more physical target man who would win balls that he could latch onto. He played in a role like that for Scotland a few times and he could get in behind defences and score goals.

Another top wide man for me was Bobby Prentice, who was a wizard on the left wing. He could be a real match winner on his day, or sometimes a bit frustrating when he was below par, but overall he was one of the greatest wingers ever seen at Tynecastle. Like Willie Johnston did a few years later, Bobby played on the edge. He was always one pass away from being an absolute genius and he was not afraid to try things. He was mesmerising when he was on his game and the fans used to sing, 'There goes Bobby, Bobby Prentice, on the wing, on the wing'. Bobby grabbed the fans' imagination as he was a charismatic character and on form he was a joy to behold, but like a lot of wingers if it wasn't going for him he would frustrate and sometimes anger the fans. In full flow he was absolutely magnificent, to the extent my family still have great memories of watching Bobby play.

Our former midfielder Cammy Fraser tells a great story that sums up Bobby. During a home match against Falkirk he swears Bobby took the ball off Jim Cruickshank in the left-back position and ran the length of the park, beating one man after another. He got to near the corner flag and came back the other way, beating them all again before passing the ball back to Cruickie! His first goal for Hearts came on 23 September 1973 in a 3-0 win over Rangers at Ibrox, with Drew Busby getting the other two. He scored lots of other great goals during his six years at Tynecastle before he left to join Toronto Blizzard in 1979.

Another wide man who could also play in midfield and who made a huge contribution to Hearts was John Colquhoun, who had blistering pace as well as an ability to look up before crossing and put superb balls onto the heads of strikers. To this day I can't understand why Celtic allowed him to sign for us for just £50,000 before the start of the 1985-86 season as he was still just twenty-three years old at the time and still had a lot to give. In that first season when we finished runners-up in the league, John was a revelation. He was the only outfield player to start every one of the thirty-six games and got eight goals in the process. Because of John's talent he was the target of some dreadful tackling, for back in the 1980s creative players like him were not as well protected by referees. Fair play to John, he always came back for more and never let defenders who were not as talented as him put him off his game.

He returned to the club in July 1993 from Sunderland and although he wasn't as sharp as he was during his first stint at the club, he still showed that form is temporary and class is permanent. In his first season back he showed his consistency by playing in thirty-eight of the forty-four league games. Only Tosh McKinlay, who played in all bar one, played more. John came close to making my Dream Team as he was such an outstanding player but after a lot of deliberation I have decided to go with a front three that would be a joy to watch and who would bang in the goals.

If there can be any criticism of my choices, it is that they all enjoyed playing in the opposition penalty area and there would be a fight between them to get into the six-yard box first. Also my choices aren't the tallest but that isn't much of a drawback considering their talent.

First up is a man I am proud to call a friend and who is a Hearts legend. John Robertson was a very intelligent striker. He was an all-round footballer and not just a finisher. You don't help create opportunities for midfield players unless you are a clever striker, which Robbo was, and as you will maybe have guessed he was one of my easiest Dream Team picks.

I don't think Hearts will ever have someone as prolific as John Robertson from now until the end of time. I would love to be proved wrong, as that would mean we would get another world-class striker, but I am confident wee Robbo will remain the main man.

I first met and played against Robbo when he was at Parson's Green Primary School and I was at Balgreen Primary School. We then played at Salvesen Boys Club together for one year at Under-11 level. When I moved up to Under-12 Robbo stayed behind in the Under-11s because he was still qualified for that age grade but he wanted to give it a go elsewhere and moved to Edina Hibs. That was a bad loss for Salvesen at the time. We played at Edinburgh Primary School and Edinburgh Secondary Schools select teams together. At secondary school level Robbo played for Portobello High School along with Dave Bowman, while I took them both on when I played for Tynecastle High School. These were real tough games with no quarter asked for or given.

Because he was a year younger than me, we didn't end up playing in the same Scotland Schoolboy Under-15 team. I played in the same team as Bryan Gunn, Dave Bowman, and Paul McStay. Paul was still eligible to play the following year when he was in the team, along with Robbo, who played in the famous 5-4 game that England won at Wembley when Paul Rideout scored a hat-trick for the home side. Looking back, I think the fact that Robbo and I played together and against each other might have given us that great understanding we had at professional level.

Although Robbo was wee at 5 feet 7 inches, I never felt concerned about him coming up against big defenders. He could always look after himself and was a tough wee bugger. He learned from Sandy Clark and Jimmy Bone how to use his body to keep defenders at bay and he could really mix it if he needed to against bigger, physical guys.

The only disappointment I had for Robbo and his family was that he lost his father at a young age. His dad had witnessed a bit of his football development but never got the chance to watch him at his prime, which was a tragedy. If he was looking down, his dad would have been very proud of how his son turned out. It was a very emotional moment when Robbo put his hand over his heart and looked to the heavens in recognition of his dad when he picked up his Hearts winners' medal after the Scottish Cup win over Rangers in 1998.

Robbo made his debut on 17 February 1982 when he came off the bench against Queen of the South in a 4-1 win. He joined his brother Chris who wore number eleven that day, and the only surprising thing is that Robbo did not score. The goals that day came from his brother Chris, Roddy MacDonald, Pat Byrne and another really talented player, Peter Marinello, who spent the later years of his career at Tynecastle.

When I was eighteen and Robbo was seventeen in 1982-83 we finished second behind St Johnstone in the old Scottish First Division. I remember Robbo scored twice at what was the old Boghead Stadium to clinch our promotion back to the Scottish Premier League with a 4-0 win over Dumbarton. That season I played twenty-six league games and scored six goals. Robbo played nineteen times and scored twenty-one goals. The following year back in the top flight we started with five consecutive league victories, and Robbo was in blistering form. He hit fifteen goals in thirty-four league games, which was a superb return considering it was our first season back among the big boys. I played twenty-nine times and got four goals. In 1985-86, the year we ran Celtic close for the league championship, he was simply magnificent again with twenty goals in thirty-four matches. Out of them all, the one that sticks in my memory was one of his two against Dundee United in the fourth last league game of the season.

As I said earlier, there was a lot more to Robbo's game than just being in the penalty box, although it was his second home. On this occasion he picked up a loose ball nearly thirty yards out and hit a left-foot shot into the top right-hand corner. I still maintain that was one of his best ever, and I had a lot to pick from. Sandy Clark got our other goal at Tannadice that day in what was one of our best-ever performances that season.

What will always endear Robbo to the Hearts faithful more than anything is his great goal-scoring record against Hibs. To be called 'The Hammer of the Hibs' when his older brother George, who is a great lad, was a big Hibs supporter must have caused some real great wind-ups in the Robertson household after games! Twenty-seven goals against the deadly rivals. What an incredible record. Robbo just couldn't stop scoring against Hibs, which was absolutely fine by me! I remember Jim Jefferies and Billy Brown's first game against them at Easter Road in October 1995 very well because I got sent off for doing something stupid yet again when we were 2-1 down. I was alone in the changing room, head in my hands, when Robbo scored to equalise. After that match Robbo came out with the immortal line to the press, 'It's not over until the fat striker scores.' On the Monday Jim and Billy said they were fining me for being sent off but I am sure it wasn't as much as it would have been if wee Robbo hadn't saved my bacon and scored the equaliser.

Robbo was among the strongest players mentally that I played alongside. He could retain focus with the fans on his back and defenders nipping at his heels. He wasn't naturally athletic but he was a natural goal-scorer who had the knack of being in the right place at the right time. I know Robbo had a year at Newcastle United and in a way I am pleased it didn't work as it meant Hearts got even more of his goals. I have Robbo to thank for securing me win bonuses almost single-handedly at times with all his goals and for that I will be eternally grateful. Also for all the joy Robbo gave to all the

Hearts fans he deserves all the praise that can be bestowed upon him.

For as long as the name of Heart of Midlothian is mentioned the name of John Robertson will be mentioned. He is part of the history of the club and one of the greatest players ever to grace Tynecastle. He is the ultimate iconic figure of the modern era. The Dave Mackays and the Willie Baulds are the iconic figures of a previous generation but wee Robbo is the man who most fans nowadays can identify with. Robbo would have been pleased in the first instance to have been given the chance to manage Hearts but he will have been disappointed not to have been given longer in the job. I am sure he would have been able to have made as big a name for himself as Hearts manager as he did as a player if he had been given a fair crack of the whip and not removed from his post so swiftly.

Unfortunately his time was much shorter than it should have been. My regret, and one I know that is shared by many Hearts fans, is that we didn't protest more at the time at his sacking. The warning bells should have been ringing when Robbo was replaced but we did not act and maybe that led to Mr Romanov thinking he could always have things his way.

One of the men I would play Robbo with up front is one of the most urbane, intelligent, interesting men I have met either in football or outwith the game. Donald Ford was at Hearts when they weren't doing too well yet he still played so superbly that he was in the extended Scotland squad for the World Cup in what was then West Germany back in 1974. He didn't play in any of the three games but to come so close in an era when Scotland had some other great strikers like Denis Law, Peter Lorimer and Joe Jordan showed his worth.

What I liked about Donald is that he never left Hearts when he was at his peak and I am sure he would have got a lot of offers. He joined in 1962 from Bo'ness United and made his debut in a 4-2 home win against Celtic on 26 September 1964.

He stayed until 1976 when he left to join Falkirk for a season before he retired.

Donald is a player I developed a decent relationship with off the park once he retired as I saw a lot of him as he was an accountant and did a lot of work for my mum and dad when they had their pub. We became friends from there and he was behind Wallace Mercer coming into the club and I presented him with his Hall of Fame Award. I actually requested I could present that award because he was a real iconic figure to the Hearts support and I would have made the same request if Jim Cruickshank had ever picked up a similar award as he meant so much to me.

Both were not as iconic figures for me as my hero Ralph Callachan, but to the vast majority of Hearts fans of that particular generation nobody came close to matching Donald Ford or Jim Cruickshank in terms of their ability or loyalty to the club.

I was twelve when Donald left Hearts but through my childhood both Donald and Jim were real huge heroes to me, along with Ralph of course. Although he was only 5 feet 7 inches tall – just like John Robertson – he was quick on his feet and was a bit like that famous German striker Gerd Muller who could sniff goals out. Donald is a real gentleman whose first talent may have been football but he had many other strings to his bow. He was a qualified chartered accountant who served on the Scottish Sports Council and also was elected as a councillor in his hometown of Linlithgow. On top of that he was a useful cricketer.

If you are looking for some Trivial Pursuit questions to ask your Hearts mates ask them who is the only player – at least to the best of my knowledge – to score a hat-trick of penalties for the club. The answer is Donald, who got three against Morton at Cappielow on 1 September 1973 in a 3-2 victory. What made Donald such a star to my family, among his other scoring exploits, was the fact that he was involved in one of the greatest Hearts fightbacks they had ever seen. Trailing 2-0 against Aberdeen at Pittodrie on 27 November 1971 with just seventeen minutes left and down to ten men, Donald took control. In front of the shocked home support in the 21,000 crowd he had scored twice before he popped up with the winner with just two minutes left.

The favourite single Donald Ford goal for my family came in the Scottish Cup against Rangers at Tynecastle on 13 May 1968. Hearts had drawn the first match at Ibrox and 44,000 people had packed the ground for the replay. There were only a couple of minutes left when Donald drifted past Dave McKinnon, the Rangers defender, and put the ball into the net. According to members of my family who were there, the place erupted like Tynecastle never had before. There was a wall of sound.

There were other Scottish Cup games I have talked to Donald about and he fondly remembers a match against Partick Thistle on 16 February 1974. What was unusual about the fourth-round replay was that the game was played on a weekday afternoon because it was the time of industrial unrest and there were power cuts, which meant the floodlights may have cut out if the game had been played in the evening. There were still 12,000 inside Tynecastle to watch Hearts win 4-1 and to witness Donald score a hat-trick.

Ask Donald and he will tell you his favourite time in a Hearts jersey was during the 1973-74 season when he scored eighteen goals in twenty-nine games, mainly thanks to Rab Prentice providing the ammunition. After he retired Donald became a respected photographer who had a gallery in South Queensferry before he moved to Carnoustie where he has a reputation as one of the best photographers of golf courses. He still gets up at ungodly hours to capture the courses at their best and his work has been shown all over the world.

My final Dream Team choice is a man who has mythical status at Tynecastle. I first met Willie Bauld at the old Telecoms Club in Chesser in Edinburgh and he had a real aura about him. I knew I was in the presence of a special man. When I used to look through the history books of him in action or watched old newsreels it looked like he always went up in the air to head the ball in a real graceful manner and, by heck, he could score goals. He was called by that generation of fans 'The King of Hearts' and you couldn't really argue with that one little bit.

He signed for Hearts in May 1946 but only after a tussle with Sunderland, who also wanted to sign him. Sunderland tried to get his registration from Musselburgh but the deal collapsed as the English club did not offer enough compensation to the east of Scotland team. Davie McLean, who was Hearts manager at the time, stepped in with enough money for Musselburgh and a decent enough signing-on fee to get Willie to sign for Hearts. From there he was sent to Newtongrange Star for experience before being loaned out to Edinburgh City, who were struggling in the old Scottish Second Division. He returned to the club with a vengeance a year later and made his competitive debut against East Fife at Tynecastle on 9 October 1948 in the League Cup when he scored a hat-trick in a 6-1 win, and as I said earlier, this was the first time the Terrible Trio played together. A week later he got another hat-trick in a 4-0 win over Queen of the South, with Alfie Conn getting the other.

He didn't score in the next win, a 2-0 victory over Rangers, where Conn and Jimmy Wardhaugh got the goals, but he was on the score sheet again the following week with a double against Clyde. He also scored in his next three matches to make it twelve goals in his first seven matches for Hearts. In that season he had scored twenty-four goals in thirty matches in all competitions, more than Jimmy Wardhaugh who got thirteen in twenty-six games and Alfie Conn who netted seventeen in twenty-eight games. The next season he was in even more remarkable form with an incredible forty goals in just thirty-eight games. Out of that figure he got thirty goals in just twenty-nine league games. That, by any stretch of the imagination, is an incredible goal-scoring record, especially as Hearts just finished third in the league that season and lost seven matches.

What I find amazing is that a talent like Willie only won three Scotland caps – scandalous in my opinion. He deserved to get a lot more. A number of knee injuries curtailed his appearances later in his career but he still got 183 league goals, which was only bettered at the time by Jimmy Wardhaugh's contribution of 206. Overall he played 414 competitive games for Hearts and scored a total of 277 goals in all major competitions. He won the Scottish League Championship twice and the Scottish Cup and Scottish League Cup once before retiring in May 1962 and opening a newspaper shop near Tynecastle.

I have spoken to a few of my older friends who have researched Willie Bauld's career at length and they tell me his great hat-trick against Airdrie in the 6-4 Scottish Cup quarter-final win at Tynecastle in the 1951-52 season was one of his finest moments. He also scored twice in the emphatic 5-1 Scottish League Cup final win over Partick Thistle on 25 October 1958. His strangest goal ever came two months later in a 5-1 win over Aberdeen at Tynecastle. Jimmy Murray ignored someone shouting to leave the ball thinking it was an opponent trying to put him off. It had been in fact Willie who had made the call and they both rose to head the ball into the net at the same time. Both Willie and Jimmy were strong characters and refused to give the other the goal as both had scored twice in the game and both wanted their hat-tricks. In the end it took a toss of the coin in the dressing room to put Willie's name on the goal that was among his twenty-six that season. The following year he scored Hearts' one hundredth goal of the season in the last minute of the second-last league game to earn a 4-4 draw against St Mirren, although the team got another two in a draw in the final league match against Raith Rovers in the year they won the league.

I am not quite sure why so many top stars like Jim Cruick-shank were alienated by the club for whatever reason, but it seems Willie fell into that same category. He was awarded a testimonial against Sheffield United in November 1962 that was played in front of 15,000 fans, but Willie was left angry at the way he was treated by the club directors that day. The pettiest thing they did, which I find shocking to this day, was the fact that they charged Willie, one of the club's greatest ever servants, for the match ball that was used. In total the club deducted £1,000 for staging the game from the £2,800 raised. It left Willie so bitter that he didn't return to Tynecastle for nearly thirteen years. When he did return it was only briefly in January 1975 at the invitation of former team-mate Bobby Parker, who was chairman at the time. He still took some persuasion and what seemed to swing it was that his young nephew was named as the Hearts mascot for that game against Kilmarnock that ended in a 1-1 draw. He got a rousing welcome in what was an emotional moment.

When he died at the age of just forty-three through heart failure it was a tragic moment in the history of Hearts Football Club and thousands lined the streets to pay their respects. On 12 March 1977 a group of members from various Hearts social clubs located at the rear of the Tynecastle stand organised a collection for flowers for his funeral. The response was so great that they formed a Willie Bauld Memorial Fifty Club that purchased a trophy to be played for in his honour. On top of that they started up a Willie Bauld Memorial Dinner that I have attended on numerous occasions and is still going strong to this day. It was only right and proper that Hearts named one of its function suites the Willie Bauld Suite in honour of his memory. He has also been inducted into the Scotland Hall of Fame, which also shows how highly he is thought of throughout the country.

So there you have my Dream Team forward line. Robertson, Ford and Bauld. Can I say, they are named in no particular order as they were all legends, not just of Hearts but also of Scottish football. With a trio like that up front no defence would be safe.

With Rudi Skacel, Dave Mackay and Steve Fulton in midfield and a back four of Walter Kidd, Craig Levein, Sandy Jardine and Tosh McKinlay, with Jim Cruickshank in goals, that is a formidable side.

Just in case they were struggling to gain the upper hand, which I know is hard to believe, I would make full use of the seven-man substitute rule and pack them with other club legends. I would name Gilles Rousset as my reserve goalkeeper, Steven Pressley as my centre-back cover, Colin Cameron and John Cumming as my midfield back up with John Colquhoun in there to either play in the middle of the park or out wide if we needed to stretch teams. Alfie Conn and Jimmy Wardhaugh would be my reserve Dream Team strikers. With Alex MacDonald working out the Dream Team tactics, I would think the fans would be in seventh heaven watching that lot.

FAMOUS FANS' DREAM TEAMS

Now I realise football is a game of opinions, and I would like to think my Hearts Dream Team selections have stimulated debate. To get a few alternative views, I asked some well-known and highly respected Hearts fans to name their team. Their choices have been fascinating and maybe a few of you might think some of their choices are better than mine! Make up your own mind from the team selections below, written by members of the Hearts family.

KEN STOTT

Ken Stott is a lifelong Hearts supporter. He is a hugely respected actor of stage and screen who played Rebus (a Hibs supporter!) in the television adaptation of Ian Rankin's famous novels about the Edinburgh detective. His latest major role is in *The Hobbit: An Unexpected Journey*, a film from Academy Award-winning director Sir Peter Jackson.

Ken: What about this? Choose your Hearts Dream Team and it'll go into a book where we can celebrate a Hearts legend who has forgotten more about football than you will ever know! Brilliant. What an honour . . . and so easy, I thought.

Well, whilst I think I've finally done it, I can tell you it's been quite a task. You see, I've followed the Hearts for over fifty years now and having seen so many fine players grace the maroon shirt, it's obvious that there could be three or more contenders for each position. However, the 1966 season saw the introduction of substitutes to the Scottish game, so I'm going to take full advantage of this rule and include seven illustrious arses on my bench!

Now, one serious point I'd like to make is that what unifies my selection is the belief that those who didn't represent their country should have, and those who did should have on many more occasions.

And so here goes.

Ken Stott's Hearts Dream Team (Formation: 4-4-2)

Goalkeeper: Craig Gordon
Though Jim Cruickshank came close – he was fantastic. As a boy I prayed to him at night. 'Please stop everything that Jim Forrest, Bobby Lennox or Pat Stanton can throw at you,' and most of the time, Cruickie did.

Although when the whistle blew at the end of extra time and it went to penalties against Gretna, I experienced a calmness which I hadn't felt at any other time during that afternoon because I knew that we had Craig Gordon in goal. I've never seen a better Hearts keeper, so he's my number one.

Defence:
Full-backs: Davie Holt and Chris Shevlane
Davie once told me that when he was a player, the job of the full-back was clear and simple: Take possession of the ball from the attacker, bring it up to the half-way line and distribute it accordingly. He was a master of this and I happily watched him do it week in and week out. While he was doing this on the left, **Chris Shevlane** was doing it equally well on the right.

194

Centre-backs: Steven Pressley and Craig Levein

My centre-backs are Steven Pressley and Craig Levein. This was when it started to get a bit difficult because a fair number of names come to mind: Alan Anderson, Roy Barry, Alan McLaren and Dave McPherson, for example. I think the last twenty-five years in particular have provided some of the best centre-backs so this isn't easy but I'm just going to have to dive in.

Steven Pressley has a place in my team for his leadership and bravery, both on and off the field on behalf of Hearts. His contribution to the club in footballing terms though is what interests me here and that I think was immense. Alongside him, a man whose playing career should have been long and glorious but was sadly cut short by injury, **Craig Levein**. As a centre-back he was infallible, and as a footballer I thought him majestic.

Midfield:

Eamonn Bannon: Occupies a berth just in front of this line. He will deliver short or sweeping passes with pinpoint accuracy and we will marvel at his coolness under pressure. His move to Chelsea broke my heart and his subsequent move to Dundee Utd depressed me even more. It all left me wondering how different things could've been, but these were financially difficult times for the club and sadly, this is a situation that every generation of Hearts supporters has had to endure.

Beside Bannon I would like to see **Colin Cameron**: his attacking runs through the middle causing mayhem. On the right wing is **Roald Jensen**: known in his hometown as *kniksen* (the Juggler). He is still the most famous footballer in Norway and on his day, he was better than anyone I had ever seen, with maybe the exception of the great Jimmy Johnstone. On the left wing is **Johnny Hamilton**. He was one of the greats who had played alongside Wardhaugh, Conn, Bauld and Sloan, and although he was approaching the end of his career when I saw him you could still see the magic. By now not the fastest, but his delivery was still excellent and he had a lethal shot.

Forwards:
John Robertson: Now if it's goals you want, it's got to be John Robertson. I definitely want goals so John Robertson it is.
Willie Hamilton: I leave the final place in this team to the man who has no fellow contenders, his talent was matchless. When he received the pitiful one and only international call up, Jock Stein sent him a telegram which simply read, 'Show the world'. Alex Ferguson described him as the best he had ever seen. It is of course, Willie Hamilton. When I first saw him he was playing for Hibs before he rejoined us in 1967, and I remember shuffling along in a huge crowd going to a New Year's Day game and fans of both sides were chatting excitedly to each other (yeah I know) about whether the great man would play that day.

He embodied the game at the time. By today's standards he was no athlete, even then he was considered out of shape, and he was, but it was of no matter because he put on a show which was full of brilliance and humour. He was an entertainer and it was him that the crowds came to see.

I was lucky enough to catch a glimpse of him before he retired, and 'the science of football' took over.

My bench is:
Jim Cruickshank – The Great.
Arthur Mann – Calm and stylish. The art of defending.
Alan McLaren – His determination, strength and spirit would slam the door on any attacker.
Gary Mackay – His love for Hearts is so well documented that it often overshadows the real reason why he has made more appearances than any other in maroon and white: he had the enthusiasm to infect his comrades with passion and pride, and a football and goal-scoring talent that could inspire any team to victory.

John Colquhoun – Imagine as a defender how demoralising it must be to see him getting ready to come off the bench!

Alan Gordon – Now this is a bit personal. He went to a 'good school' and he happened to be taught English by my father at George Heriot's and the now famous words of Eddie Turnbull, 'Your trouble is, yer brains are in yer heid', made an impact on me because I realised that it is in fact possible to be bright and be an abundantly gifted sportsman.

Willie Wallace – He was such a hero of mine. John Robertson would I know have quite a problem holding on to his place amidst such competition. When he moved to Celtic I was distraught. I was twelve years old and I didn't know that that sort of thing was allowed. Ah well . . .

Gary: What a team Ken has picked. It is a Dream Team packed full of talent and with some very interesting choices. Holt and Shevlane were before my time but I can see how they would work well with Levein and Pressley. With Bannon sitting and spraying passes from in front of the back four, Cameron just ahead of him in the centre of midfield and Jensen and Johnny Hamilton out wide, it is a formation that would be fascinating to see in action. Up front wee Robbo and Willie Hamilton, playing further forward than usual and in a free role, would be a joy to behold. All in all, Ken has picked a Dream Team that captured my imagination big time.

FIRST MINISTER ALEX SALMOND

When not working, First Minister Alex Salmond enjoys football – supporting Scotland and Heart of Midlothian – horse racing, golf and reading. He gets along to Tynecastle whenever his busy schedule allows and keeps an eye out for their results regardless of where he is.

His most enduring football memory, certainly in terms of games he has actually attended, is as a youngster watching Hearts defeat Kilmarnock at Hampden in October 1962 to lift the League Cup, when his dad told him there would be many more similar triumphs for Hearts in the years ahead. There have been a few more such occasions over the years of course – especially the 2012 Scottish Cup final win over Hibs – but perhaps not quite as trophy-laden as he imagined that day, despite some great players turning out in the maroon.

First Minister Alex Salmond's Hearts Dream Team (Formation: 4-3-3)

Goalkeeper: Jim Cruickshank

A great goalkeeper, who while not the tallest, made up for it with great athleticism and courage. He was also a renowned shot-stopper, especially of penalties, a skill which he demonstrated in one New Year derby against Hibs by not only parrying the spot-kick but also saving two rebound efforts! He made a nervous start to his first Scotland game, but didn't let his country down on any of the half-dozen times he was selected to play in the dark blue – it should have been many more.

Defence:

Jim Jefferies: Jim will perhaps be best remembered by some Hearts fans for his spell as manager, with the highlight the 2-1 Scottish Cup final triumph over Rangers in 1998. But he was also a great servant as a player, a strong, committed presence at the back who made over 300 appearances for the club.

Davie Weir: A true Scottish footballing legend, Davie was a late developer as a player, playing college football in the US before returning to Scotland and arriving at Hearts in 1996. He was a member of that great 1998 Scottish Cup-winning squad and also played for Scotland in our last – to date – major finals appearance at the France '98 World Cup. Davie has gone on to represent his country many times, and to continue his playing career into his forties is a truly remarkable feat.

Eddie Thomson: A stalwart presence at the back for the Jambos for seven seasons, Eddie played at Tynecastle during an era which was not the best for the club, but he was one of the finest defenders in Scotland at the time, before deciding to try his luck in playing and management in first the United States and then Australia.

Andy Lynch: Although used by Hearts as an attacker in a left-wing position in his time at Tynecastle, none other than Jock Stein spotted his ability as a left-back, which is the position Lynch made his own once he moved to Celtic later in his career, and he would fill this position admirably in an all-time Hearts eleven.

Midfield:

Dave Mackay: One of the all-time legends of the Scottish game. A ferocious competitor, who combined a no-nonsense style with some sublime skills, Dave went on to have a huge impact on the English game during his time with Tottenham. No less a figure than George Best probably summed it up better than anyone when he described Mackay as 'the hardest man I have ever played against – and certainly the bravest'.

John Cumming: While Dave Mackay might be remembered as the man who taught Billy Bremner to be a hard man, it could be argued that John 'Iron Man' Cumming taught Dave Mackay the art of hard but fair tackling. The most decorated and successful player in the club's history, and a one-club man for his whole senior career, he was one of the Hearts team I watched from the Hampden terraces along with my dad when they won the 1962 League Cup final.

Tommy Walker: The most successful boss in the club's history during the glory years, Tommy Walker would be my ideal player–manager. Although I never saw him play myself, he was a legendary midfielder, who my dad has assured me is the greatest player Hearts and Scotland have ever produced.

Forwards:

John Robertson: The wee man was the ultimate poacher, always on the end of a headed knock-down or a rebound somewhere in or around the edge of the six-yard box. You always knew Hearts were in with a shout in any match in which Robbo was playing, such was his lethal finishing ability. The club's all-time record goal-scorer and also a great servant for the national cause who pulled on the dark blue sixteen times, he is a must-pick for my Dream Team.

Donald Ford: Notable as one of the only two Hearts players to be capped in the 1970s, alongside Jim Cruickshank, Ford was another fine striker who spent most of his top-flight career at Tynecastle and is rightly regarded as a Jambos legend. It speaks volumes that, at a time when the club was struggling, he was selected as part of Scotland's 1974 World Cup squad for the finals in West Germany. If needed, he could be used as a winger rather than an out-and-out striker.

Willie Bauld: A free-scoring striker in the old-fashioned mould, he was a key part of the Hearts team that enjoyed such great success in the late '50s, winning all three domestic trophies in his time at Tynecastle. A true great and another definite for the starting eleven.

Substitutes: The subs' bench of those who nearly, but not quite, make into my Dream Team would be made up with goalkeeper Craig Gordon, defender Craig Levein, midfielders Rudi Skacel and Jim Townsend, and striker Rene Moller.

Gary: The First Minister has picked a team that any football fan, regardless if they supported Hearts, would pay good money to watch. The only selection he has made that I would categorically disagree with is at right-back where he has picked Jim Jefferies. As a manager I can see why he would be a Dream Team candidate. As a player? I am sorry, Jim and Mr Salmond, absolutely not. Not good enough.

His centre-back pairing is the most interesting I have seen out of all the Dream Teams and an absolutely fascinating one that, once I studied it closely, came to the conclusion that the First Minister had picked a great combination. I watched Eddie Thomson as a player and he was a real self-assured character while I was fortunate enough to play alongside David Weir, and the pair of them would fit together well.

On the left flank he has picked Andy Lynch and he has been very clever with his decision. Andy liked to get up the pitch and I can understand why, for the balance of the team that the First Minister has picked, he has put him there as he was an out-and-out left-sided player who could get to the by-line to provide crosses to the front three.

I did not see the three lads he has put into his midfield in the flesh but obviously I have heard about their quality from others and it is hard to argue with his choices. People who are steeped in the tradition of Heart of Midlothian, which clearly the First Minister is, would always tell you that the three in his midfield are legends and who could argue with that. His front three are also all class acts and are out-and-out strikers and they would certainly get a lot of goals for you.

You could not argue with his bench. Craig Gordon won't let you down; Craig Levein is a top-class defender; Rudi Skacel is someone who has been idolised twice at the football club. Jim Townsend was a really good servant to Hearts and I am delighted that Rene Moller gets a mention, as I too remember him with great affection. He was a top player.

DAVID MCLETCHIE, MSP

Conservative MSP David McLetchie is a Hearts season ticket holder who has been following the team all of his life. He attended Leith Academy and George Heriot's School before graduating in law from Edinburgh University in 1974. He has held numerous positions within the Scottish Conservative Party at constituency and national level and was president of the Scottish Conservative and Unionist Association from 1994-1997.

In September 1998 he was elected to lead the party's campaign in the first election to the Scottish Parliament held in 1999. He was returned as a regional list member for Lothians. In the 2003 election he won the Edinburgh Pentlands constituency, which he held with an increased majority in 2007. In 2011 he was returned on the regional list for Lothian. David was the leader of the Scottish Conservative MSPs from 1999-2005 and their Chief Whip and Business Manager from 2007-2011 and is now their spokesman on Justice and Constitutional Affairs.

David McLetchie MSP's Hearts Dream Team (Formation: 4-4-2)

Goalkeeper: Craig Gordon

The position of goalkeeper is the hardest to fill in my Hearts Dream Team of the last fifty years because we have had some outstanding keepers in that period from Jim Cruickshank through Henry Smith, Gilles Rousset and Antti Niemi to Craig Gordon. In my book, Craig just edges it because of his combination of shot-stopping ability with sound defensive organisation and a mastery of the angles. Of all our goalies he has gone on to play at the highest club level and won the most international caps for Scotland, so better judges than me rate him highly. I look forward to seeing him back in a Scotland shirt again and maybe even a return to Tynecastle in the final stages of his career.

Defence:

Alan McLaren: Alan was a solid, reliable player, an excellent tackler and sound distributor of the ball from the back.

Craig Levein: Craig showed a maturity that belied his years from the moment he walked into Tynecastle. He was an outstanding reader of the game as a player and is a man who speaks with intelligence and authority and demands high standards of himself and others. It is no surprise that he is now the Scotland team manager.

David Weir: He has had the lengthy career which injury denied Craig but, that apart, they share many of the same qualities and I think that in time he too will prove to be an outstanding manager and coach.

Gary Naysmith: He played alongside David in the 1998 Scottish Cup-winning team and subsequently in the English Premier League with Everton.

Midfield:

Neil Berry: In my opinion, there was no better ball winner for Hearts than Neil Berry, another stand-out player from the team of '86 who did so much of the unselfish hard work that helped others to play. Julien Brellier and Stefano Salvatori deserve honourable mentions in this role as well.

Colin Cameron: He will always be best remembered for scoring a penalty after two minutes of the 1998 Scottish Cup final but is chosen for his all-round play and ability to make goal-scoring late runs into the penalty box. A live-wire player with a terrific engine.

Paul Hartley: In a seventeen-year playing career spanning ten clubs Hearts fans undoubtedly saw the best of Paul Hartley as the midfield general of the 2006 team. The hat-trick against Hibs in the 2006 Scottish Cup semi-final would win him a Dream Team place on its own but that would not do justice to the enormous contribution he made to winning many other games.

Eamonn Bannon: To complete my midfield I ought to pick Gary Mackay because, in my time, I have seen him play more games for Hearts than any other player and his dedication to the club, ability and consistency deserve selection. However, as my mid-field four is a bit lacking in width to supply my strike force, I am going to pick Eamonn Bannon instead, who was a magnificent crosser of the ball and an intelligent all-round footballer.

Forwards:

John Robertson: Robbo is impossible to ignore given his goal-scoring record, and he was too often dismissed as just a penalty-box player who only scored goals, as if that was a crime. He is a man who should have been awarded many more caps for Scotland.

Sandy Clark: Sandy was the perfect partner up front for John Robertson. A strong and fearless centre-forward who could not only score goals but was selfless in what he did for Robbo and the rest of the team.

Manager: Alex MacDonald

He made a great contribution to Hearts and built a great side that just missed out on the 1986 Scottish League title.

I had to think long and hard to work out my best team as other contenders for my back four were Andy Webster, Christophe Berra, Steven Pressley, Sandy Jardine, Paul Ritchie and Tosh McKinlay. Jardine is best known for his career at Rangers but in his time at Hearts he played an influential role as a sweeper and was part of the management team with Alex MacDonald, who rebuilt the club under Wallace Mercer's chairmanship after the horrors of the late '70s and early '80s.

Among the others competing for selection in my midfield were Thomas Flögel, Steve Fulton, Ralph Callachan, Kenny Black, Rudi Skacel and the late Willie Hamilton, who played in that

League Cup final in 1962 and is regarded by many in Edinburgh as the finest midfield player to play for both Hearts and Hibs.

In selecting my team, I accept I am short of wingers and we have had some great ones in my time, so thanks to John Colquhoun, Allan Johnston, Neil McCann and Bobby Prentice for all the memories of their exciting play. I would also like to recognise the contributions of Drew Busby, Willie Gibson and Donald Ford. Gibson scored some of the scruffiest goals I have ever seen but certainly knew how to find the net and reputedly never missed a penalty. Donald Ford was an energetic, speedy centre-forward and Drew Busby's presence, power, hard work and not a little skill has won him a legendary status even among fans who never saw him play.

Finally, in my fifty years of supporting Hearts I have watched more games in the company of my son James and my good friend Alasdair Loudon than any others. Thanks to James and Alasdair for all the memories and good times we have shared watching the Boys in Maroon.

Gary: I think what I like about David's team is the wonderful balance to his back four. His goalkeeper is different class and the physicality of Alan McLaren is well needed there, as David Weir and Craig Levein had other qualities – David reading the game, Craig using his pace. Gary Naysmith on the left side of defence was a top performer as he was always reliable, as is David's holding midfield player Neil Berry. Neil came into my thoughts when I was working out my Dream Team as he was a player's player and you cannot give a bigger accolade to a football player. Having him in the team would allow the industry and guile of Cameron and Hartley to come to fruition. He has picked a great front three, with Robertson and Clark being the best I ever played alongside. That partnership was outstanding. To put Eamonn Bannon in there would allow quality balls into the box and Eamonn also had a decent record of getting goals from the wide area.

It is a really well-balanced team from someone who is a lovely man, a true Hearts fan, but someone who does not have the same political allegiance as I do. David, I think after going through your Dream Team your politics is the only thing I am going to disagree with you over.

MARTIN GEISSLER

TV news reporter Martin Geissler grew up just a mile or so from Tynecastle and fell in love with Hearts at an early age. He has, in the words of the song, 'travelled far, by bus and car' to watch the Jam Tarts play. Present at all the main highs (and lows) over the past thirty-odd years and a veteran of many European road trips, his Hearts supporting credentials are impeccable. These days he works as a correspondent with ITV News, covering major news events all around the world (he compiled this Dream Team while filming with British troops in Helmand Province, Afghanistan). But he hasn't lost his passion for the club and will still fly home from far-flung places to make it to Tynecastle for an 'unmissable' match.

Martin Geissler's Hearts Dream Team (Formation: 4-4-2)

Goalkeeper: Henry Smith
You need a certain something to be a really charismatic goal-keeper and Henry Smith had it in spades. A real maverick who first earned a living down the coalmines of Yorkshire, he was capable of genuine brilliance and heart-stopping blunders, often coming within just minutes of each other. You could argue with some confidence that better goalies have pulled on a Hearts jersey, Antti Niemi for one, but you just can't pick them over this guy. It's not right. A true fans' favourite, no one else was quite like him. For a decade and a half, we had a goalie called Henry, and that alone was pretty cool.

Defence:

Walter Kidd: Every great team needs a no-nonsense grafter, and Walter is mine. When I close my eyes I can still take myself back to the Shed in the early eighties. Zico commanded the corner in front of us with a pride and determination that won him universal respect.

Craig Levein: Simply the most accomplished player I've ever seen in a Hearts shirt. Composed and commanding, Craig exuded authority not just over the back line he marshalled but over opponents, too. After injury put paid to his playing days, Craig brought the same class and intelligence to the dugout. Mild mannered and calm on the surface, but beneath the velvet glove there was a fist of steel. Just ask Graeme Hogg!

Dave McPherson: I can't think of anyone better to partner Levein at centre-half, and vice-versa. A commanding presence in either box and the never-say-die attitude of a true winner. Slim gets the call-up to my Dream Team with one specific instruction: more of those mazy runs, please – they might not have been pretty (or effective, much of the time), but they got me out of my seat!

Tosh McKinlay: Joe Jordan tried to bring an Italian-style of play to Tynecastle when he arrived in 1990 and in some respects, at least, he succeeded. He wanted to achieve a free-flowing model using attacking full-backs and Tosh completely understood the brief. His pace and flair were recognised with a regular place in the Scotland team. On the down side, he wasn't a great fan of his own right foot – but I'll forgive him that!

Midfield:

John Colquhoun: On his day he was our Diego Maradona. Well, maybe my memory's a little rose-tinted, but he had pace, energy, balance and the accuracy and timing to deliver a killer cross. JC was a key part of a great team. And, after twenty-odd years, I've just about forgiven him that miss in the Olympiastadion, Munich, that night in '89!

Gary Mackay: Gary broke through at Tynecastle amid a crop of exciting young talent around the time I first started following Hearts. For the next seventeen years, he was at the heart of the club in every sense. In his time in maroon, they burst from the gloom of the second tier to challenge for the Premier League and win respect across the continent. Gary was the keystone of one of the greatest periods in Hearts' history. No one has pulled on the maroon jersey more often and, given the nature of modern football, no one ever will. Unquestionably the captain of my Hearts Dream Team.

Drew Busby: Every great team needs a real cult hero, and the Buzz-bomb is mine. Robust and rough around the edges, when the crowd sang, 'he'll drink all your whisky, your Newcastle Brown', there was a sense that it might actually be true . . . but boy did he know where the goal was. A fierce shot and a fine 'tache, he gets a place in my Dream Team as a true crowd-pleaser. I'm playing him in midfield, incidentally, as opposed to his preferred striking role, but there was no way I was leaving him out.

Rudi Skacel: When the final history of Hearts is written (hopefully not for some considerable time), those twelve remarkable games under George Burley should be given a chapter all to themselves. Whatever really happened between Burley and the board, the explosive excitement of those few weeks was unforgettable. Rudi Skacel epitomised the swagger of the side Burley assembled and the wonderful lack of respect they showed the so-called heavyweights of the Scottish game. I couldn't pick a side without a nod to that extraordinary period, so Rudi gets a place. Also, how could I not include the man who scored against the Hibs in our Scottish Cup final win of 2012 in my Hearts Dream Team?

Forwards:

John Robertson: Right. I'll keep this brief. I love watching Hearts beat Hibs. There are few things I enjoy more, in fact. So for that reason, and so many, many others, step forward, John Robertson, and claim your place in my side.

Willie Gibson: He might not feature in everyone's Hearts Dream Team, but Willie Gibson helped me fall in love with the club. He was the player I pretended to be, aged eight or nine, kicking a ball around the street or the school playground. There's a short period in your life when football either hooks you in or passes you by. When I got drawn along for the ride, Willie was the talisman striker at Tynecastle and my first real hero in maroon. I had a poster of him, from *Shoot*, I think, on my bedroom wall. His distinctive features peered down at me for years. I still have that poster somewhere. But my wife forbids it from our bedroom these days.

Manager: Jim Jefferies

Jim could quite easily have made it into my team as a player but his qualities in the dugout and the dressing room surpass even his performances on the pitch. Jim has all the attributes required to succeed in management: a formidable, demanding, often combative character, he commands respect and repays it with the kind of loyalty that really pulls a squad together. He brought us a Scottish Cup for the first time in almost half a century and for that alone he joined the ranks of the true Hearts legends. His love for the club is genuine and reciprocated. With a Dream Team on the pitch, you'd want his snarling, grimacing, grumpy face barking instructions from the side-line, wouldn't you?

It's a difficult but wonderful task, putting together your club's Dream Team. It brings back all the old memories and stirs up so much healthy debate. I've restricted myself to selecting players I saw represent Hearts. Obviously Conn, Bauld, Wardhaugh, Dave Mackay and others would march into an all-time Hearts side but as I never saw them play I don't feel the same connection I have with the players listed. So, my starting eleven are all players who got my blood racing, my fist pumping or my larynx rattling.

As with everything in life, the more time passes, the more romantic your memories become. As I write this, I'm back smelling the hops from the brewery, the Bovril from that funny little wooden pie-stand half-way up the school-end terrace, and the waft from what passed for a gents toilet behind the wall at the top of the Shed. In my mind's eye, I'm watching Ian Ferguson blast home his rocket against Bayern Munich (on my eighteenth birthday), or José Quitongo jinking and twisting in the ninety-third minute to rob Celtic of two points. And I'm working my way through the eleven players, re-living the wonderful moments that won them all a place in Hearts' history and a starting berth in my team.

Gary: That Hearts team would do Martin justice most definitely. When you look at the team it is packed with modern-day stars that excited the crowds through the years. It is good to see he has picked Henry Smith, a fans' favourite as Martin says, who won us more games than he lost. His two centre-backs, McPherson and Levein, played for Hearts and Scotland in the World Cup and are a well-tried and trusted pairing. Tosh McKinlay, when he left Hearts, represented Scotland in a World Cup and Walter Kidd was someone who epitomised what Hearts supporters love in a player in that he gave full commitment.

It would be a privilege to captain Martin's Dream Team, and although I always preferred to get forward from the midfield in my later years, I played a holding role under Jim Jefferies and Billy Brown. I did not always enjoy playing in that position but I would be delighted to hold in the midfield that Martin has picked. That is because there is so much quality on either flank from Colquhoun and Skacel, players who could get crosses into the box, beat people and also score important goals. Then you have Drew Busby who could do all your tackling and also get in the box to score goals. Maybe Martin is looking a bit through rose-tinted glasses but as a lifelong Hearts fan he has every right to say John Colquhoun was as a good as Maradona at times, but the wee Argentine may have something to say about that! Also for Martin to remember John's miss in the Olympic Stadium is fair going for someone of Martin's vintage and shows his love of the Hearts.

I have to say I am delighted he has picked Willie Gibson in his Dream Team. Willie was great with the young guys like myself when I first started out at Tynecastle and would have been a prolific scorer in Martin's Dream Team. I can see why he has put Willie next to Robbo because both would feed off the kind of terrific service you would get from your wide men Colquhoun and Skacel.

MIKE AITKEN

Mike Aitken is a former chief football writer and Chief Sports-writer of *The Scotsman*. He continues to attend as many Hearts matches as he possibly can and has a column in the match day programme.

Mike Aitken's Hearts Dream Team (Formation: 4-3-3)

Goalkeeper: Craig Gordon
The first Hearts player to win the Scottish Football Writers' Player of the Year award since Sandy Jardine in the '80s, Gordon was an influential member of the side which finished second in the SPL and won the Scottish Cup in 2006. A wonderfully intuitive shot-stopper, Craig also commanded the penalty box and built a solid understanding with his centre-backs.

Defence:
Bobby Parker: A fearless defender who never shirked a tackle and struck free-kicks with as much ferocity as any player in the

club's history, Bobby served the club with distinction as player, captain, trainer, coach, scout, chairman and director for half a century.

Craig Levein: Blessed with fantastic pace, keen intelligence and a high level of ability, Levein formed an understanding with Jardine, which was the outstanding defensive pairing in Hearts' history.

Sandy Jardine: Scotland's Player of the Year on two occasions with Rangers and Hearts – he was the first footballer to earn this distinction with different clubs – Jardine was a cultured full-back at Ibrox and a composed centre-back during his spell at Tyne-castle.

John Cumming: One of the club's greatest servants, he won more medals – four League Cups, two Championships and one Scottish Cup – than any other Hearts player. Although he was a half-back for most of his career rather than a full-back, I've cheated only a little by including him at left-back, a position he first played for the club after deciding he didn't have a future as a left winger.

Midfield:

Alex Young: Young enjoyed a fantastic scoring rate for Hearts, contributing seventy-one goals in 155 league appearances. He glided through games and stroked home goals. He's fondly remembered at Tynecastle as a creative footballer with a deft touch who was also idolised at Everton as 'the Golden Vision'.

Dave Mackay (captain): Mackay was a natural leader. He ran the game from midfield as a force of nature and won a clean sweep of honours with Hearts – the Scottish Cup in 1956, the Championship in 1958 and the League Cup in 1954 and 1958. The finest Hearts' player of the post Second World War era, Mackay also became a legend with Spurs.

Willie Hamilton: An astonishingly alert inside-forward with quick feet and an even faster football brain, Hamilton was

212

regarded by Jock Stein as an even more gifted maverick than either Jimmy Johnstone or Jim Baxter. Of all the players honoured in this list, Hamilton was the most extraordinary.

Forwards:

John Robertson: The greatest finisher in the club's history, Robertson demonstrated from an early age an uncanny sense of calm in front of goal. The club's record league goalscorer with 214, he scored twenty-seven of those goals against Hibs.

Willie Bauld: The King of Hearts might only have been 5ft 8ins tall, but he was supreme in the air and a prolific goalscorer. He won Championship, Scottish Cup and League Cup medals and was arguably the most popular footballer in the club's history.

Jimmy Wardhaugh: Jimmy scored 206 goals in 304 league appearances for Hearts. All in all, Wardhaugh scored 375 goals for the club and formed thrilling partnerships with Willie Bauld and Alfie Conn and Jimmy Murray and Alex Young.

Manager: Tommy Walker

Regarded as Britain's best footballer in the '30s, Walker returned to Hearts as a player–coach after the Second World War and went on to become the club's most successful manager.

Substitutes: Jim Cruickshank, Steven Pressley, Gary Naysmith, Gary Mackay, Willie Wallace, Donald Ford, Rudi Skacel.

Gary: I still see Mike at Hearts games to this day and he has a wealth of experience to draw upon. I agree with him that you have to find positions for the top players and although Johnny Cumming may not be happy playing at left-back, he would get on with the job and is too good to leave out.

Alex Young is well respected at Hearts but became a bigger idol at Everton Football Club. When you look at his record again you will find he had an incredible goal-scoring record for someone coming from the wide area. As for Willie Hamilton, well, I have listened to Mike and others speak about him in the past, and I can't argue with the fact that he appears to have been a great inside-forward with great vision who could score goals.

There is no question about the quality of his front three and his overall team selection. Would it be a successful side and is it maybe too attack-minded? It could be, but I for one would pay good money to watch them play.

BRIAN SCOTT

Brian Scott is the former chief football writer with the *Scottish Daily Mail*, where he still writes a regular Saturday column.

Brian Scott's Hearts Dream Team (Formation: 4-4-2)

Goalkeeper: Craig Gordon

Long before most of us had ever heard of him, people within the game were talking about Craig Gordon's potential. When, finally, he made his breakthrough with Hearts, we found out why. He impressed as being mature beyond his years and proceeded to display all the attributes required by an international goalkeeper.

Defence:

Bobby Kirk: More than half a century has elapsed since Bobby was winning medals in the most successful team ever assembled at Tynecastle, yet I doubt if the club have fielded a better right-back than him. In contrast to his immediate forerunner in the '50s, Bobby Parker, he didn't have a physical presence. Rather, he was nimble and a good footballer.

Dave McPherson: His height alone (6'3") made him stand out in even the best of company although, for such a towering figure, he was well balanced and remarkably comfortable with the ball at his feet. Just as he gave Hearts a sense of assurance in defence, he could make his presence felt at the opposite end of the field. A good guy to have around.

Craig Levein: He and McPherson operated virtually as one when they played alongside one another in the '80s. Craig was very astute in the way he operated, reading the game well and able to control the ball in the tightest of situations before using it to the team's advantage. We may be sure that, had it not been for injury, he would have won more than sixteen caps.

Davie Holt: I was sorely tempted to pick George Thomson, a defensive ally of Bobby Kirk's, at left-back. He was ahead of his time in the way he got forward on the flank. Yet I've gone for the man who succeeded him circa 1960, Davie being a real stoic who could stand up to the very best of wingers who played in opposition to him.

Midfield:

John Colquhoun: Decisions, decisions! I thought immediately of Alex Young for this role. He was a very fine footballer, albeit well short of his peak when he played for Hearts in the late 1950s. But, finally, I opted for JC who could tease opposing defences with something like the same degree of skill and sling over good crosses.

Dave Mackay: Those who never saw him play maybe can't appreciate just how good he actually was. The only negative thing I could say about him is I saw him once make a pig's ear of taking a penalty at Tynecastle. Dave was the ultimate competitor, fearsome in the tackle and forever driving others on. But he had a high level of skill also and could pass the ball with a rare precision.

Jimmy Wardhaugh: Jimmy, a member of Hearts' Terrible Trio, was classed as an inside-forward. In the modern game, he would be an attacking midfielder. I did think very seriously of Gary Mackay for this role, then went for Jimmy on account of the fact he was a prolific goal-scorer as well as a tireless worker between the penalty boxes.

John Cumming: Virtually without a challenger, in my view, to play on the left side of midfield. Dave Mackay is reported to have said John was the best wing-half he ever played with which, coming from him, ranks as the ultimate compliment. Nobody has won more medals with Hearts than this stalwart of yore. He tended to play deep but, having begun as a winger, he had the capacity to get forward.

Forwards:

John Robertson: His scoring record for Hearts guaranteed him a place in my Dream Team selection. Defenders, invariably far bigger than he was, hated playing against this wee fella. Those who questioned what he did outside the penalty box surely missed the point that he wasn't cut out so much to make chances as to take them, which he did with outstanding regularity.

Willie Bauld: No Hearts side of all-time greats could be without the regal presence of the King himself. Though hardly the tallest, his heading ability was uncanny. I can see him yet: hovering on high, just waiting to head in yet another cross. He was two-footed, as well, with a deft touch on the ball. Willie had charisma, at a time when few besides scholars of Greek were familiar with the term.

Manager: Alex MacDonald

He had a way of teasing the very best out of players and was desperately unlucky to finish THAT season (1985–86) without a trophy to show for it. Alex's public persona, after he quit playing, was somewhat understated. But those who worked for him will attest to the strength of his man-management.

Gary: Brian has put together a side that will appeal to all generations of Hearts fans. Bobby Kirk and Davie Holt I was told about by my grandfather and you can't argue with them playing the full-back roles either side of McPherson and Levein. Brian has a good balance to his midfield and with Jimmy Wardhaugh supporting the front two and John Colquhoun giving you the width, it is an exciting team. Brian, I know for a fact, watched these players at close quarters for years and I am sure John Colquhoun will be humbled by the fact that he was picked by Brian in his Dream Team ahead of the great Alex Young. Robertson and Bauld up front is a fantastic partnership and, as Brian says, although Willie wasn't the tallest he scored nome great goals with his head. I am pleased someone like Brian picked Alex MacDonald as his manager as the bug bear for some people was that he never won anything. But when you think of the state of Hearts when he came into the club and the way he turned it around, it makes him a good choice.

STUART BATHGATE

Stuart Bathgate has been a Hearts supporter since 1965 and a sportswriter for *The Scotsman* since 1996.

Stuart Bathgate's Hearts Dream Team (Formation: 4-4-2)

Goalkeeper: Craig Gordon
Jim Cruickshank performed heroics in a poor Hearts side, and more recently Antti Niemi was exceptionally talented, but for me Gordon's agility and concentration was even more impressive. When your team are in a penalty shootout, how many other goalkeepers would leave you totally confident of victory?

Defence:
Walter Kidd: One of half a dozen players in this selection who

could captain the side, the right-back was a vital member of the team which re-established itself in the top division after the yo-yo years.

Sandy Jardine: Played much of his career at right-back but was at the heart of defence (and pushing forty) when he was voted Scotland's Player of the Year in 1986. And whatever position he played in, you could always rely on him to be completely calm, yet also totally committed. A model professional.

Craig Levein: The fastest man in the game in his day, but read the game so well that he never looked hurried. One of the most skilled central defenders the country has produced – who knows how good he would have become had injury not curtailed his career?

Takis Fyssas: The Greek left-back was far from being the most acclaimed member of George Burley's side, but he was a crucial component in it nonetheless. His ability to slide in, win the ball, get back to his feet and start a counter-attack seemed to be performed in one fluid movement, and he could play at a relentlessly high tempo.

Midfield:

John Colquhoun: Many remember him primarily as a right-winger, but he was just as effective as a finisher – remember his goal against Dundee United in the 1986 Cup semi-final?

Julien Brellier: Selfless, tenacious and a real team player, the French holding midfielder was a joy to watch during his brief time at Tynecastle. Whenever there was a loose ball in the defensive third of the field, you could be sure Brellier would get there and tidy things up.

Gary Mackay: With Brellier as the anchor, Mackay would be free to concentrate on what he did best, taking the play to the opposition with his direct running. 'Playing for the jersey' is a tired old cliché, but in Mackay's case it was true for every one of his 737 or so appearances.

Rudi Skacel: When George Burley took over as Hearts manager he had less than a full team of registered players. Weeks later he had one of the most talented squads ever assembled at the club, and Skacel was the pick of the bunch; a lethal finisher in his own right, he also brought the best out of Paul Hartley.

Forwards:
Donald Ford: A quick and intelligent striker, he helped Hearts keep their heads above water during the long and painful decline that set in from the mid-1960s. One of the club's greatest servants and a gentleman on and off the pitch.
John Robertson: With Robbo up front alongside Ford you wouldn't play too many high balls into the box, but they would make a great predatory pair, and any loose balls in the box would be sure to end up in the net.

Manager: Tommy Walker
I've confined my choice of players to those I've seen myself, but in choosing a manager I'll have to go for someone from before my time and nominate Tommy Walker. He ended a trophy drought that had lasted nearly half a century, and went on to preside over the most successful team in the club's history.

Substitutes: Can we have thirty or so? There are so many I'd love to see in this squad, with Pasquale Bruno, Colin Cameron, Bobby Prentice and Roald Jensen near the top of the list.

Gary: Stuart's team has a fantastic balance to it, particularly in the midfield area. I feel that when Julien Brellier played under George Burley he gave master class after master class as to how to play a holding midfield role. He won the ball, gave it to other people to play and had a great football brain. You have Colquhoun and Skacel to go and provide the spark and inspiration, while I would just be delighted to be part of Stuart's midfield and would try and support the front two as best I could. It would be great to play balls into the feet of Robbo and Fordy and go link up with them, safe in the knowledge that someone like Julien would be there to give cover for me. The difficulty for Fordy would be he would be puffed out by the time he got into the box because he would have been doing all Robbo's running for him, as Sandy Clark and Jimmy Bone would testify from when they played alongside the great man.

IAIN MERCER

Iain Mercer is the son of the late Wallace Mercer, who was chairman and owner of Hearts between 1981 and 1994. He is a former news and sports radio journalist and now runs the family property development and investment company based in Edinburgh. Iain is a season ticket holder at Tynecastle and follows the fortunes of his club avidly.

Iain Mercer's Hearts Dream Team (Formation: 4-4-2)

Goalkeeper: Craig Gordon
From the late Jim Cruickshank to Henry Smith, Gilles Rousset to Marian Kello, the player wearing the number one jersey at Hearts has, more often than not, been a safe pair of hands. My choice was a close call between Antti Niemi and Craig Gordon, but I opted for the latter. 'World class' is an over-used term in football, but I believe some of his saves truly were that. His talents yielded a £9 million transfer fee from Sunderland in 2007, becoming the club's most profitable export from the Youth Academy.

Defence:
Walter Kidd: Tough, fearless and uncompromising are three words I would use to describe Walter Kidd. He was part of a rare

breed of professional who spent virtually his entire career at one club (fifteen years), making 356 appearances for Hearts in the process. His no-nonsense approach to the game made him a favourite with the fans who affectionately nicknamed him 'Zico' after the Brazilian midfielder

Craig Levein: Like a gazelle across the pitch, one of Craig's best attributes was the pace he possessed. During his 401 appearances in maroon, he won the SPFA Young Player of the Year Award twice (the first player ever to retain it). Had he not endured a terrible run of knee injuries, which ended his playing career prematurely, then without doubt he would have gone on to play at the highest level in Europe, and earned many more than just sixteen caps for his country.

Dave McPherson: Dave McPherson's height (6'3") ensured he was a commanding presence for club and country, both in defence and attack. Despite his lofty stature he was quite an adept dribbler, and many Hearts fans will recall one of his devastating runs leading to a goal in a 4-2 Scottish Cup win over Rangers in 1995. His time at Tynecastle saw him assume the position as club captain and firmly establish himself as a regular with Scotland.

Takis Fyssas: Takis Fyssas. A classy left-back who was brought in by George Burley at the start of the 'Romanov Revolution' in 2005. Capped by Greece sixty times and a 2004 European Championship winner, we can be thankful to Romanov for bringing a player of his calibre to Tynecastle in what was the winter of his career. I always think you can tell a good player by the amount of time he has on the ball, and Takis always seemed to have bags of it, no matter who he was up against.

Midfield:

Rudi Skacel: Rudi was a vital player in the Cup-winning year of 2006 – the year we split the Old Firm in the league – and also in 2012 when we famously beat Hibs. He quickly earned himself cult status amongst the supporters with his seventeen goals during that term, not least with his strike against Gretna in the Scottish Cup final. His return to the club in 2010 was a welcome surprise for every Jambo, and he quickly re-established his hero status finishing as top scorer.

Paul Hartley: Like many Hearts fans, I was a bit underwhelmed with Paul when he first joined the club in 2003 from St Johnstone. I suppose the fact that he was an ex-Hibee worked against him, but when he went on to torment them so many times in a Hearts strip, it meant he became a Tynecastle idol pretty quickly! For me, his crowning glory was not lifting the Scottish Cup in 2006, but his fantastic hat-trick (his first ever as a professional) against Hibs in the semi-final. I would love to see him back as manager one day.

John Colquhoun: John was a good old-fashioned winger blazing down the flanks at any given opportunity. He was the third prong in the Robertson, Clark and Colquhoun strike force, which enjoyed so much league and European success in the mid-1980s. In his two spells at the club he made 345 appearances for Hearts, scoring sixty-six times in the process, but had an assist in hundreds of other goals. It was a shame that he was only capped twice by Scotland.

Lothar Matthäus (but I suppose I'll have to make do with Gary Mackay!):

The only player in my Dream Team who hasn't played for the club, although he has been linked with the manager's position once or twice, is the great German who used to be one of my heroes. He was the complete midfielder and I recall his sparkling performances for West Germany at the World Cup finals in 1990. That summer I tried to encourage Dad to sign him for Hearts but I seem to recall the response as being, 'He's far too expensive. We'll have to make do with Gary Mackay!' I suppose in my Dream Team if I am being serious, I too will have to do with Gary Mackay.

Forwards:

John Robertson: The club's record goal-scorer, this man will forever be a legend in Gorgie, primarily due to the twenty-seven goals he scored against Hibs during his two spells at the club. Following his £800,000 transfer to Newcastle United in 1988, I can exclusively reveal I had a hand in his return 'home' only eight months later. Transfers of players were often discussed amongst the family and when Dad asked, 'Shall we bring John back?' I answered with, 'Can you really afford not to?' In truth, the decision had already been made, but it is something I remind Robbo of from time to time!

Ricardo Fuller: Ricardo had a massive impact on Hearts during the short time he was at the club on loan from Preston. His goal (which started from inside his own half) against Motherwell in December 2001 will go down as one of the all-time great strikes at Tynecastle. In this team he would be the perfect foil for wee Robbo due to his height, but also his ability to create the unexpected.

Manager: Jim Jefferies

This was a difficult choice and in the end came down to two former Hearts players: Alex MacDonald and Jim Jefferies. The former is remembered for revitalising Hearts in the early 1980s, almost winning the League and Cup double in 1986 before leading the club to the quarter-finals of the UEFA Cup in 1989. But Jefferies went one step further to lift the Scottish Cup in 1998 thus ending a forty-two-year drought in the competition. After leaving the club in 2000 he returned for a second spell as manager in 2010.

I picked this team because many, if not all, of the players represent special memories for me, whether it be when Hearts went so close to a League and Cup double in the 1985-86 season, the run to the quarter-finals of the UEFA Cup in 1989 or the Scottish Cup triumphs of 1998, 2006 and 2012. All of these players have played their part in the tremendously rich history of our famous football club. Alongside them there are many others I have not included. The likes of Antti Niemi, Alan McLaren, Gary Mackay, Colin Cameron, Sandy Clark, David Weir and Stephane Adam are just a few who would be worthy of a place in this team.

Gary: Iain's attempts to pick Lothar Matthäus made me laugh out loud. At the time when he tried to get his dad to sign him, Lothar would have been at the top of his game and Iain, as any young lad would, would have tested his dad as to what his ambition would be. Thank God we didn't get him, as I wouldn't have had a look in if he turned up! Now if Iain only put me in his Hearts Dream Team because he couldn't get Kenny Black then I would be a bit angry. But to make me second pick behind Matthäus is okay.

I like the look of Iain's team overall and it is interesting he has picked Ricardo Fuller as he is a name that doesn't crop up at all elsewhere in the Dream Teams, yet Iain is correct in suggesting having him alongside wee Robbo might just work.

GEORGE FOULKES

George Foulkes, Baron Foulkes of Cumnock, is a member of the House of Lords and a former chairman of Hearts who is a season ticket holder at Tynecastle.

George Foulkes's Hearts Dream Team (Formation: 4-4-2)

Goalkeeper: Craig Gordon
While Craig might not have been the longest-serving keeper at Hearts, at his best he was phenomenal and thoroughly deserved the accolade of Scotland's number one. A commanding, athletic and unflappable figure between the sticks, he instilled total confidence in his defence. It was a blow for the Hearts fans

when he left to go Sunderland for the record British transfer fee for a goalkeeper at the time of £9 million.

Defence:
Walter Kidd: Zico was a top-class defender for Hearts who was Mr Consistency himself. His experience at the back was invaluable and he always looked like he had time on the ball. He hardly wasted a pass and some of his runs from deep were a joy to behold.

Steven Pressley: Pressley was a commanding and inspirational defender. He played at Hearts over eight seasons and gained thirty-two Scotland caps to become our most capped Scotland player of all time. 'Elvis' was also the second longest-serving club captain after Bobby Parker and captained Hearts to Scottish Cup success in 2006 against Gretna.

Craig Levein: Craig was one of the most intelligent and talented defenders to grace the Tynecastle turf. He spent fourteen years at Hearts and gained sixteen Scotland caps during this time. Had it not been for serious injuries he would have achieved many more games for both Hearts and Scotland. He also presided over a successful period as manager of Hearts as well.

Andy Anderson: Andy 'Tiger' Anderson was a skilful and hugely popular Hearts and Scotland left-back who played for Hearts from 1929 until 1939 when he retired at just thirty years of age. He won twenty-three caps for Scotland between 1933 and 1938 and captained the national team in four of those games.

Midfield:
Gary Mackay: Gary pips Robbo for the most appearances for the Jam Tarts with an incredible 737 games from 1980 to 1997. A stylish, attacking midfielder he is one of the longest-serving Hearts players of all time. Mackay was the toast of Ireland for his goal against Bulgaria that helped them qualify for their first ever finals.

Dave Mackay: While he only played 180 competitive games for Hearts, he was remembered affectionately by the Jambos for his hard tackling, no-nonsense style. He won all three domestic trophies at Hearts and went on to win the double with Spurs in 1961. Brian Clough claimed in 2003 that Mackay was Tottenham Hotspur's greatest-ever player and George Best asserted that he was the hardest man he ever played against.

John Cumming: John Cumming was a fearless player for Hearts. He was a tough-tackling midfielder whose quote 'Blood doesn't show on a maroon shirt' from after the 1956 Cup final is immortalised in the player's tunnel at Tynecastle. He was a one-club man, having spent his entire career at Tynecastle and notching up 505 appearances. He has won more winners' medals than any other Hearts player with a total of seven medals to his name.

Jimmy Wardhaugh: Jimmy scored 272 goals in 416 games during his illustrious career, forming one part of the Terrible Trio that terrorised defences with Willie Bauld and Alfie Conn. He was nicknamed 'Twinkle Toes' and was Hearts' top league goalscorer for forty years until overtaken by John Robertson.

Forwards:

John Robertson: The 'Hammer of Hibs' is an automatic selection for this team with 271 goals in 631 appearances during his two stints at Hearts, including twenty-seven goals against Hibs. He finally won a winners' medal in the momentous 1998 Scottish Cup victory, as an unused substitute. It was never over with Hearts while he was playing until the 'fat striker scored'.

Willie Bauld: Willie Bauld was truly the 'King of Hearts' and remains one of the most revered players ever to play at Tynecastle Park. He scored a few more goals than Robbo and Wardhaugh, with 277 in all competitions and this was achieved in 415 appearances. Despite this phenomenal record, he was only awarded three full Scotland caps.

Manager: Tommy Walker

Tommy would most likely be in the Dream Team having scored an amazing 222 goals in 216 competitive games for Hearts, as well as several famous goals for Scotland against England. However, it was his time as manager that cemented him as one of the greatest Hearts legends of all time. His managerial tenure was the most successful period in our history although he inherited the team from Davie MacLean. During his time as manager the Jambos won the league twice which included the incredible 1957–58 season with a record sixty-two points and 132 goals scored (still the Scottish top league record). In addition to this he won the Scottish Cup and the League Cup four times.

There are a lot of players who would grace any Hearts team and were hard to leave out. Indeed one of Hearts' greatest players of all time was Bobby Walker, who played from 1896 to 1914. Hearts have also been blessed with some great keepers, such as 'Wembley Wizard' Jack Harkness, Jim Cruickshank, Henry Smith, Antti Niemi, and Gilles Roussett.

In addition to these, there are legends like Alex Massie, Freddie Glidden, Barney Battles, Bobby Prentice, Bobby Parker, Alfie Conn, Alex Young, Jim Jefferies, Donald Ford, Drew Busby, Donald Park, who graced the maroon and were also very difficult to omit. Other more recent favourites of mine who also just miss out and were key players in great Hearts teams include Walter Kidd, John Colquhoun, Davie McPherson, Colin Cameron, Gary Naysmith, Paul Hartley, Gary Locke and Stephane Adam.

Gary: George's Dream Team brought a smile to my face, as his side, I would guess, would play open, entertaining football. Now I'm not just saying that because I am in it but because there are lots more talented players in that team than me who could spray passes all over the pitch. The one pick of George's that fascinated me more than any other was his choice of Andy 'Tiger' Anderson at left-back. He may not be well known to the younger generation of Hearts fans but it is great that George has given him the recognition he deserves.

JOHN JEFFREY

John Jeffrey is a former Scotland rugby internationalist who was part of the legendary 1990 Grand Slam-winning side. He was also a member of the successful British Lions squad that won the Test series 2-1 over Australia in 1989. He remains an important figure within world rugby and is a member of the International Rugby Board. He farms just outside Kelso and gets along to Tynecastle to watch his boyhood heroes whenever his busy schedule allows.

John: I've selected my Dream Team from players that I have actually seen in the flesh, with the notable exception of Hearts' greatest-ever player, Dave Mackay. Every Hearts team would HAVE to be built round him.

John Jeffrey's Hearts Dream Team (Formation: 4-4-2)

Goalkeeper: Jim Cruickshank
An absolutely fantastic player and a legend in my book. Hearts have always been blessed with top-class goalkeepers through the years, like Gilles Rousset, Antti Niemi and Craig Gordon, but not one of them came close to Cruickie.

Defence:
Walter Kidd: Zico was an incredible player that was one of my first Dream Team picks. A dependable right-back who could go

228

on some mazy runs. Maybe he wasn't the most talented but he was dependable and worked hard for ninety minutes.

Craig Levein: An absolute real class act who always seemed to have acres of space. The fact he gave Graeme Hogg a dunt put him up in my estimation. That is nothing against Graeme Hogg, it was just that Craig was such a classy, smooth guy I always wondered if he had a hard edge. The way he put him down that day made me realise he was tough. One of my heroes.

Alan McLaren: Alan was another player who was always comfortable on the ball and not one of those guys who would just hoof it up the park.

Jim Brown: A real unsung hero of many a Hearts side. Jim was one of the most consistent players in the history of the club and he would never let you down. He was versatile as well and could play on either side of the back four.

Midfield:

Dave Mackay: What Hearts team would be complete without Dave Mackay? That picture of him holding Billy Bremner up by the shirt will live in the memory forever. If you were in an under-age team and wanted one over-age guy in it to bring some steel and leadership you would pick Dave every time. An all-time great not just of Hearts but of Scottish football.

John Colquhoun: Hearts were never really renowned for having tricky wee wingers until he came along. He had a sparkle and brought something different to the team.

Eamonn Bannon: Bannon is the same age as me and I met him at a party when we were sixteen and wondered why all the girls were flocking around him; then I realised it was because he was a Hearts player. I watched him play a lot at Tynecastle and he had talent in abundance. I was gutted when he went to Chelsea. Even more gutted when he came back and signed for Dundee United before he came back to us. He could make the right passes and scored some quality goals. I may never have been as good a

footballer as Eamonn and although the girls didn't flock to me like they did him when I was sixteen, at least I still have my hair!
Drew Busby: The Buzz-bomb. I loved his energy. He was a nuisance. A hard guy. Whenever he went into the tackle the crowd used to hold its breath as he used to go in hard as hell.

Forwards:
Donald Ford: Drew may have been tough but Donald was a sophisticated guy. What a player and what a servant of Hearts. He played in a poor period in the history of the club but still got goals and became a real hero.
John Robertson: Robbo. What can you say? Everyone of a certain generation surely must have Robbo down as their favourite ever player. An absolute legend. Never the greatest athlete but the way he banged in the goals, especially against Hibs, puts him into the superstar bracket.

Manager: Jim Jefferies
Jim would be my manager for the way he brought success to the club. I felt he always handled himself well when it came to Hearts' matters. A man who retained his dignity throughout his two spells as Hearts manager.

Gary: I don't know what John's background is in managing rugby teams but after picking such a cracking Hearts Dream Team I have to say he would be well capable of managing a football team and working out tactics. JJ is a great rugby man, too big for me to argue with for not putting me into the team, but the balance of this team is absolutely magnificent so I can't have any real complaints about not getting a mention. You can see where he is coming from in every aspect of his selection. He has picked a team of wonderful players and has set them up in a manner that would appeal to what Hearts supporters like in a team. There is real solidity in the back and midfield players who can get forward and put great crosses into the box. His team has two outstanding strikers but you also have Drew Busby in the hole behind them ready to link up whenever he can. I am delighted JJ has picked Jim Brown as I always felt he was one of the unsung heroes of Hearts. Although he committed the ultimate sin of moving to Hibs, he was an outstanding player. I can understand why he has chosen Jim Jefferies, as Hearts had not won a trophy for thirty-six years but when you look closely at JJ's team he has picked five guys from Alex MacDonald's time in charge. He was put together a fascinating team that tactically is as strong as any I have seen.

CHARLES AND DAVID FALCONER

The former Lord Chancellor and his brother David have been Hearts fans all their lives. Growing up in Edinburgh they remember the great sides of the 1960s where legends like Willie Hamilton caught their attention. Although Charles moved south and was at the heart of politics and a minister in Tony Blair's government for all of its ten-year life, Lord Chancellor for the last four years, he always kept an eye out for Hearts results regardless of the pressure of work. He liaised with his brother David, who has lived in Edinburgh all his life and been a regular at Tynecastle during that time, before coming up with his Hearts Dream Team.

Charles and David Falconer's Hearts Dream Team (Formation: 4-4-2)

Goalkeeper: Craig Gordon
It was a tough choice but he just gets the nod ahead of Jim Cruickshank. He made stunning saves in his two years prior to his transfer to Sunderland. He was also a Hearts supporter and played for our youth team.

Defence:

Takis Fyssas: I know Takis Fyssas was very left-footed but he was such a class act we had to get him into our team somewhere. I loved his enthusiasm for Hearts and although playing on the right would not come naturally to him, I make no apologies for picking him as he could get up the park and come back onto his left foot to put crosses into the box.

Craig Levein: Technically Hearts' finest defender we've ever seen. Fast, great in the air, with fantastic ball skills. Let down by being injury prone, hence the nickname of 'Shergar' among some of the fans.

Sandy Jardine: Played under Alex MacDonald till his late thirties and read the game beautifully. He gave Levein a great apprenticeship.

Gary Naysmith: A fast attacking wing-back who could defend as well.

Midfielders:

John Colquhoun: A great servant to Hearts who scored goals and made loads of assists. Bought from Celtic and was one of Hearts' best purchases.

John Cumming: He was the main man in the Hearts engine room when we first went to watch Hearts with our dad against Kilmarnock in 1959. David was nine years old, and I was seven. He shored up the defence from midfield and played through a lot of injuries, hence his nickname 'Iron Man'.

Willie Hamilton: The most technically talented player we've ever witnessed to wear a maroon jersey. Jock Stein, who managed Willie Hamilton when he played for Hibs after Hearts, said he was the best player he'd ever managed and this was from a man who won the European Cup with Celtic. Tragically Willie died in his thirties in Canada from alcohol abuse. We both feel privileged to have watched such a great player at his peak.

Rudi Skacel: A man with a love for Hearts and a magic left foot. Appears lazy in play at times but will always come up with an assist or a goal or two, as he showed in the Scottish Cup final win over Hibs in 2012.

Forwards:
Willie Bauld: Crowned King of Hearts in the 1950s and we were lucky enough to see him play in 1959 when watching the Kilmarnock match. Hearts had won the championship twice in the '50s, thanks to the contribution of Cumming and Bauld.
John Robertson: Scored over 200 goals for Hearts and a great six-yard box player and incomparable scorer against Hibs. He is an icon for all Hearts supporters.

Manager: Alex MacDonald
Did a fantastic amount of work in reviving Hearts and put together a fantastic team.

Gary: In terms of attacking, this is a top-class side. I particularly like the look of Charlie and David's midfield, which has a great balance to it. John Colquhoun, Willie Hamilton and Rudi Skacel and with John Cumming in a holding role is probably the best unit I have seen selected. Up front Willie Bauld and John Robertson would get the goals, while a centre partnership of Craig Levein and Sandy Jardine is a magnificent choice. Although I knew Gary Naysmith would be fine at left full-back, I wasn't too sure to begin with about Takis Fyssas, who was very left-footed, being named at right-back. After corresponding with them I can understand their thinking, which is top class. Takis was a member of the Greek team that won Euro 2004, and as Charlie and David pointed out, he is experienced enough to show wingers inside so he could tackle them on his favoured left foot. Where he would really come into his own would be in attack. He would be behind their right midfielder John Colquhoun, who would provide enough crosses into the box with his right foot. Takis could get up the line, cut inside and put in crosses with his left for a bit of variation. Charlie and David have picked a very attacking formation, which would have pleased their Dream Team manager Alex MacDonald, who would have loved working with the players they have selected.

12

STATS ATTACK

I thought it would be interesting to give a breakdown of the
Hearts careers of my Dream Team as they show the great service
each and every one of them gave to the club.

Can I thank Davy Allan of London Hearts for painstakingly
putting together the statistics for each and every one of them. His
work and that of other loyal members of London Hearts can be
found on their world-class website www.londonhearts.com. As a
football website, regardless of what club is involved, it is the best
and most comprehensive around.

Join the Hearts Dream Team debate by visiting
Gary Mackay's Hearts Dream Team page on Facebook!

Player Records

Willie Bauld

Season	League				Scottish Cup				League Cup				Europe				Texaco/A-Scottish Cup				Total				Goals/Game
	Starts	Sub	Total	Goals	Starts	Sub	Total	Goals	Starts	Sub	Total	Goals	Starts	Sub	Total	Goals	Starts	Sub	Total	Goals	Starts	Sub	Total	Goals	
1948-49	24		24	17	4		4	1	2		2	6									30		30	24	0.800
1949-50	29		29	30	3		3	2	6		6	8									38		38	40	1.053
1950-51	30		30	15	3		3	2	6		6	3									39		39	20	0.513
1951-52	29		29	14	7		7	5	6		6	8									42		42	27	0.643
1952-53	23		23	10	4		4	2	5		5	5									32		32	17	0.531
1953-54	21		21	10	3		3		6		6	4									30		30	14	0.467
1954-55	25		25	21	4		4	6	9		9	12									38		38	39	1.026
1955-56	20		20	15	5		5	3	3		3										28		28	18	0.643
1956-57	24		24	12	1		1		6		6	3									31		31	15	0.484
1957-58	9		9	5					6		6	5									15		15	10	0.667
1958-59	20		20	15	2		2		8		8	9	2		2	2					32		32	26	0.813
1959-60	17		17	10					6		6	3									23		23	13	0.565
1960-61	11		11	3	3		3		4		4	3	1		1						19		19	6	0.316
1961-62	11		11	6	1		1	1	3		3	1	2		2						17		17	8	0.471
	293	0	293	183	40	0	40	22	76	0	76	70	5	0	5	2	0	0	0	0	414	0	414	277	0.669

Jim Cruickshank

Season	League				Scottish Cup				League Cup				Europe				Texaco/A-Scottish Cup				Total			
	Starts	Sub	Total	Clean Sheet	Starts	Sub	Total	Clean Sheet	Starts	Sub	Total	Clean Sheet	Starts	Sub	Total	Clean Sheet	Starts	Sub	Total	Clean Sheet	Starts	Sub	Total	Clean Sheet
1960-61	4		4	1	1		1	1			1										5		5	1
1961-62	5		5	1	1		1	1													7		7	2
1962-63	6		6	2																	6		6	2
1963-64	34		34	9	3		3	1	6		6	2	3		3						46		46	12
1964-65	34		34	6	4		4	2	6		6										44		44	8
1965-66	34		34	1	4		4		6		6	1	5		5	1					49		49	12
1966-67	34		34	8	1		1		6		6	1									41		41	9
1967-68	2		2	2	5		5	1	3		3										28		28	3
1968-69	31		31	6	2		2		5		5	1									38		38	7
1969-70	29		29	13	3		3	1	6		6	3									38		38	17
1970-71	32		32	11	2		2	1	6		6	1					8		8	2	48		48	15
1971-72	2		2	5					6		6						2		2	1	28		28	7
1972-73	11		11	2	7		7														11		11	2
1973-74	11		11	5																	18		18	5
1974-75	27		27	7	4		4	2	5		5	2									31		31	9
1975-76	35		35	12	9		9	4	3		3						3		3		52		52	18
1976-77	27		27	3	6		6	3					2		2						38		38	6
	358	0	358	93	52	0	52	17	59	0	59	12	10	0	10	1	13	0	13	3	528	0	528	135

Donald Ford

Season	League				Scottish Cup				League Cup				Europe				Texaco/A-Scottish Cup				Total				
	Starts	Sub	Total	Goals	Starts	Sub	Total	Goals	Starts	Sub	Total	Goals	Starts	Sub	Total	Goals	Starts	Sub	Total	Goals	Starts	Sub	Total	Goals	Goals/Game
1964-65	2		2						4		4	2									7		7	2	0.286
1965-66	9		9	2	2		2	2	6		6	2	2		2						17		17	2	0.118
1966-67	5		5						6		6	4									5		5		n/a
1967-68	29		29	11	6		6	3	6		6						8		8	8	41		41	16	0.390
1968-69	23	4	27	6	2		2	6	6		6	2					2		2		31	4	35	10	0.286
1969-70	24	5	29	8	3		3		6		6	3					4		4		33	5	38	8	0.211
1970-71	32		32	11	2		2	2	6		6	2					4		4		48		48	23	0.479
1971-72	30		30	15	3		3	1	6		6	3									41		41	19	0.463
1972-73	32		32	9	2		2	1	6		6	2									44		44	12	0.273
1973-74	29	1	30	18	7		7	6	8		8	5					1		1	1	46	1	47	29	0.617
1974-75	21	1	22	13	2		2		6		6	5					1	1	2	1	32	2	34	19	0.559
1975-76	2		2	2	1		1		6		6	2					1		1		10		10	3	0.300
	243	11	254	93	30	0	30	13	60	0	60	27	2	0	2	0	20	1	21	10	355	12	367	143	0.390

Steve Fulton

Season	League				Scottish Cup				League Cup				Europe				Texaco/A-Scottish Cup				Total				
	Starts	Sub	Total	Goals	Starts	Sub	Total	Goals	Starts	Sub	Total	Goals	Starts	Sub	Total	Goals	Starts	Sub	Total	Goals	Starts	Sub	Total	Goals	Goals/Game
1995-96	26		26	2	4		4														30		30	2	0.067
1996-97	25	4	29	1	4		4		2	2	4	1									31	6	37	2	0.054
1997-98	36		36	5	3		3	1	3		3		1		1						43		43	6	0.140
1998-99	27		27	2	1		1		3		3	1	1		1	1					32		32	4	0.125
1999-00	16	10	26	1	1		1		2	1	3										19	11	30	1	0.033
2000-01	23	1	24	1	1		1		2		2		2		2						28	1	29	1	0.034
2001-02	27	8	35	3	2		2		1		1										30	8	38	3	0.079
	180	23	203	15	16	0	16	1	13	3	16	2	4	0	4	1	0	0	0	0	213	26	239	19	0.079

Sandy Jardine

Season	League				Scottish Cup				League Cup				Europe				Texaco/A-Scottish Cup				Total				
	Starts	Sub	Total	Goals	Starts	Sub	Total	Goals	Starts	Sub	Total	Goals	Starts	Sub	Total	Goals	Starts	Sub	Total	Goals	Starts	Sub	Total	Goals	Goals/Game
1982-83	39		39	2	4		4		10		10										53		53	2	0.038
1983-84	36		36		2		2		7		7										45		45		n/a
1984-85	34		34		5		5		5		5		1		1						45		45		n/a
1985-86	35		35		5		5		3		3										43		43		n/a
1986-87	34		34	1	3		3		1		1		2		2						40		40	1	0.025
1987-88	9		9						3		3										12		12		n/a
	187	0	187	3	19	0	19	0	29	0	29	0	3	0	3	0	0	0	0	0	238	0	238	3	0.013

Walter Kidd

Season	League Starts	League Sub	League Total	League Goals	Scottish Cup Starts	Scottish Cup Sub	Scottish Cup Total	Scottish Cup Goals	League Cup Starts	League Cup Sub	League Cup Total	League Cup Goals	Europe Starts	Europe Sub	Europe Total	Europe Goals	Texaco/A-Scottish Cup Starts	Texaco/A-Scottish Cup Sub	Texaco/A-Scottish Cup Total	Texaco/A-Scottish Cup Goals	Total Starts	Total Sub	Total Total	Total Goals	Goals/Game
1977-78	22	2	24		3		3		3		3	1									28	2	30	1	0.033
1978-79	29	1	30		4		4										2		2		35	1	36		n/a
1979-80	27	7	34	2	2		2				2						2		2		30	7	37	2	0.054
1980-81	25		25	1	3		3				3										32		32	1	0.031
1981-82	29	1	30		2	1	2				3						2		2		33	2	35		n/a
1982-83	37		37		10		10				10										50		50		n/a
1983-84	31		31	1	7		7				7										40		40	1	0.025
1984-85	33		33	1	5		5		2		2		2		2						44		44	1	0.023
1985-86	28		28		2		2		2		5	1									35		35	1	0.029
1986-87	33	2	35		1		4		2		2										40	2	42		n/a
1987-88	16	2	18		3		1				3										20	2	22		n/a
1988-89	20		20		1	1	2		6		6										28	1	29		0.091
1989-90	12	5	17	1	1	1			1			1									16	6	22	2	0.091
1990-91	1	3	4		1	1				1	1										2	5	7		n/a
1994-95			1							1	1										1		1		n/a
	344	23	367	6	41	3	36	0	10	1	44	3	4	0	4	0	4	0	4	0	434	28	462	9	0.019

Craig Levein

Season	League Starts	League Sub	League Total	League Goals	Scottish Cup Starts	Scottish Cup Sub	Scottish Cup Total	Scottish Cup Goals	League Cup Starts	League Cup Sub	League Cup Total	League Cup Goals	Europe Starts	Europe Sub	Europe Total	Europe Goals	Texaco/A-Scottish Cup Starts	Texaco/A-Scottish Cup Sub	Texaco/A-Scottish Cup Total	Texaco/A-Scottish Cup Goals	Total Starts	Total Sub	Total Total	Total Goals	Goals/Game
1983-84	17	2	19		2		2		5		5	1									19	2	21		n/a
1984-85	35	1	36	1	4		4		5		5		2		2						46	1	47	2	0.043
1985-86	33		33	2	5		5		3		3										41		41	2	0.049
1986-87	12		12						1		1		2		2						15		15		n/a
1987-88	21		21																		21		21		n/a
1988-89	8	1	9		2		2						2		2						12	1	13		n/a
1989-90	35		35		3		3		3		3										41		41		n/a
1990-91	33		33	4	3		4		3		3		4		4						40		40	4	0.100
1991-92	36		36	2	4		4		3		3										43		43	2	0.047
1992-93	37		37	3	3		3		3		3		3		3	1					46		46	4	0.087
1993-94	30		30	3	3		3		2		2		2		2						37		37	3	0.081
1994-95	24		24		4		4		2		2										30		30		n/a
1995-96	1		1																		3		3		n/a
	322	4	326	15	30	0	30	0	27	0	27	1	15	0	15	1	0	0	0	0	394	4	398	17	0.043

Dave Mackay

Season	League				Scottish Cup				League Cup				Europe				Texaco/A-Scottish Cup				Total				Goals/Game
	Starts	Sub	Total	Goals	Starts	Sub	Total	Goals	Starts	Sub	Total	Goals	Starts	Sub	Total	Goals	Starts	Sub	Total	Goals	Starts	Sub	Total	Goals	
1953-54	4		4																		4		4		
1954-55	25		25	2	4		4		7		7	1									36		36	3	0.083
1955-56	28		28	4	6		6		2		2										36		36	4	0.111
1956-57	31		31	5	1		1		6		6										38		38	5	0.132
1957-58	28		28	12	3		3		6		6										37		37	12	0.324
1958-59	19		19	4	2		2		5		5	1	2		2						28		28	5	0.179
	135	0	135	27	16	0	16	0	26	0	26	2	2	0	2	0	0	0	0	0	179	0	179	29	0.162

Tosh McKinlay

Season	League				Scottish Cup				League Cup				Europe				Texaco/A-Scottish Cup				Total				Goals/Game
	Starts	Sub	Total	Goals	Starts	Sub	Total	Goals	Starts	Sub	Total	Goals	Starts	Sub	Total	Goals	Starts	Sub	Total	Goals	Starts	Sub	Total	Goals	
1988-89	17		17	1	3		3						2		2						22		22	1	0.045
1989-90	29		29	1	2		2														31		31	1	0.032
1990-91	31	2	33	2	1		1		3		3		4		4						39	2	41	2	0.049
1991-92	37	2	39	2	5		5		3		3										45	2	47	2	0.043
1992-93	32	2	34	1	3		3		3		3	1	4		4						42	2	44	2	0.045
1993-94	43		43		3		3		2		2		2		2						50		50		n/a
1994-95	11		11		1		1		1		1										12		12		n/a
	200	6	206	7	17	0	17	0	12	0	12	1	12	0	12	0	0	0	0	0	241	6	247	8	0.032

John Robertson

Season	League St	Sub	Total	Goals	Scottish Cup St	Sub	Total	Goals	League Cup St	Sub	Total	Goals	Europe St	Sub	Total	Goals	Texaco/A-Scottish Cup St	Sub	Total	Goals	Total St	Sub	Total	Goals	Goals/Game
1981-82		1	1	1																		1	1	1	n/a
1982-83	19	4	23	21	1		1		3	1	4										23	5	28	21	0.750
1983-84	34		34	15	5		5	1	2	2	4	4									41	2	43	20	0.465
1984-85	33		33	8	5		5	2	5		5	1	2		2	2					45		45	13	0.289
1985-86	34	1	35	20	3		3	4	5		5	1									42	1	43	25	0.581
1986-87	31	6	37	16	1		1	2	6		6	1		2	2						38	8	46	19	0.413
1987-88	39		39	26	3		3	2	4		4	3									46		46	31	0.674
1988-89	8	7	15	4		1	1		2		2			1	1						10	9	19	4	0.211
1989-90	25	7	32	17	3		3	4		1	1	1									28	8	36	22	0.611
1990-91	31		31	12	3		3	1	1		1		3		3	3					38		38	16	0.421
1991-92	42		42	14	3		3	4	6		6	2									51		51	20	0.392
1992-93	41	1	42	11	2		2	1	5		5	2	4		4	1					52	1	53	15	0.283
1993-94	32	4	36	8	2	1	3	3	2		2		2		2	1					38	5	43	12	0.279
1994-95	27	4	31	10	2		2	1	5		5	3									34	4	38	14	0.368
1995-96	28	5	33	12	4	2	6	2		1	1										32	8	40	14	0.350
1996-97	25	2	27	14	1	1	2	2	4	2	6	3		1	1						30	6	36	19	0.528
1997-98	10	11	21	6		1	1		1	2	3										11	14	25	6	0.240
Total	459	53	512	214	38	6	44	29	51	9	60	21	11	4	15	7	0	0	0	0	559	72	631	271	0.429

Alex MacDonald As Player

Season	League St	Sub	Total	Goals	Scottish Cup St	Sub	Total	Goals	League Cup St	Sub	Total	Goals	Europe St	Sub	Total	Goals	Texaco/A-Scottish Cup St	Sub	Total	Goals	Total St	Sub	Total	Goals	Goals/Game
1980-81	28		28	3	2		2	1	4		4	1									34		34	5	0.147
1981-82	15	1	16	1					4		4										19	1	20	1	0.050
1982-83	29	2	31	5	3		3	1	9		9	3									41	2	43	9	0.209
1983-84	19	5	24	1	1		1		3		3										23	5	28	1	0.036
1984-85	14	8	22	2		1	1		4	2	6										18	11	29	2	0.069
1985-86		1	1																			1	1		n/a
Total	105	17	122	12	6	1	7	2	24	2	26	4	0	0	0	0	0	0	0	0	135	20	155	18	0.116

Gary Mackay

Season	League Starts	Sub	Total	Goals	Scottish Cup Starts	Sub	Total	Goals	League Cup Starts	Sub	Total	Goals	Europe Starts	Sub	Total	Goals	Texaco/A-Scottish Cup Starts	Sub	Total	Goals	Total Starts	Sub	Total	Goals	Goals/Game
1980-81	11	1	12		2		2			1	1	1									13	2	15		n/a
1981-82	10	7	17	2		1	1		2		2										12	8	20	2	0.100
1982-83	26	8	34	6	4		4		2	1	3										32	9	41	6	0.146
1983-84	29	2	31	4	2		2		7	1	8	2									38	3	41	6	0.146
1984-85	16	1	17	2	5		5	4					1		1						22	1	23	6	0.261
1985-86	30	2	32	4	5		5	2	2		2										37	2	39	6	0.154
1986-87	31	5	36	7	5	2	7	2	1		1		2		2						39	7	46	9	0.196
1987-88	40	1	41	5	4		4	2	3		3	1									47	1	48	8	0.167
1988-89	29		29	2	3		3		4		4	2	6	2	8						42	2	44	4	0.091
1989-90	31	2	33	1	1	1	2		2		2										34	3	37	1	0.027
1990-91	27	3	30	3	1		1	1	3		3		1	1	2						32	4	36	4	0.111
1991-92	41	2	43	1	3		3	1	3		3										47	2	49	2	0.041
1992-93	36	1	37	2	4		4		3		3	1	4		4	1					47	1	48	4	0.083
1993-94	34	2	36	1	2		2		2		2		2		2						40	2	42	1	0.024
1994-95	21	13	34	2	4	1	5		1		1										26	14	40	2	0.050
1995-96	21	5	26	2	5		5		3		3										29	5	34	2	0.059
1996-97	20	7	27	1	1	2	3		5		5		2		2						28	9	37	1	0.027
	453	62	515	45	51	7	58	12	43	3	46	6	18	3	21	1	0	0	0	0	565	75	640	64	0.100

Rudi Skacel

Season	League Starts	Sub	Total	Goals	Scottish Cup Starts	Sub	Total	Goals	League Cup Starts	Sub	Total	Goals	Europe Starts	Sub	Total	Goals	Texaco/A-Scottish Cup Starts	Sub	Total	Goals	Total Starts	Sub	Total	Goals	Goals/Game
2005-06	33	2	35	16	4		4	1		1	1										37	3	40	17	0.425
2010-11	27	2	29	13																	27	2	29	13	0.448
2011-12	19	10	29	12	6	1	7	5	1		1	0	1	2	3	1					27	13	40	18	0.450
	79	14	93	41	10	1	11	6	1	1	2	0	1	2	3	1	0	0	0	0	91	18	109	48	0.440

Player records in summary

	League				Scottish Cup				League Cup				Europe				Texaco/A-Scottish Cup				Total				
	Starts	Sub	Total	Goals	Starts	Sub	Total	Goals	Starts	Sub	Total	Goals	Starts	Sub	Total	Goals	Starts	Sub	Total	Goals	Starts	Sub	Total	Goals	Goals/Game
Willie Bauld	293		293	183	40		40	22	76		76	70	5		5	2					414		414	277	0.669
Jim Cruickshank	358		358		52		52		59		59		10		10	0	13		13		528		528		n/a
Donald Ford	243	11	254	93	30		30	13	60		60	27	2		2	0	20	1	21	10	355	12	367	143	0.390
Steve Fulton	180	23	203	15	16		16	1	13	3	16	2	4		4	1					213	26	239	19	0.079
Sandy Jardine	187		187	3	19		19	0	29		29	0	3		3	0					238		238	3	0.013
Walter Kidd	344	23	367	6	35	1	36	0	41	3	44	3	10	1	11	0	4		4	0	434	28	462	9	0.019
Craig Levein	322	4	326	15	30		30	0	27		27	1	15		15	1					394	4	398	17	0.043
Dave Mackay	135		135	27	16		16	0	26		26	2	2		2	0					179		179	29	0.162
McKinlay Tosh	200	6	206	7	17		17	0	12		12	1	12		12	0					241	6	247	8	0.032
John Robertson	459	53	512	214	51	9	60	29	38	6	44	21	11	4	15	7					559	72	631	271	0.429
Rudi Skacel	79	14	93	41	10	1	11	6	1	1	2	0	1	2	3	1					91	18	109	48	0.440
Alex MacDonald	105	17	122	12	5	1	6	2	24	1	25	4	1	1	2	0					135	20	155	18	0.116
Gary Mackay	453	62	515	45	51	7	58	12	43	3	46	6	18	3	21	1					565	75	640	64	0.100

Wallace Mercer as Chairman

season	League						Scottish Cup						League Cup						Europe						Total					
	G	W	D	L	F	A	G	W	D	L	F	A	G	W	D	L	F	A	G	W	D	L	F	A	G	W	D	L	F	A
1981-82	39	21	8	10	65	37	2	1	0	1	4	2	6	2	1	3	5	9	0	0	0	0	0	0	47	24	9	14	74	48
1982-83	39	22	10	7	79	38	4	2	1	1	5	6	10	6	1	3	20	10	0	0	0	0	0	0	53	30	12	11	104	54
1983-84	36	10	16	10	38	47	2	1	0	1	3	2	8	3	3	2	10	10	0	0	0	0	0	0	46	14	19	13	51	59
1984-85	36	13	5	18	47	64	5	2	2	1	9	3	5	3	0	2	8	5	2	0	1	1	2	6	48	18	8	22	66	78
1985-86	36	20	10	6	59	33	5	4	0	1	10	7	3	2	0	1	5	3	0	0	0	0	0	0	44	26	10	8	74	43
1986-87	44	21	14	9	64	43	7	3	3	1	8	5	1	0	0	1	0	2	2	1	0	1	3	3	54	25	17	12	75	53
1987-88	44	23	16	5	74	32	4	3	0	1	9	3	3	2	0	1	9	5	0	0	0	0	0	0	51	28	16	7	92	40
1988-89	36	9	13	14	35	42	3	2	0	1	7	3	4	3	0	1	11	4	8	5	1	2	10	4	51	19	14	18	63	53
1989-90	36	16	12	8	54	35	3	2	0	1	7	4	3	2	0	1	9	3	0	0	0	0	0	0	42	20	12	10	70	42
1990-91	36	14	7	15	48	55	1	0	0	1	1	2	3	2	0	1	3	3	4	2	1	1	7	6	44	18	8	18	59	66
1991-92	44	27	9	8	60	37	6	3	2	1	9	3	3	2	0	1	5	1	0	0	0	0	0	0	53	32	11	10	74	41
1992-93	44	15	14	15	46	51	4	3	0	1	11	2	3	2	0	1	4	3	4	1	0	3	4	5	55	21	14	20	65	61
1993-94	44	11	20	13	37	43	3	2	0	1	3	3	2	1	0	1	2	1	2	1	0	1	2	4	51	15	20	16	44	51
	514	222	154	138	706	557	49	28	8	13	86	45	54	30	5	19	91	59	22	10	3	9	28	28	639	290	170	179	911	689

Alex MacDonald as Manager

season	League						Scottish Cup						League Cup						Europe						Total					
	G	W	D	L	F	A	G	W	D	L	F	A	G	W	D	L	F	A	G	W	D	L	F	A	G	W	D	L	F	A
1981-82	21	14	1	6	45	21	2	1	0	1	4	2	0	0	0	0	0	0	0	0	0	0	0	0	23	15	1	7	49	23
1982-83	39	22	10	7	79	38	4	2	1	1	5	6	10	6	1	3	20	10	0	0	0	0	0	0	53	30	12	11	104	54
1983-84	36	10	16	10	38	47	2	1	0	1	3	2	8	3	3	2	10	10	0	0	0	0	0	0	46	14	19	13	51	59
1984-85	36	13	5	18	47	64	5	2	2	1	9	3	5	3	0	2	8	5	2	0	1	1	2	6	48	18	8	22	66	78
1985-86	36	20	10	6	59	33	5	4	0	1	10	7	3	2	0	1	5	3	0	0	0	0	0	0	44	26	10	8	74	43
1986-87	44	21	14	9	64	43	7	3	3	1	8	5	1	0	0	1	0	2	2	1	0	1	3	3	54	25	17	12	75	53
1987-88	44	23	16	5	74	32	4	3	0	1	9	3	3	2	0	1	9	5	0	0	0	0	0	0	51	28	16	7	92	40
1988-89	36	9	13	14	35	42	3	2	0	1	7	3	4	3	0	1	11	4	8	5	1	2	10	4	51	19	14	18	63	53
1989-90	36	16	12	8	54	35	3	2	0	1	7	4	3	2	0	1	9	3	0	0	0	0	0	0	42	20	12	10	70	42
1990-91	3	0	1	2	2	6	0	0	0	0	0	0	3	2	0	1	3	3	0	0	0	0	0	0	6	2	1	3	5	9
	331	148	98	85	497	361	35	20	6	9	62	35	40	23	4	13	75	45	12	6	2	4	15	13	418	197	110	111	649	454

BIBLIOGRAPHY

Believe! Mark Donaldson with Gary Mackay. Mainstream Publishing.

Flawed Genius. Stephen McGowan. Birlinn.

Great Tynecastle Tales. Rob Robertson and Paul Kiddie. Mainstream Publishing.

Gritty, Gallant, Glorious: History and Complete Record of Hearts 1946–1997. Norrie Price.

Hands On Hearts. Alan Rae with Paul Kiddie. Luath Press Limited.

Heart to Heart. Mike Aitken and Wallace Mercer. Mainstream Publishing.

Hearts in Art. Andrew Hoggan. Mainstream Publishing

'Images of Sport'. Heart of Midlothian. Tempus.

The Dave Mackay Story. Dave Mackay with Martin Knight. Mainstream Publishing.

The Gary Mackay Story. Gary Mackay with Mark Donaldson. Fort Publishing Limited.

The Jim Jefferies Story. Jim Jefferies with Jim McLean. Mainstream Publishing.

The Management. Michael Grant and Rob Robertson. Birlinn.

The Willie Johnston Story. Tom Bullimore with Willie Johnston. Know The Score.